Preliminary Edition Notice

You have been selected to receive a copy of this book in the form of a preliminary edition. A preliminary edition is used in a classroom setting to test the overall value of a book's content and its effectiveness in a practical course prior to its formal publication on the national market.

As you use this text in your course, please share any and all feedback regarding the volume with your professor. Your comments on this text will allow the author to further develop the content of the book, so we can ensure it will be a useful and informative classroom tool for students in universities across the nation and around the globe. If you find the material is challenging to understand, or could be expanded to improve the usefulness of the text, it is important for us to know. If you have any suggestions for improving the material contained in the book or the way it is presented, we encourage you to share your thoughts.

Please note, preliminary editions are similar to review copies, which publishers distribute to select readers prior to publication in order to test a book's audience and elicit early feedback; therefore, you may find inconsistencies in formatting or design, or small textual errors within this volume. Design elements and the written text will likely undergo changes before this book goes to print and is distributed on the national market.

This text is not available in wide release on the market, as it is actively being prepared for formal publication. Accordingly, the book is offered to you at a discounted price to reflect its preliminary status.

If you would like to provide notes directly to the publisher, you may contact us by e-mailing studentreviews@cognella.com. Please include the book's title, author, and 7-digit SKU reference number (found below the barcode on the back cover of the book) in the body of your message.

The Story of Sociological Theory

Contextualizing Social Thinkers

Preliminary Edition

David G. LoConto

New Mexico State University

cognella
SAN DIEGO

Bassim Hamadeh, CEO and Publisher
Mazin Hassan, Acquisitions Editor
Tony Paese, Project Editor
Abbey Hastings, Production Editor
Asfa Arshi, Graphic Designer
Greg Isales, Licensing
Natalie Piccotti, Director of Marketing
Kassie Graves, Senior Vice President of Editorial
Jamie Giganti, Director of Academic Publishing

cognella | ACADEMIC PUBLISHING
3970 Sorrento Valley Blvd., Ste. 500, San Diego, CA 92121

ACTIVE LEARNING

This book has interactive activities available to complement your reading.

Your instructor may have customized the selection of activities available for your unique course. Please check with your professor to verify whether your class will access this content through the Cognella Active Learning portal (http://active.cognella.com) or through your home learning management system.

Table of Contents

Preface

Twenty years ago, I was interviewing for a position at a university. The university did not advertise for any particular areas of specialization. However, when I arrived for the interview, while having lunch with one of the faculty, he asked if I could or would be willing to teach theory. I stated that "teaching theory would be fun." He responded, "I don't think I've ever heard someone use the words 'theory' and 'fun' in the same sentence." I had already been teaching theory and always had a nice time with it. Students enjoyed the class. I did not see this opportunity as odd or unusual. Theory was a critical area for which I had some passion. Why shouldn't it be fun?

Regardless, in all the years teaching theory, one area that I found challenging was selecting a textbook the students could understand. Ideally, I would prefer students to read the actual works of social theorists, not what others said or little snippets from actual works. I mean, is it possible to understand Durkheim by reading 10 pages of original works out of a couple thousand pages he wrote? I do not think so. So that left the textbook. In the classroom I would always be told by students that their understanding of the material came through attending lecture. It did not come from the textbook. During the COVID-19 pandemic, lectures were not as easy to come by. When talking one afternoon with a friend of mine, Risa Garelick, regarding postmodernism and how I explain it in the classroom, she asked me to write down what I told her so she could use it. Then, somehow, we got into a conversation about writing a textbook. Risa said I should write a theory textbook. Several months later, here it is.

This textbook is largely targeting undergraduate students. I do not claim to explain every element of every theory or theorist. The aim is to provide enough information that would cover 15 weeks of material. I would hope that faculty would supplement the textbook with lectures, videos, or other materials that would assist in filling out the story of social theory. In addition, the method of writing is more approachable, as I try to avoid the jargon that can be so alienating in theory textbooks. Hopefully, through this method of writing, students will come to enjoy or at least appreciate theory a little more. At the end of each chapter are suggestions for additional reading. I would hope, if you find the chapters interesting, that you take the time to read more on the topics. Reading entire works or even books by some of the theorists is far more comprehensive and actually enjoyable.

Regardless, like any textbook, there will be some information students will like over others. I am hopeful that this text will assist in providing knowledge of some social theory and theorists. Ultimately, in understanding theory, the next step is to apply the theory to some phenomena. That is when the theory turns to practice and comes to life. I hope that this textbook opens that door.

Chapter 1: The Need for Sociology

The World in Which We Live

One of the joys of being a sociologist is that no matter what is occurring in the world, there is never a shortage of things to study. As I am writing this section, it is November 4, 2020. A national election was held yesterday, and currently, the world awaits the results. There is an atmosphere of anticipation, uncertainty, and trepidation. As a sociologist, 2020 has at times felt overwhelming in terms of subject matter. There were times when I just had to turn off mentally and emotionally. There has been too much tragedy, stress, and social turmoil. Between friends and family dying or being hospitalized and many of us having our sole human interaction via Zoom as our escape back to the so-called real world, it is no wonder that many people are experiencing extreme anxiety.

That is life in the 21st century. Whether the focus has been on voting rights, COVID-19, journalism, popular culture, or crime rates, there is always something occurring, and its emotional range is from pure enthusiasm, joy, and boredom to dread and tragedy. The students have changed as well. We are victims of the times in which we grow up, and this generation is no different. They have been shaped in part by the hypervigilance of the media and the corresponding mass amount of information that gets shared. One of those areas involves the concept of *fact,* **which is a truth known by experience or observation**. Students have always questioned the validity of material presented in classes, but now it is different. The problem has not been in the questioning, however, but in flat-out denial. That is new. Too often now, students are denying facts—denying truth. We see this in everyday life as well. A friend of mine was on an ABC news show. When discussing the Black Lives Matter social movement, he cited the FBI Uniform Crime Reports to point out there were and are inequities in the criminal justice system in how groups of Americans are treated. The FBI Uniform Crime Reports are the gold standard in data. They are cold hard facts. A person (nonprofessional, nonacademic) on the show with him dismissed what my friend stated by simply saying that "anyone can come up with numbers." When people have this point of view, it makes it difficult to ever prove a point. Yet this is the place in which we find ourselves in the United States. Our citizens live in different worlds. Numbers are the easiest forms of data to demonstrate. Yet, whether we are talking about crime in the United States or the 2020 election results, people are denying facts. I expect this will continue for some time before we reach an agreement as a people regarding what is real, what is fact. Until we get there, however, a roller coaster existence will probably continue to be the norm.

For myself, I grew up in the 1960s and 1970s. I remember the Watts Riots, the student demonstrations, the Kent State University and Jackson State University shootings, the moon landing, and the Woodstock music festival. I remember the immense grief following the assassinations of John F. Kennedy, Martin Luther King Jr., and Robert Kennedy. I remember watching Robert Kennedy getting shot and killed. I was watching it happen live on TV with my mom. Over 50 years later, it still resonates with me. These kinds of experiences helped shape me. In part because of these experiences, it seemed rather normal that I should major in sociology.

I learned in sociology classes that our lives are indeed influenced by the society in which we live. Social rules and conventions do influence our lives. They create the parameters within which our choices are made. We begin to learn these parameters before we can talk, and they are reinforced, altered, or contradicted every time we enter a social situation. By the time we get to college, these rules are such a part of us that we obey them without thinking. They are normal. We do not even think of them unless someone breaks those very rules. My point is that our environment shapes who and what we are. Any of you who have travelled around the country or world can attest to this fact.

Through sociology, we also learn how or why we connect with some people and not others. Although we may not recognize them, there are reasons for our social behavior, and a knowledge of these reasons is useful in our personal lives and occupations and in recognizing and understanding trends in the world around us. At its best, an understanding of sociology can bring to light an entire new dimension of social forces that influence us constantly. Put another way, sociology can assist people to become more successful in life.

As mentioned above, in the 21st century, we are bombarded by so much information. In sociology, we refer to this as *multiphrenia*, **the idea that technological developments have increasingly exposed people to multiple opinions, values, and ways of life**. The results of this are that people get drawn into potentially larger arrays of relationships, projects, and commitments. Further, in this socially saturated condition, the person is immersed in an extended world of *ought*, or criteria for social acceptability (as in, this is what you ought to do). As a result, the traditional ideal of a single, coherent self is replaced by a sense of self as fragmented and decentered. We are pulled in so many directions that it makes it difficult to commit to any one thing, idea, or identity.

The term "multiphrenia" was used, in particular, to refer to people's experiences of conflict in values, ideals, opinions, and motives. In other words, with this multiphrenic state, it is more difficult to feel centered about things, and potentially, people will feel more swayed over the course of any particular day, month, or year. People are increasingly feeling threatened by not being able to have a stable sense of self. Too much information and too many different stories lead to us being thrown off balance. Considering how many people are tied to their cell phones and constantly being notified of one thing or another, multiphrenia is indeed part of life in the 21st century. More importantly, however, what are the consequences of multiphrenia? If we struggle to commit due in part to the mass amount of information we are inundated with, then fragmentation of a civilization can occur rather easily. We have seen that in recent years within the United States. The fragility of our union has not been this apparent since the late 1850s.

What Is Sociology?

So what exactly is sociology? There are several answers to this question. The dictionary might tell you that it is the study of social relationships, social institutions, and society. The term itself, often credited to Auguste Comte (1798–1857), the founder of the study of sociology, is derived from two root words: *socius*, which means "companion" or "associate," and *logos*, which means "word." At its most basic, then, it means "words about human associations or society." Others may tell you sociology is simply the scientific study of society.

Another way to find out what sociology is would be to observe sociologists at work. Some may spend most of their time looking over volumes from the census bureau or traveling to the deserts of the Southwest to find documentation of the atom bomb testing done in the 1950s and 1960s. Some may use a survey to investigate sexual behavior or study health disparities along the US-Mexico border. Others may look into how college students perceive their professors or how Harry Potter fans become social activists. Obviously, there is a wide range of topics we can study.

If you pursued all these approaches, you would probably find yourself with a bewildering variety of ideas about sociology. What do they have in common? They all suggest that sociology is concerned with every aspect of the social world because everything, in some manner, impacts the thoughts or actions of everyone. As stated by the American Sociological Association (ASA, n.d., para. 1), *sociology* **"is the study of social life and the social causes and consequences of human behavior."** The term "social life" encompasses all interpersonal relationships, all groups or collections of persons, and all types of social organizations. The phrase "causes and consequences of human behavior" encompasses how these relationships, groups, and organizations are interrelated; how they influence personal and interpersonal behavior; how they affect and are affected by the larger society; how they change or why they remain static; and what the consequences are of these factors. This definition reflects the belief that people can be understood only in the context of their contacts, associations, and communications with other people. The very heart of sociology is its concern with the complexities and subtleties of human social life. This makes sociology a discipline that is highly relevant not only to professional sociologists but also to people in virtually every line of work and at every level. If you were to take an engineering or computer science course, you may use the same or similar quantitative methods in doing analyses. The difference is that in sociology you will address how the meanings associated with data impact human beings. How does the phenomena being studied impact humanity? This is an easy, though often overlooked, question in many of the physical sciences. This difference comes in handy when applying for jobs and serves sociology majors well.

Some other areas investigated by sociologists include such things as racial and ethnic relations, prejudice and discrimination, power and politics, and how they relate to and impact jobs and income. The impact is felt on families and family life, school systems and the educational process. Social control is also involved in various organizations, bureaucracies in terms of groups and group dynamics. Sociologists also study leisure, health care systems, military systems, and women's and labor movements. The stratification of people by wealth, education, power, and such differences as gender or age may also be examined. As you can see, sociology is an extremely broad field. It provides knowledge that directly applies to occupations that involve evaluation, planning, research, analysis, counseling, and problem solving. In its most comprehensive sense, sociology can be regarded as including every aspect of social life. Its causes, its forms and structures, its effects, and its changes and transformations.

Why Study Sociology?

In addition to its specific content areas, sociology is also a perspective, a way of looking at society and social behavior. Like the blind men who described the elephant differently depending on where they touched the elephant, everyone regards the world from their own point of view. That is, even when we agree on facts, how we experience those facts differs based on a series of variables, such as age, income, level of education, type of education, gender, where we live, political party, our sources of news, and so on. For instance, one of my cousins just recently came out of a 2-week induced coma due to COVID-19. Until that time, my cousin knew no one who got sick other than minimal symptoms, much like a head cold, or was asymptomatic. He did not disagree that COVID-19 existed; he simply did not think it was that bad. He thought it was exaggerated. Then my cousin got sick. Confirming this belief, he had mild to no symptoms. Around the 14th day, he felt fine and went back to work. Three days later, he was in the hospital being put in a coma. Fortunately, he is going to make it, although he will have to learn how to walk and take care of himself again. It will be months before he is close to normal in terms of his health. He may never return to full health. After his experience, he recognized COVID-19 was not a hoax. While I have had several friends be hospitalized and die, and others suffering the effects of coronavirus months after diagnosis, I have other friends who know no one who has been diagnosed with COVID-19. Our thoughts about facts vary depending upon various factors that will influence how we experience those very facts. The subjective aspect of facts is how we experience something; the objective is knowing something did occur. Inevitably, though, it is important that we understand that there are patterns despite the uniqueness of every person. We tend to follow patterns of speech, attitudes, values, as well as behaviors. We can group people along variables, such as age, gender, political affiliation, sexuality, and so much more. For all our uniqueness, we tend to act, think, and feel like those around us. To understand this phenomenon, we use a sociological perspective.

What is this sociological perspective? It is a conscious effort to question the obvious and to remove oneself from familiar experiences and examine them critically and objectively. This sort of empirical (i.e., concerned with or verifiable by observation or experience rather than theory or pure logic) investigation enables us to determine whether our generalizations about society are accurate. These investigations could involve asking questions about poverty in a wealthy nation, about the social forces leading to unionization, or about the effects of divorce on family life and on children. It will also lead us to understand that the processes involved in human behavior are the same or similar whether people are organizing and demonstrating for human rights or organizing and demonstrating to have the first space shuttle named after the starship *Enterprise*. There are patterns.

This perspective also entails efforts to see beyond individual experiences. The sociologist tries to interpret *patterns*, **meaning the regular, recurrent aspects of social life**. An awareness of interaction patterns and group processes can help us to understand the relationship between our personal experiences and the society in which we live. Human behavior is, to a large extent, shaped by the groups to which people belong, social interactions, and the surrounding social and cultural context. Apart from the social and cultural context, for example, it may be difficult to understand the anger of people in a neighborhood when children are bussed to a school in a different neighborhood. Behaviors such as these reflect the group, the institution, and the society in which they occur. Because individual behavior can be understood more fully in its social and cultural context, the sociological perspective considers the individual as part of the larger society. It notes how the society is reflected in individuals and attempts to discover patterns in behaviors and regularity in events.

Families are studied at three levels: macro, micro, and meso. The difference relates to the size of the unit of analysis. *Macrosociology* **deals with large-scale structures and processes: broad social categories, institutions, and social systems (e.g., war, unemployment, divorce, etc.).** Solutions to these problems are sought at the structural or organizational level. *Microsociology***, on the other hand, is concerned with how individuals behave in social situations**. The social problems of a veteran, an unemployed worker, or a divorcée would be subjects for microsociological research. Solutions would be sought at the personal or interpersonal level. The sociological perspective involves investigations of problems on both scales.

Perhaps the distinction between macrosociology and microsociology can be clarified by elaborating on the issue of divorce. At a macro level, we can observe how divorce rates vary crossculturally by degree of societal modernization or how divorce rates are related to various systems of mate selection, lineage, or place of residence. Those methods will not provide us the details of the divorce or how the people involved were impacted emotionally. When studying divorce at the micro level, we can observe spouses in interaction and note that divorce is more likely to occur if the persons involved cannot agree on important issues, if one person takes a rigid or inflexible stance, or if the personalities of the persons involved are incompatible. At the micro level, sociologists could also understand how the divorce impacted individuals on an emotional level. There would also potentially be opportunities to address friendship networks and how the divorce impacted feelings and behavior associated with friendships. This cannot be achieved at the macro level.

Some sociologists find it impossible and unwise to discuss separately the macro and micro levels, as these levels are interconnected. You cannot have one without the other. Therefore, these sociologists see reality as process—that is, mesosociology. In *mesosociology***, everything is interconnected, so people's language, values, attitudes, and everything else about individuals are determined or strongly influenced by the environment and associations that these individuals had, has, and will have throughout their lives**. The same holds true for societies. They are comprised of everything and everyone within them. In other words, everything is what it is due to the interconnectedness with everything else. To isolate something out from the whole undermines the complexities of life. Therefore, those using this perspective would always integrate and contextualize what they are studying and the implications for their findings. This is particularly of importance when conducting research and reporting findings if the research wants to facilitate change in policy. Otherwise, the research would be too one-sided, and if policy was affected, it might not yield the desired results.

Auguste Comte was born on January 20, 1798. He was a philosopher who is also considered the father of sociology. He wanted to use scientific evidence to identify causes for human behavior. He wanted to develop a system of analysis that would create a better world. He eventually developed what he called "a system of positive philosophy" in which logic and mathematics, combined with sensory experience, could better assist in understanding human relationships and actions in the same way that the scientific method had allowed for an understanding of the natural world.

Comte divided sociology into two main fields, or branches: *social statics*, or the study of the forces that hold society together; and *social dynamics*, or the study of the causes of social change. By using certain tenets of physics, chemistry, and biology, Comte extrapolated what he considered to be a few irrefutable facts about society—namely, that since the growth of the human mind progresses in stages, so too must societies. He claimed the history of society could be divided into three different stages: theological, metaphysical, and positive, otherwise known as the law of three stages. The theological stage reveals humankind's superstitious nature, one that ascribes supernatural causes to the workings of the world. The metaphysical stage is an interim stage in which humanity begins to shed its superstitious nature. The final and most evolved stage is reached when human beings finally realize that natural phenomena and world events can be explained through reason and science. As part of this last stage, humans would develop a moral doctrine that was separate from religion. People would work together to build a better world: a utopia. As part this process, Comte coined the term *altruism*, which is the idea of true selflessness. By living a life that is selfless and working for the benefit of those around us, Comte believed people would create a perfect society.

This view guided many of the sociologists in the late 1800s and early 1900s and is still somewhat of a belief today; that is, most sociologists major in sociology because they want to help make the world a better place. How we get there, however, as you will see throughout this book, varies by the theory or theorist.

What Is Social Theory?

Social theory **is a system of ideas intended to explain something, especially one based on general principles independent of the thing to be explained.** Social theories differ on four points: First is the subject matter, such as micro, meso, and macro, as was covered above. Second are assumptions about human nature. Are our lives determined or nondetermined? If our lives are determined, then we have little to no freedom of choice. We become victims of our surroundings. Prediction becomes easy. Everything becomes cause and effect. If life is nondeterministic, then people create and construct everything in how they interact with the world. People will differ on how they see and experience the world. Their values, interests, and so many other variables influence how people go through life. Life, then, is a negotiation. Therefore, understanding humans would mean getting to know the people one is studying, thereby creating a more thorough understanding of them. Sociologists would then need to understand how people perceive the world around them and how they negotiate not only life's obstacles but also how the obstacles are defined and recognized. I mean, why do some people find science fiction so inspiring while others find it boring? Or why is it that some people think studying for 5 hours a day is ridiculous while others find it necessary and important? Studying people correctly is as important as the topic of the research.

The third difference involves methodology (i.e., the methods of arguments and research). These are deductive and inductive. ***Deductive research* begins with a general idea, a hypothesis, and uses logical reasoning to deduce its empirical implications to draw conclusions as to what happens in the real world**. This is the traditional scientific method of study. In deductive research, one would start with a hypothesis, such as "Children who come from high-socioeconomic status (SES) households will make more money as adults than those who do not." This is easy to test. ***Inductive research*, on the other hand, is when you assert, derive, or induce statements from direct observation of the subject matter. Researchers start without clearly defined hypotheses**. People who use this form of methodology are suspicious of those who solely use quantitative data because they think it is too distant from the subject matter. When looking at the differences between economic outcomes of children from high-SES and low-SES families, those practicing inductive research might choose to search out how the outcomes are influenced. Instead of using hard, numerical data, they might use in-depth interviews and see how those from both economic classes experience life. Those who solely use quantitative data are suspicious of those who use qualitative data because the information can be viewed as being too subjective or anecdotal.

Fourth, and lastly, are differences in objectives. Is the focus of the inquiry on description or explanation? Description involves understanding and comprehension. To describe phenomena requires more than something superficial; it would involve in-depth knowledge of the social phenomena. One friend told me that she has an assignment where she asks students how to make a peanut butter and jelly sandwich. Most students say, "Put peanut butter and then jelly on two slices of bread and put them together." There's no mention of where the peanut butter is, what kind to use, the differences involved, or how to access the peanut butter. The same is true for the jelly. And how do you apply the peanut butter? With your hands, a fork, or a spoon? Where do we get the bread? Do we slice it ourselves? How do we do that? In all, making a peanut butter and jelly sandwich is a detailed process, and usually, we take most of that for granted. It is habit. The same is true when describing any other form of human behavior. It can be quite detailed and nuanced.

Explanation, on the other hand, involves reinterpretation of things to different and more general concepts. Explanation provides a foundation from which the building blocks of investigation can be furthered. If you give an explanation of something that has happened, you give people reasons for it, especially in an attempt to justify it. What is the purpose of a peanut butter and jelly sandwich? Obviously, there are a number of ways to go. I have even heard parents say, "To get my son to shut up."

The History of Social Theory

The history of social theory cannot be discussed without talking about the history of social thought leading up to the advent of sociology in the 19th century. Social theory has its roots in questioning authority. Inevitably, what we see when looking at sociological thought is that sociologists have continually drawn upon views that questioned authority in their day. You have probably noticed that in your sociology classes. The professors show how the system or systems take advantage of people. Sociologists ***debunk* (expose the falseness or hollowness of a belief)** common views held in society. We do this through theory and method. There were several people and phenomena that influenced this aspect of sociology.

René Descartes demonstrated that rationalistic control over phenomena could be obtained through a rigorous use of the mathematical method. Careful observation and clarity of expression served the purpose of the pursuit of knowledge. Sir Isaac Newton combined his religious beliefs and science, believing that the two complemented each other and that the scientific method could be used to find God's will. From here, reason became more and more prominent. God's creation (the world and those who inhabit it) could be understood by rational analysis, and through this, people could see God's plan in motion. Inevitably, this reason began to address the relations of people, one to another, and suggest that there are natural laws that govern human behavior. However, they also began to see that God's creation could shape the structure of human relations. Therefore, we become products of the social.

Philosopher Immanuel Kant (1784) said:

Enlightenment is man's leaving his self-caused immaturity. … Such immaturity is self-caused by lack of intelligence, but by lack of determination and courage to use one's intelligence without being guided by another. … Have the courage to use your own intelligence! Is therefore the motto of the Enlightenment. … All that is required for this enlightenment is freedom; and particularly the least harmful of all that may be called freedom, namely, the freedom for man to make public use of his reason in all matters.

The appeal to reason over authority and tradition: the claim that the individual can take control by means of the critical faculty of the intellect; the powerful idea that freedom and truth are complimentary, mutually reinforcing principles in life. There needs be no contradiction among truth, freedom, individual development, and social good.

Kant also argued that we were moral subjects, separate from the natural world, and we had free choice to act in a moral or immoral manner. A civilized society permits and encourages individuals to act morally. But morality is an act of free will. In other words, a person is a natural object but also a moral subject.

Because of this, sociologists could never judge humans because they were not completely governed by the natural. Humans are free from causal determinants of behavior. Therefore, what we garnered from Descartes, Newton, and Kant was the need to step outside ourselves and use acceptable research methods, a critical eye, and the ability to frame social phenomena in a manner that elicits an objective understanding of the world.

Similarly, something as simple as human migration contributed greatly to sociological exploration and understanding. In Europe between 1500 and 1800, there was a tremendous amount of expansion and discovery both in science and exploration. However, Germany was floundering at a time when other European powers were ascending. Provincialism and the many wars that occurred in the middle of Europe between 1500 and 1800 splintered the German peoples. Business initiatives folded under the weight of political disunity. Local governments were springing up everywhere. With all the chaos around them, a social movement based on a different philosophical orientation to the world around them developed. Germans were fed up with British imperialism, French rationalism, and the overall pragmatic philosophy of the West. What became known as "German idealism" developed through the desire to transcend nation, class, and religion. They spoke in the name of humanity. Some pleaded for religious tolerance on the basis of a common system of ethical values to which all people could subscribe. Others spoke of the unique character and meaning of each culture and how they contributed to the richness of humanity. Idealists challenged the ideas of classical beauty. They found that they offered an alternative to the narrow-minded thought found in everyday life. Along with the development of idealism, Germans began hearing stories of a far-away land people were going to where they could be both free and supported by a central government—the United States of America. In America, they thought they would be able to implement their philosophical beliefs. They thought they could relocate to America, the New World, and in so doing be allowed to carve out a new life for themselves. But instead of assimilation and acculturation, they sought out America as a place where they could continue their cultural traditions.

Lester Ward was born in Joliet, Illinois, on June 18, 1841, and passed away in Washington, DC, on April 18, 1913. He earned bachelor's and master's degrees from George Washington University in 1869 and 1873, respectively. He did considerable research in geology and paleobotany but became interested in sociology as an emerging discipline. His published works in sociology were so well received that, without an academic position, he was elected president of the American Sociological Society in 1906 and 1907. In 1906, Ward was made professor of sociology at Brown University. At a time when sociologists were attempting to integrate social Darwinism into sociology's fledgling canon, Ward stood up against it.

He approached human society from two perspectives. First, he analyzed developments in social organization in terms of how we expend our time and energy. This part of his work is featured in his *Dynamic Sociology* (1883) and *Pure Sociology* (1903). But Ward also emphasized the role of feelings, motives, and will in social affairs, which influenced the social psychology of one of his students, Edward Alsworth Ross, and other social psychologists, such as Charles A. Ellwood (see Cleveland, 2006; LoConto & Jones-Pruett, 2006).

Like many social thinkers of the 19th century, Ward sought to integrate the ideas of Darwin into the understanding of humanity by suggesting an evolution of social order through conflict and resolution of conflict by means of compromise and cooperation. This in many ways was consistent with John Dewey's theory of functional psychology that was developing in the 1890s. This theory asserted that the fruits of previous social achievements made possible the ability of people to direct further evolution by rational effort and acquired intelligence.

Ward opposed the conservative, laissez-faire approach to government. He regarded education as the primary foundation for human progress. In short, Ward anticipated the development of modern governmental responsibilities that manifested themselves during the Great Depression, particularly the expansion of formal education as a funnel for maximum participation by citizens in public affairs.

Hence, in the 1700s, they arrived in Pennsylvania where William Penn had promised them religious freedom. They also arrived in the south and in New York. There, they lived in small, tightly knit ethnic enclaves away from the rest of the communities. They spoke German, ate German foods, married other Germans, practiced their religion (at that time, Lutheran), and had their own newspapers and businesses. They resisted outside interference. Eventually, the colonists began to fear that the Germans would always resist them and the American ways. Colonists feared that, eventually, instead of Germans becoming Americanized, Americans were going to become Germanized. Their only allegiance, philosophically, was with the pluralistic attitudes of the Quakers. This was especially troublesome in the 1700s as Americans tried to gain independence from England. They needed a military, but it seemed the Germans couldn't care less. Germans wanted their privacy and to protect their way of life. They did not want to be bothered by politics and found plenty of land in which they could exercise their freedoms away from the central cities of colonial America. Yet they inevitably did influence the development of American society. Through their behaviors, attitudes, and values, they not only contributed to the United States but also laid the foundation for what would become sociology. We see various levels of German philosophy that all contribute to what sociology is about:

- The Enlightenment facilitated the philosophy of a counterculture revolution that questioned tradition and authority.

- They held that reason would clue us in to God's creation and God's will.

- They thought reason should be used to understand the world and being.

- They believed that science was something pure, objective, and rational.

- Many also thought that humans were part of this creation and were natural beings.

- Others thought humans were moral subjects.

- Expansion brought comparative analyses and ethnocentric themes.

- German idealism brought with it the "separate but equal" doctrine.

- Darwin's thoughts, which are often misinterpreted as only "survival of the fittest," were integrated into various schools of thought that blended rationalism, reason, and evolution, which equated the status quo in terms of process as being good, natural, and a sign of progress.

- Sociological investigation was influenced by both.

However, throughout our history, social theory has been plagued from both ends of the spectrum, with some theorists being very advocacy oriented and others preferring to just sit back and watch. Steven Seidman suggested that we are in a state in which sociology is comprised of those who write sociological theory and those that write social theory. *Sociological theory* intends to uncover a logic of society; it aims to discover the one true vocabulary that mirrors the social universe. Sociological theorists typically claim that their ideas arise out of humanity's self-reflection as social beings. They position theory in relation to a legacy of social discourse, as if theorizing were simply humanity's continuous dialogue on the social. They seek to find a universal language, a universal connectedness, that eliminates the contextual embeddedness. The hope is to add to the common stock of knowledge. In short, sociological theory does not attempt to facilitate change. It is simply an explanation of the social.

Seidman argued that *social theory* is typically associated with social conflicts and public debates. They aim to clarify an event or a social configuration but also to shape its outcome perhaps by legitimating one outcome or imbuing certain actors, actions, and institutions with historical importance while attributing malicious and demonic qualities to other social forces. Social theory relates moral tales that have practical significance; they embody the will to shape history. Social theories attempt to represent the truth, but they arise out of ongoing contemporary conflicts and aim to affect them. Their moral intent is never far from the surface. They are typically evaluated in terms of their moral, social, and political significance. When we look at Karl Marx, and *The Communist Manifesto*, we see him writing with the intention to facilitate change by exposing how the seemingly natural relationship between classes of people can be changed, which would in turn create a utopian society. Similarly, Max Weber, in *The Protestant Work Ethic and the Spirit of Capitalism*, is trying to stimulate the German middle class to motivate them to seize power. Émile Durkheim, in *The Division of Labor in Society,* was trying to protect his government from the attacks of both the left and the right. All three of these early sociologists were trying to use theory to facilitate change—change for the better (because they had some knowledge that others did not).

Since World War II, with the exception of a select few in the 1950s and early 1960s (specifically, the structural functionalism theory of Talcott Parsons), social theory has been the dominant mode of theorizing. You probably see that in your sociology classes. Social theory is used as a means to an end. It is used to explain and facilitate change. In *The Sociological Imagination* by C. Wright Mills (1956), he states that the promise of sociology was to make personal troubles public issues. He suggested that we need to understand that the life of an individual and the history of a society cannot be understood without understanding both. Yet we as a society typically do not define our troubles in terms of historical change or institutional contradiction. People are often not aware of the influences of history on our lives. What Mills (1956) suggests is that through sociology, people can develop a "quality of mind that will help them to use information and to develop reason in order to achieve lucid summations of what is going on in the world and what may be a variety of individuals" (p. 5). Through sociology, we are able to grasp the relationship between history (society) and biography (individual).

Summary

In this chapter, five overarching topics were addressed: (a) the world in which we live; (b) What is Sociology?; (c) Why study Sociology?; (d) What is Social Theory?; and (e) the history of social theory. All work together to lay the foundation for the rest of the book. To understand social theory, we must understand the world in which we live. Too often, people think that the rest of the world is just like their own experiences. Without knowing what is really occurring in the world, we make incorrect assumptions. In knowing what sociology is, we can understand why it is so important for life in the 21st century. Sociology helps us parse out and deconstruct all the various elements of everyday life. We can understand not only how or why an individual makes a decision or acts the way they do but also how patterns of thoughts and behaviors develop, continue, and pervade a society. By understanding social theory, we then move toward methods of explanation, understanding that simply saying "That is just the way people are" or "They are liberal" is not sufficient for explanation. Theories help us frame human behavior and allow us to better understand what is occurring.

We must also understand that social theories are living entities in the sense that they are always adjusting and adapting, changing with the ever-changing world in which we live. You will see in the coming chapters how various theorists have approached social life in a variety of manners, looking at genetics, consensus, interaction, conflict, and the language used in everyday life. These theories also are connected with methodology, which is so key. How we collect data goes hand in hand with the theories we use. In today's world, where we now have the opportunity to access millions of items of data in a matter of seconds or minutes, how we use theory with method is more and more important. Using the wrong methods for a theory weakens the explanation. Pairing the right methods with theories leads to a richer experience with human behavior and social life in general. It allows for a greater understanding and provides the foundation for prediction. All these can lead to helping ourselves and others to make better choices.

Comprehension Questions

1. What would be a deductive piece of research you would like to do? What is an inductive piece of research you would like to do?

2. What are the differences between sociological theory and social theory? Which type of theory is taught in your sociology courses? Which type of theory do you prefer, and why?

3. Explain how microsociological research fits with inductive research.

4. Which type of research would you prefer, micro, meso, or macro? Explain each, but also identify and explain why would choose that direction.

5. Explain the sociological perspective. How does this perspective use empirical methods to debunk false beliefs?

Critical Thinking Questions

1. What is multiphrenia? How is this phenomena or process part of your everyday life?

2. What are facts, and what are the issues we are facing today in the United States in regard to people believing facts? What contributes to the disagreement on facts?

3. How did the Enlightenment influence German idealism? Explain how the ideas associated with the Enlightenment are being addressed in American society today.

4. What falsehoods that are being talked about today in everyday life need to be debunked? Please explain your answer.

5. How has German idealism shaped American society?

6. Explain how the idea of our lives not being predetermined changes how we approach human behavior.

Additional Recommended Reading

Bogardus, E. S. (1940). *The development of social thought*. Longmans, Green and Company.

House, F. N. (1936). *The development of sociology*. McGraw-Hill.

Small, A. W. (1916). Fifty years of sociology in the United States. *The American Journal of Sociology, 21*, 721–864.

Small, A. W. (1924). *Origins of sociology*. Russell & Russell.

Ward, L. F. (1883). *Dynamic sociology*. Appleton.

References

American Sociological Association. (n.d.). *What is sociology?* https://www.asanet.org/about/what-sociology

Kant, I. (1774). *What is enlightenment?* Retrieved May 8, 2021, from http://www.columbia.edu/acis/ets/CCREAD/etscc/kant.html

Chapter 2: Genetics and Sociology

Trying to Find a Way

When sociology began, the goal was to demonstrate its necessity and *validity* (being factually sound). Émile Durkheim's study on suicide (see Chapter 3) was one of the first empirical studies conducted to demonstrate that point. That study demonstrated the promise sociology held. But the validity of the findings was suspect in the scientific community. Durkheim's study and those of other sociologists were often accused of being subjective and anecdotal. There was pressure among sociologists to use accepted methodologies found in the physical sciences. It was believed and advocated that by utilizing those methods, it would be much easier to determine the validity of the findings. Sociologists were trying to find their way theoretically as well. Linking to theories addressing genetics seemed a plausible path. In the field of psychology, the inclusion of alleged instincts was accepted as fact at the time. Therefore, focusing on genetics to understand human behavior was not unusual. In the late 1800s, there was no greater influence than Charles Darwin. Beyond the influence on genetic-driven theories within sociology, you will see in Chapter 4 that he had great influence in processual theories in sociology and philosophy, such as symbolic interactionism and pragmatism. For this chapter, the focus will be on his alleged ideas as they relate the use of a genetic argument for human behavior in what became known as social Darwinism. I state "alleged" ideas simply because Darwin's claim to understanding humanity was never stipulated in *On the Origin of Species*, or at least never clearly laid out. His ideas were interpreted incorrectly, often to the chagrin of Darwin himself.

No sociologists utilize social Darwinism any longer, but for a brief time in the late 1800s and very early 1900s, it was a popular perspective in parts of Europe and the United States. In the United States, we learn the ideas of Charles Darwin incorrectly. We associate "the survival of the fittest" with Darwin when that is not the case. Social Darwinism "evolved," if you will, from a misinterpretation of Darwin by Herbert Spencer. Darwin disagreed with social Darwinism and did not like his name being used to identify it. Nevertheless, social Darwinists believed that people were ranked genetically and were placed in groups, typically in racial groups (Hofstadter, 1944/1992). However, during that time a racial group was defined much differently than today. Typically, any ethnic or national group was considered to be a separate race. For instance, not only were Italians defined as a separate race but there were also two races of Italians, southern and northern (LoConto, 2004). In Ireland, there was such animosity toward Irish Catholics that Irish Protestants were able to create a new race of people by calling themselves Scotch-Irish. It is important to understand that based on scientific analyses in the 21st century, there are no statistically significant biological differences that exist within those groups or any other ethnic groups.

Social Darwinists would use statistical analyses to identify which groups were more genetically evolved. They would do so by measuring (a) income, (b) wealth, and (c) IQ. Their logic was that the more evolved a group of people were collectively, the higher would be their income, wealth, and IQ. These numbers were easy to identify and were an easy way in which to demonstrate the differences. We demonstrate these differences using those same measures today (substituting level of education for IQ) but interpret the findings differently. Here in the United States in the late 1800s and early 1900s, for instance, the numbers demonstrated that those from western Europe (English and French), as well as some northern Europeans (not Irish Catholics) had the highest levels of these three indicators. Social Darwinists concluded that these groups were more evolved compared to other groups, such as Italians, Greeks, and Poles.

Income and wealth were biased, as typically people were emigrating to the United States because they were struggling to survive where they had currently lived. Those already in the United States had time to build a life, buy property, and develop economic stability. IQ also was biased. The belief now is that IQ is heavily based on cultural knowledge. Therefore, people coming from a distinctly different culture would be at a disadvantage. In addition, often the IQ test was given in English to non-English-speaking people. By the second generation for these groups, ironically, their IQs would match other American citizens. Genetics played no role in income, wealth, or IQ. The methods used to reach those conclusions were terribly flawed; nevertheless, these conclusions were used to justify discrimination both socially and legally. The 62nd Congress in 1911 determined that people who were of southern Italian descent were "too nervous a race" and should not be allowed to do dangerous jobs, as people would die (LoConto, 2004). Beliefs like that served to make discrimination commonplace and influenced immigration policies. The goal in the United States was to limit the amount of non-Western and non–northern Europeans into the country (see https://www.migrationpolicy.org/sites/default/files/publications/CIR-1790Timeline.pdf). Nevertheless, there had to be scientific backing for these beliefs.

From Herbert Spencer's point of view, with the persistence of force, anything that is *homogeneous* **(being the same)** is inherently unstable. That is, living in a world that is diverse by nature, some "thing" that is **constantly the same, or static**, cannot adapt or adjust to the changing world in which one lives or exists. This is due in part to the fact that the persistence of force is not consistent to all parts of the whole. Therefore, something that is homogeneous cannot sustain itself. The organism dies. With diversity, however, such as civilization, it can adapt and adjust. For example, say a group of five people were brought together to solve a problem that involved an understanding of gardening. If you have a diverse group, there is a chance that there would be a person within that group who has experience with gardening. They can use their skills to solve the problem. They may even take the lead. But if all people were the same, that is came from New York City, were all hockey players, and had never had any experience with gardening, they would struggle more to solve the problem. Hence, diversity can provide for more abilities to adapt and adjust. Of course, too much might lead to a lack of organization as well. In nature, there would need to be a balance. However, in civilizations that are more diverse, they can adapt. This can eventually lead to the civilization becoming a **utopia (a perfect world)**. Adaptation is the key to evolution. It indicates change. Therefore, to remain static is to die in the eyes of Herbert Spencer and social Darwinists. This adaptation, however, cannot be orchestrated through human laws, because human laws are static. They are not flexible. Instead, the role of the state should be to ensure that peoples' freedoms do not become curbed artificially. Accordingly, then the civilization develops consistent with nature, which would make it the strongest and as well developed as possible.

Social Darwinism had its fans among Christians. Between the time of Galileo and Comte, many Christians had come to believe that science validated Christianity (LoConto & Jones-Pruett, 2014). In the late 1800s, many still had this view. Mainly found among those who believed in predestination, they believed that life was hard and demanding. Those who worked hard were shown to be approved by God. They were the faithful, the saved. Those who spent their time in leisure and waste were looked down upon. Therefore, "economic life was construed as a set of arrangements that offered inducements to men of good character, while it punished those who were … negligent, shiftless, inefficient, silly, and imprudent" (Hofstadter, 1944/1992, pp. 10–11).

It was clear then from a Christian perspective, specifically Calvinism, that God had created natural laws and that it was the role of humans to recognize these laws (LoConto & Jones-Pruett, 2014). Natural selection applied to all things, including humans. The more prudent method of identifying those who were the chosen peoples were those found to be the wealthiest. The fact that many of these individuals were recipients of inheritance only bolstered the argument that these individuals were the result of good breeding. Both Spencer and William Graham Sumner, as well as other social Darwinists, advocated "personal providence, family loyalty and family responsibility, hard work, careful management, and proud self-sufficiency" (Hofstadter, 1944/1992, p. 12). The belief that these rules or laws were handed down from God only demonstrated even more that these individuals were not only the best of the best but also the most qualified to lead the country and discern the norms by which people would live. Of course, by the early 1900s, it became obvious that there was little science to back up these claims. Social Darwinism died out in the United States.

Guiding Questions:

1. How do social Darwinists view state interference?

2. How does the evolutionary process impact views toward the poor?

3. What is laisse-faire, and what are the consequences of such an ideology?

4. What is the role of socialization for social Darwinists?

5. How do or might social Darwinists view foreign policy?

6. What are the key differences between social Darwinists and eugenicists? Please explain.

Herbert Spencer

Herbert Spencer (1820–1903) was born in England, the son of a schoolteacher. He received considerable training in mathematics and the natural sciences but little in history and none in English. Feeling unfit for a university career, he worked as a railway engineer, a draftsperson, and finally as a journalist and writer. One of Spencer's major concerns was with the evolutionary nature of changes in social structure and social institutions (Barnes, 1948; Ellwood, 1939). He believed that human societies passed through an evolutionary process like the process Darwin explained in his theory of natural selection. It was Spencer who coined the phrase "survival of the fittest" and believed that human societies evolved according to the principles of natural laws. This was not an unusual perspective at the time, though other social thinkers, such as Lester Ward and Charles Ellwood, went in other directions. Just as natural selection favors particular organisms and permits them to survive and multiply, societies that have adapted to their surroundings and compete will survive. Those that have not adapted and cannot compete will encounter difficulties and eventually die.

Spencer's theory did, however, at times parallel Darwin's theory of biological evolution. He believed that societies evolved from relative homogeneity and simplicity to heterogeneity and complexity. As simple societies progress, they become increasingly complex and differentiated. Think of this process as the development of a village into a city. If you have experienced that, you see how the introduction of more and more people into the village or small community leads to massive change regarding traffic, crime, friendships, and attitudes. Spencer viewed societies not simply as collections of individuals but as organisms with a life and vitality of their own. The idea of survival of the fittest led Spencer to argue for a policy of noninterference in human affairs and society. We refer to this as *laissez-faire*, **which states that governments should not interfere in the daily lives of people and that natural laws should be allowed to proceed unencumbered**. The goal for sociologists in this school of thought would be to demonstrate how trying to solve social problems caused more problems and inevitably led to the weakening or destruction of the society. Spencer opposed legislation designed to solve social problems, believing it would interfere with the natural selection process. He also opposed free public education, assuming that those who really wanted to learn would find the means. Just as societies that could not adapt would die out, Spencer contended that individuals who could not fit in did not deserve to flourish.

If this sounds familiar, yes, a laissez-faire philosophy is consistent with conservatism, a view that gained popularity for a short time in the Republican Party during the Ronald Reagan administration and continues to a small degree today. When you hear some politicians talking about the need for less government, that view is one of laissez-faire. Therefore, from this point of view, if people are poor, it is the result of their inability to improve economically, not the result of something structurally wrong with the system. From the laissez-faire perspective then, there would be no need to interfere by changing the system. In addition, in the late 1800s and early 1900s, being poor was viewed as a disease or defect, called *pauperism*, which stated that people were poor because of genetics (Davis, 1997). Since social Darwinists believed this inability to be genetic, there was no need to try and help poor people. The "cream would always rise to the top," you might say. Again, as stated above, this impacted immigration policies as well as shaped social interaction among people. To social Darwinists, segregation seemed natural and should not be outlawed.

As you can imagine, Spencer's ideas had the support of people of wealth and power. His theories strengthened the position of those who wanted to keep most of the population impoverished and minimally educated. His ideas also tended to support discriminatory policies. A natural evolutionary law kept people unequal. Spencer thought that conflict and change were necessary parts of the evolutionary process. Unlike social thinkers like Karl Marx (see Chapter 5), however, Spencer believed that planned change would disrupt the orderly evolution of society, which he thought would eventually improve the social order. If we let people move forward naturally, the dominant individuals would prove their worth at the expense of the weaker individuals. The weak would die off … literally.

Methodologically, Spencer was one of the earlier writers to be concerned with the specific problems of subjectivity in the social sciences. He devoted attention specifically to the problem of bias and other difficulties that sociologists face in their work. It was very common in the early teachings of sociology for these sociologists to buy into the view that humans fall into the natural order; therefore, there must be similarities, or the same principles that govern both human society and the rest of the natural world. This is seen throughout the writings of Herbert Spencer but also can be found in some degree in many of the other early sociologists' work. It can also be found in many schools of thought, specifically that of the University of Chicago, with Robert Park leading the way as he documented the continual evolution of cities (Park & Burgess, 1967).

Spencer (1897/2017) identified four parallels between biological and social organisms. It also must be noted that *symmetry*, **or the quality of being made up of exactly similar parts, is very important from this perspective**. Spencer saw humans as symmetrical to other life forms. The four parallels are:

1. Both begin as small organisms and increase in size (mass) through slow, insensible development.

2. Both begin as simple structures and become more structurally complex in the course of their growth.

3. Both begin with parts that are loosely organized and, with a minimum of mutual dependence and increased growth and complexity, become increasingly integrated and mutually dependent.

4. Both biological and social organisms have a life span that is greater than those of their respective units.

But Spencer also found four fundamental differences:

1. Biological entities have a specific and fixed observable external form, whereas societies do not.

2. The units (cells and organs) of a biological entity are physically connected to each other, whereas the members of a society may be spread over great distances without direct physical contact.

3. The parts of a biological organism are more or less fixed and stable in their proximate positions to one another, whereas the individuals who compose a society are not stationary but are capable of physical mobility from one place to another, rearranging their spatial relationships.

4. Consciousness is located in only one part of the biological entity—the brain—whereas each individual in the social organism is capable of independent consciousness of reality.

This last point was an area where Spencer deviated from the rest of the early functionalists from France (e.g., Comte and Durkheim). Here, Spencer suggested that individuals can and will differentiate themselves from the collective whole, while people like Comte and Durkheim stated that the individual would subordinate themselves to the collective whole. This view from Spencer suggested that as societies grew and developed, there would be greater opportunities for differences in choices in all aspects of life. People would move toward difference, increasing the opportunities for adaptation and adjustment. Durkheim allowed for that but saw it as a weakness.

Like functionalists, Spencer felt that as society grew more complex, each of the parts would increasingly become more and more dependent upon each other. However, he felt that this growth would occur slowly over time and would always adjust toward equilibrium. He pointed to the thousands of years it took to get rid of slavery and the hundreds of years it took to get out of pictorial writing as evidence that social evolution took place over long periods of time. However, he stated that as societies evolved, this evolution was fairly uniform, replicating that of the biological organism. But as society evolved, the changes were uniform in their constant increase, and that change begat change. He saw similar changes occurring globally among populations that had no contact with each other. For instance, humans globally went through similar processes of planting seeds to grow plants for food rather than relying entirely on the wild plants and animals they could gather or hunt. They began recognizing seeds from plants with particular traits and planted those seeds in the next growing season. Through this process of artificial selection, they created a variety of crops with characteristics particularly suited for agriculture where they lived. Events like these served to support Spencer's views.

Spencer (1897/2017) argued that since natural change proceeds because of persistent long-run forces, any attempts by the government to facilitate change were foolish and likely to cause more harm than good. He felt that governments were likely to upset the natural order of things. For Spencer, social change or evolution was unidirectional. Societies evolved in the direction of greater geographical and population size; greater density of population, separation, or differentiation into a larger number of parts; greater functional specialization or groups and regions; and increased integration and communication between parts of society. And over time, these societies would develop greater abilities to operate cooperatively with each other and adapt to their environment. For Spencer, natural social evolution was progress.

In addition, while Spencer saw groups serving functions, he believed that once in existence, groups could change their function or lose their function altogether. For instance, Spencer saw the aristocrats originally serving a military function, then to a political function, and then to no function whatsoever. At that point, the aristocrats were no longer functional for the development of society.

However, that does not mean that every society would evolve the same way or in the same direction. He made distinctions between various types of societies. One's physical environment would shape the types of adaptations that people would make. Living in Hawaii requires different adaptations than those for people living in Alaska. Inevitably, foods, clothing, customs, values, and attitudes would be influenced as adaptations to the physical environment. And changes in the physical environment could lead to the destruction of the society. That has been evident with the indigenous peoples of Chaco Canyon in New Mexico or the Maya civilization in Mesoamerica where in both cases drought destroyed civilizations or led to the civilizations leaving the areas. Wars also serve as potential hazards for civilizations, leading to the destruction of entire infrastructures. Therefore, while Spencer saw societies progressing and moving forward, natural and social events could lead to the demise of societies.

Franklin Henry Giddings, son of Edward Jonathan Giddings, a prominent Congregational minister, and Rebecca Jane Fuller, was born in Sherman, Connecticut, on March 23, 1855. Giddings spent most of his time with his two grandfathers who taught him the skills of surveying and mechanical drawing. In high school, teacher Henry H. Scott introduced Giddings to the works of Herbert Spencer, Thomas Henry Huxley, Charles Darwin, and John Tyndall. These scholars would later influence much of his writings in sociology, as they focused on the genetic influences or suggestions regarding human behavior.

Giddings built his reputation as a leading quantitative sociologist, behavioralist, and theorist. He was one of the scholars responsible for transforming American sociology from a mere division of philosophy into a research science. Giddings's work became the foundation for the neopositivism defended by subsequent sociologists. Though little of Giddings's quantitative work was original, his prolific works and programmatic statements paved the way for later scholars working in the field. He developed the idea of *consciousness of kind*, or innate collective feelings of similarity and belonging. Committed to an evolutionary view of society, Giddings believed that human nature is prone to be either progressive or conservative, either of which can be dominant depending on the time and social environment. He also felt that emotion has played an integral part in the development of human society.

Giddings discerned four stages of human evolution: zoogenic, anthropogenic, ethnogenic, and demogenic. He asserted that in the lower stages, individuals were more susceptible to emotional forces. Modern society (in the demogenic stage) is not totally free of these forces but uses reason and critical reflection in determining its own destiny. Giddings also believed that societies could not exist without certain inequalities. In his view, inequality is a result of constitutional or genetic differences, forming the bases for class divisions. Giddings felt that these divisions were natural and led to permanent conflicts.

He served as the third president of the American Sociological Society for the years 1910 and 1911. At the 1910 annual meeting, Giddings delivered a presidential address entitled "The Relation of Social Theory to Public Policy." His influence on sociology came after he retired through his students who inevitably led sociologists to focus more on statistical analysis and not trying to change society. This was an evolution of his thought on laissez-faire. That view quickly died during the 1930s, as the social consequences of the Great Depression were too extreme for sociologists to ignore.

William Graham Sumner

Like most sociologists of his era, William Graham Sumner is largely forgotten (see LoConto & Pruett, 2006; Small, 1916; Sorokin, 1955; Turner, 1990). If Sumner is acknowledged in sociology in the 21st century, it is limited to his work *Folkways* (1906), and little is said other than his contribution to the incorporation of language in sociology that is still used to this day, such as folkways, mores, cultural relativism, and ethnocentrism. Sumner taught at Yale University and influenced his students in such a manner as to shape sociology for decades. He was originally trained as an ordained curate for the Episcopal Church. He left the ministry, however, to focus more of his attentions on the political, economic, and social forces found within society. This training, as was common for many of the early sociologists, would prove to be useful in teaching his students (Barnes, 1948; Bogardus, 1940; Ellwood, 1938). His preparation, charisma, and ability to convey a message within his lectures led students to be motivated and swayed by his teachings (Barnes, 1948; Bogardus, 1940; Ellwood, 1938). His views could be found in the early 20th century in a variety of fields that influenced or changed American policies regarding immigration, the criminal justice system, as well as social mores of right and wrong (Gould, 1996; Hofstadter, 1944/1992).

Sumner's views were evolutionary. Like many of the sociologists or social scientists of his day, he included biology, ***utilitarianism* (making choices in life that maximize happiness and minimize harm),** and their concepts into discussions of the social (see Allport, 1922; Baldwin, 1896; Faris, 1937; McDougall, 1924; Sumner, 1963, 1883/1995; Thomas, 1901; Yerkes, 1910). And like many thinkers, he picked and chose who he would read and what information he was interested in learning (Barnes, 1948). If the views were not consistent with his own, Sumner had little use for that information. While he can be grouped together with Spencer, Gumplowicz, and others in the social Darwinist camp, Sumner was not a disciple of any of these sociologists. To rely solely on the writings or views of any one individual would be uncharacteristic of Sumner (Ellwood, 1938).

As a sociologist, Sumner was someone who stressed objectivity in research. He was insistent that introducing morals into the social science discourse would be problematic for the disciplines. Like other social Darwinists, Sumner believed that if social scientists attempted influencing public policies, they would disrupt the natural order (Sumner, 1883/1995). He said that "those in the social sciences never take account of any ulterior effects which may be apprehended from the remedy itself. It generally troubles them not a whit that their remedy implies a complete reconstruction of society, or even a reconstitution of human nature" (Sumner, 1883/1995, p. 101). As someone who bought into the ideas of social Darwinism and the laissez-faire doctrine, Sumner's role was to make people aware of the natural instincts and developments of humans. He did not suggest creating legislation that would create equality or equal opportunity but instead wanted to identify natural laws and make sure legislation would not interfere with these laws.

Laws of nature do not suggest natural equality. "Class inequality is the natural result of people making the best of what is afforded them. If we are a free, self-governing people, we can blame nobody but ourselves for our misfortunes" (Sumner, 1883/1995, p. 94). Sumner believed that the best government for the United States would be one whose philosophy rested on a doctrine of laissez-faire. In his view, paternalistic tendencies weaken civilizations and remove the ability of the state to provide peace, order, and security. Sumner saw that party leaders from various philosophical presuppositions had taken control or weakened the government by placating to their own selfish aspirations. Therefore, political parties were then simply exploiting the system by changing legislation to meet their own needs. The masses were getting caught in a crossfire of legislative selfishness that corrupted the abilities of the government to function in a manner that is satisfactory for the well-being of all.

The answer then was to remove as much power from the government as possible. This would curtail political parties from obtaining power. Private enterprise could then take control, as it is more efficient than any government. Pressures to remain in business and to obtain a profit would determine the quality of services provided in society. Due to these pressures, private enterprise would never outrun its functions, because it relies on customers and products. Without customers or products, these private enterprises would cease to exist, and this would create a balance. By shrinking the affairs of the government, it then would become more manageable and more efficient. Sumner (1883/1995) had three propositions to defend his views on laissez-faire: (a) that it is morally wrong to extend state activities, inasmuch as the burdens are not distributed in accordance with the benefits received; (b) that the state is proved by history to be incompetent as compared with private enterprise, and moreover, when it extends its activities, it neglects its proper function of maintaining order and preserving civil liberties; and (c) that, since social evolution is primarily a product of nonvolitional forces, the interference of the state in an attempt to accelerate the process of evolution cannot fail to be mischievous and an impediment to progress.

Sumner used the term *speculative legislation* **as meaning something that is designed to alter the social order by direct legislation**. However, he saw this as troublesome, as it would obstruct the system found within the United States. He viewed change in the United States as slow, with historic continuity distinct from dogmatism and abstractionism. In Sumner's views, speculative legislation attacked problems as though the problem itself was rudimentary. This approach created new problems or unintended consequences, as people inherited a vast number of social ills that never came from nature. They were the complicated products of all the tinkering, muddling, and blundering of social doctors in the past. "These products of social quackery are now buttressed by habit, fashion, prejudice, platitudinarian thinking, and new quackery in political economy and social science" (Sumner, 1883/1995, p. 102). Therefore, to attack such problems would be limited in scope as to its effects and thereby may create more problems.

Charlotte Perkins Gilman (1860–1935) was a noted writer, lecturer, economist, and theorist who fought for women's domestic rights and women's suffrage in the late 1800s and early 1900s. She was born in Hartford, CT, to Frederick Beecher Perkins and Mary Fitch Westcott Perkins. Her great-grandfather on her father's side was Dr. Lyman Beecher, the renowned Calvinist preacher. Especially proud of her family lineage, Gilman revered her great-aunts Harriet Beecher Stowe, the noted novelist; Catherine Beecher, an advocate of higher education for women; and Isabella Beecher Hooker, a leader in the demand for equal suffrage. This lineage may have contributed to her belief in genetics as an influence or determinant in human behavior.

Yet at the same time, this did include her viewing genetics playing a part in women's rights. In her book *Women and Economics* (1898), Gilman argued that women could never be independent until they first had economic freedom. While many of these themes were explored through her lectures and papers (Gilman produced more than a thousand works of nonfiction), they also permeated her fiction. In 1892, she published her now-famous semiautobiographical story *The Yellow Wallpaper*. The story depicts a woman sent to rest in the bedroom of a rented summer home. The narrator's husband, a physician, does not believe she is really ill and describes her malady as hysterical tendencies. The woman, however, descends into madness. While the story received mixed reviews, Gilman contended that her purpose in writing it was to reach Dr. Mitchell and show him the failure of his treatments.

Gilman's literary reputation declined in the years before her death, and her ideas regarding women's roles seemed outmoded in the early 20th century. The advent of the women's movement in the 1960s, however, brought about a revival of attention to her work. In 1993, a poll named Gilman the sixth most influential woman of the 20th century, and in 1994, she was inducted into the National Women's Hall of Fame in Seneca Falls, New York.

In the field of education in the United States, conservative Republicans have regularly approached inadequacies with graduation rates to the accountability factor. The solution has been to have standardized tests for students to judge whether they were learning what they were intended to learn. The problem with such an approach is that all schools are not created equal and neither are the neighborhoods in which they exist. When schools fail to get enough funding because property taxes in their communities are low, they often skimp on a variety of supplies, including computers, books, and even toilet paper. For schools whose funding is tied to test scores, they have been forced to spend an inordinate amount of time preparing students to take these tests instead of learning subjects. The result is the proliferation and extension of inequities within America. This is the very thing with which Sumner was concerned. Given this type of argument, sociologists today would agree with Sumner.

Summer (1883/1995) defined laissez-faire as "mind your own business" (p. 104). This, for Sumner, was his idea of liberty. With the government or social doctors getting involved, the natural order would be upset. He never said, however, that laissez-faire would bring a utopia or any form of perfection as Spencer indicated. There are "ills which are inherent in the conditions of human life" (Sumner, 1883/1995, p. 105). Without the influence of those trying to facilitate change, the only troubles that would exist would be those influenced by nature and natural laws. Therefore, in Sumner's eyes, society and those members that comprise it, need little care or supervision.

The doctrine of laissez-faire comes to the fore especially as it relates to the middle class (Sumner, 1883/1995). According to Sumner, the middle class is the backbone of any great civilization. The middle class never asks for assistance from the government, yet in the operation of the government, it is the middle class that gives up part of their wealth to help those below them on the economic food chain. As Sumner (1883/1995) stated, "It's the 'Forgotten Man' who is threatened by every extension of the paternal theory of government. It is he who must work and pay. When, therefore, the statesmen and social philosophers sit down to think what the State can or ought to do, they really mean to decide what the Forgotten Man shall do" (p. 130). In the view of Sumner, the middle class gets taken advantage of by those in power, and thereby they give up more of their own power in return. By taking away from the middle class, civilization weakens. Sumner saw a laissez-faire form of government as beneficial in the long term, as it would protect the middle class from deprivation. Sumner, however, was simply noting what was occurring or what he believed occurred. In this sense, he was not suggesting that this is the best solution but instead suggested that those in power were virtually untouchable in their actions to control their own or anyone else's interests. Because of this, the middle class was always vulnerable to attack by those in power to provide for the poor. Sumner's model was a picture of inequality with those at the top maintaining their power bases by establishing a system of government operating to provide for the poor through the stripping of the middle class. This was made available when people forgot "that a government produces nothing at all, they leave out of sight the first fact to be remembered in all social discussion—that the State cannot get a cent for any man without taking it from some other man, and this latter must be a man who has produced and saved it. This latter is the Forgotten man" (Sumner, 1883/1995, p. 108). This is accomplished through the stripping of rights of the middle class as the "plutocrats," as Sumner refers to them, take in the name of democracy what the priests, nobles, and generals had in other forms of governments throughout history.

> There is a victim somewhere who is paying for it all. The doors of waste and extravagance stand open, and there seems to be a general agreement to squander and spend. It all belongs to somebody. There is somebody who had to contribute it, and who will have to find more. Nothing is ever said about him. Attention is all absorbed by the clamorous interests, the importunate petitioners, the plausible schemers, the pitiless bores. Now, who is the victim? He is the Forgotten Man. If we go to find him, we shall find him hard at work tilling the soil to get out of it the fund for all the jobbery, the object of all the plunder, the cost of all the economic quackery, and the pay of all the politicians and statesmen who have sacrificed his interests to his enemies. (Sumner, 1883/1995, pp. 125–126)

Instead, the politicians built palaces, provided tax cuts for the rich, or provided regressive taxes that served those with money.

> The Forgotten Man works and votes—generally he prays—but his chief business in life is to pay. His name never gets into the newspapers except when he marries or dies. He is an obscure

man. He may grumble sometimes to his wife, but he does not frequent the grocery, and he does not talk politics at the tavern. So, he is forgotten. (Sumner, 1883/1995, p. 128)

What is evident in Sumner's works is that the middle class is stuck paying for the greed of the rich and the inadequacy of the lower classes. The end result was the gutting of the rights and liberties of those whom are the backbone of the civilization. This is no more apparent than in a time of war.

Sumner does not recant from his laissez-faire position when it comes to war. War is something that should only be done as a last measure, and one in which the survival and safety of the people are involved (Sumner, 1963). This is different than the current belief in the United States, which sees conservative philosophy as "hawks" when it comes to war. Sumner's conservative philosophy saw two critical problems associated with war: People would be leaving their "own business unattended to; and second, there is the danger of impertinent interference with another's affairs" (Sumner, 1883/1995, p. 99). Imperialism or these tendencies of the United States were strongly opposed by Sumner. He viewed imperialism as imposing another's will upon a population. Restricting freedoms through conquest or other means completely outweighs any superficial benefit advocated by the nation that would be infringing upon that population. One of Sumner's concerns would surface on the pressures that would be applied to the middle class. Costs, taxes, and a restriction of liberties would threaten the very fabric of American society. "There is no state of readiness for war; the notion calls for never-ending sacrifices. It is a fallacy" (Sumner, 1963, p. 59). Whereas industrialization and the investment in capital build nations, military ventures inevitably lead to destruction. As he stated,

> It is we who are now here who have thrown it away; we have decided that instead of working out the advantages of it by peace, simplicity, domestic happiness, industry and thrift, we would rather do it in the old way by war, glory, alternate victory and calamity, adventurous enterprises, grand finance, powerful government, and great social contrasts of splendor and misery. Future ages will look back to us with amazement and reproach that we should have made such a choice in the face of such an opportunity and should have entailed on them the consequences-for the opportunity will never come again. (Sumner, 1963, p. 49)

Expansion of the state was viewed negatively by Sumner. Imperialism for the sake of exploiting people, access to resources, or expansion hurts a nation in the long term. Expansion placed pressures on valuable resources much like what is seen regarding imperialism when the victim state of such invasion fights back. The costs eventually outweigh the benefits and bring about the end or the beginning of such end to the nation attacking. Sumner referred to historical accounts of the Roman Empire and its way of life based on conquest that eventually led to an army of non-Romans. When the Roman army began to get defeated, they were comprised mainly of defeated peoples who were led by Roman generals. They could not sustain their advances, and the eventual result was the collapse of the Roman Empire. Likewise, at one time, the sun never set on the British Empire, and the Spanish Armada could only oversee so much of the world. The lesson that Sumner taught was that *imperialism* (a policy of extending a country's power and influence through diplomacy or military force) led to expansion of debt, which in turn would get placed on the middle class to pay. Eventually, countries or empires would become so overextended their infrastructure would collapse.

In addition, Sumner said that imperialism eventually led to arrogance. For Sumner (1883/1995), a common attitude that existed at the time was the belief that one's own people were better than another and that any invasion or invasive policies were based on a faulty belief that the invasive peoples were doing this for the benefit of the other country. A problem also existed for the conquered peoples; that is, should they be allowed as citizens of the dominant state or be viewed as a conquered underclass? For Sumner, in this first case, he used an argument that addressed his ideas on social organization. He suggested there would eventually be corruption and the disintegration of the economic, political, and social system, as the peoples incorporated into the new society would not have the history, values, attitudes, or way of life that would be consistent with the dominant nation, thereby calling into question the validity of the views of the dominant nation. Second, Sumner said that by reducing the oppressed to a conquered underclass the country was reduced to a military state instead of a republic. The focus was not on the people who have been conquered but instead on the interests of the dominant nation (e.g., military conquest for the sake of access to oil reserves).

This flies in the face of a laissez-faire doctrine of nongovernment interference in two main ways: (a) The dominant nation state is active and imposing their will on others; and (b) the conquered nation is forced into laws they have not voluntarily and naturally advocated. Both points address the philosophy of laissez-faire: one as it applies to foreign policy and the other at a national level. If laissez-faire was advocated in a nation-state, it would be hypocritical to attack another country unless provoked. Second, the government established in the conquered nation would be completely totalitarian and therefore the opposite of laissez-faire and contradictory of the values of the conquering nation. What would exist would be a nation that advocated laissez-faire yet imposed their will on others and established governments that were not of the laissez-faire doctrine. All the while, the middle class of the dominant nation would get straddled with the costs of such endeavors and would be socialized to believe these things are done for their own benefit in the name of safety and at the exception of civil liberties. War never produces what is wanted. As Sumner (1963) stated, that interference created unexpected new problems; therefore, war is never a rational solution to problems.

> During a period of peace, rest, and routine, powers are developed which are in reality societal variations, among which a certain societal selection should take place. Here comes in the immense benefit of real liberty, because, if there is real liberty, a natural selection results; but if there is social prejudice, monopoly, privilege, orthodoxy, tradition, popular delusion, or any other restraint on liberty, selection does not occur. War operates a rude and imperfect selection. (Sumner, 1963, p. 53)

When there is a need for more knowledge and more reason, war is the destruction of the morals that keep us alive. "We talk of civilizing lower races, but we never have done it yet; we have exterminated them. Our devices for civilizing them have been as disastrous to them as our firearms" (Sumner, 1963, p. 55).

By the end of his career and life, many of the ideas of social Darwinism had either been formally debunked or became largely ignored. However, Sumner's ideas beyond folkways, mores, and ethnocentrism were accepted into the canon of sociology. More importantly, however, Sumner provided a roadmap on how policies can influence outcomes that are unexpected or unwanted. This line of thinking pushed for sociologists to be better prepared to see the various effects of policies and how to anticipate these outcomes. In short, Sumner's work provided us an inroad to thinking past the obvious.

Ludwig Gumplowicz

Ludwig Gumplowicz (1838–1909) was born in Austria. He was one of the most prolific sociological writers of his time. Though a social Darwinist, Gumplowicz was the first avowed sociologist to emphasize the importance of the general sociological concepts of association and socialization as developmental processes (Barnes, 1948). From his point of view, sociology was the study of the interrelation of social groups. Consistent with social Darwinists, he felt that sociologists should focus on trying to identify natural laws. Specifically, however, Gumplowicz studied political groups and political associations. Often, he was listed as someone who focused on conflict, emphasizing the process of survival of the fittest. He used conflict and competition found within the social Darwinist camp as a means of interpretation of the nature, development, and functioning of the state and regarded it as adequate to explain every phase of political action and theory. Many early sociologists viewed social Darwinism as a conflict school of thought because of the writings of people like Gumplowicz and Gustav Ratzenhofer (Bogardus, 1940; Ellwood, 1938).

It was this theory or these ideas that separated Gumplowicz from his leanings toward being a strict social Darwinist. He saw complexity within the world that social Darwinists often would ignore. Gumplowicz saw the state as a social phenomenon consisting of social elements behaving according to natural laws. The state is a formal structure that combines social elements that should behave in accordance with social laws. Therefore, social laws serve to shape human behavior. It is a form of socialization. In this sense, then, social elements precede the state, but the state will then influence these social elements, inevitably leading to new social elements that match the social laws. These processes connecting socialization with social elements were consistent with Darwinian theory that influenced adjusting and adaptation. For Gumplowicz, this occurred through socialization.

However, he distinguished this from society. Society has conflicting groups that have one or more common interests. It is critical to understand that Gumplowicz focused a tremendous amount of his writing on addressing conflict between groups. These groups initially were distinguished along biological or genetic lines. These physiological differences would lead to different needs, values, and attitudes. Groups come into conflict with each other seeking economic gain and hoping to improve their lives. Originally, they killed off others. Later, it turned to political subjugation. Eventually, this would become institutionalized over time. As part of this union that occurred as societies became more organized and institutionalized, Gumplowicz used the term **syngenism, which he defined as "that phenomenon which consists in the fact that invariably in associated modes of life, definite groups of men, feeling themselves closely bound together by common interests, endeavor to function as a single element in the struggle for domination"** (Gumplowicz, 1893/2001, pp. 241–242). Therefore, diverse groups can and will come together because they have common interests to form a society. Society then becomes a group centering around common interests.

The state is a group controlled by a sovereign minority. He did not view the state as having some ethical superiority over the masses, and most likely saw it as the reverse. Gumplowicz felt that no state had ever developed without dominating or having conquest over another group. Yet after such atrocities as genocide and slavery, as things became more "civil," if you will, this instituted more class-based animosity. This would take the form similar to what Marx addressed between the bourgeoisie and the proletariat. Eventually, as states became more structured and somewhat democratic, political parties became interest groups. Gradually, rights were granted to lower classes.

As stated above regarding the evolution of the state, cultural assimilation becomes necessary to maintain some form of stability. **Cultural assimilation is the process in which a minority group or culture comes to resemble a society's majority group by largely assuming the values, behaviors, and beliefs of that group.** Cultural assimilation follows a pattern of (a) the adoption of the language of the conquerors; (b) the acceptance of their religion, manners, and customs, forming a cultural unity; and (c) there comes the physical process of intermarriage wherein an ethnic or national unity is produced. That amounts to the creation of a folk state or nation and is the outcome of social and political evolution. Gumplowicz did not feel that these states were sustainable, however. The overall processes involved in maintenance or expansion would lead to the inevitable decline of the state or the change of the state into another entity. External resistance or internal disruption would lead to this end. His influences were extreme in the sense that his ideas of an immoral state making decisions would lead to a need for overthrowing governments or, if nothing else, would lead to a monitoring of governments to best serve the people.

In this sense, then, Gumplowicz saw the need, as many social Darwinists did, for a sociologist to have a position of authority or to hold some sway. Unlike many of his day, as mentioned above, as opposed to seeing people and societies evolving and creating a utopia, Gumplowicz believed that if guided by a sociologist, it would lead to a lesser degree of institutional development that would see the continuation of social elements that would live long past the nation-state.

Though Gumplowicz was a pessimist at heart, he provided a more sociological approach to social thought than previous social thinkers, such as Spencer. His focus on the importance of socialization became a critical tenet of the fledgling field of sociology and was adopted by those in the functionalist camp as a key element in explaining human organization and civilization in general. Émile Durkheim's ideas surrounding social solidarity are consistent with the ideas of Gumplowicz when it comes to socialization. In addition, his evolutionary view of conflict leading to structure and organization also became part of what would eventually be called The Chicago School, as they analyzed cities that were booming in population in the late 1800s and early 1900s.

Eugenics and Francis Galton

Although most Americans have never heard of him, Sir Francis Galton introduced the philosophy of eugenics, which changed the world. Introduced in 1883 by Galton, the term *eugenics* is derived from the Greek word *eugenes*, meaning "well born." Although Galton originally gave eugenics a broader meaning, it has come to be applied primarily to research and programs intended to improve the genetic constitution of humans. He was instrumental in founding the Eugenics Society of Great Britain in 1908. A sister organization, the American Eugenics Society, was formed in 1926 (Barnes, 1948; Hofstadter, 1944/1992).

To an extent, the ideas of Galton and other late-19th-century eugenicists were at odds with the attitudes of the social Darwinists. The latter maintained that natural processes inherent in the human way of life would automatically select those most fit, making eugenic involvement in human reproduction needless. Nevertheless, it is safe to say that changes in immigration policies and sterilization practices were the direct result of legislators buying into the ideas of eugenics. Countries in Europe as well as the United States believed they were trying to protect the genetic composition of their citizens.

During the first quarter of the 20th century, especially in the United States, eugenicists were seen as progressive. Many of their attitudes now, however, would be classified as racist. For example, there was an implicit belief in the natural genetic superiority or inferiority of various classes and races. Many of the early-20th-century eugenicists thought that racial mixture was hazardous from the standpoint of a possible deterioration of what they called "pure racial stocks."

Galton also worked extensively on problems of inheritance, but he was concerned with characteristics such as human intelligence that are governed by numerous genes and are subject to large environmental effects, especially during the growth and development of the child. Galton's work provided evidence that superior intellect had a strong hereditary component. He found a marked tendency for the children of eminent parents also to attain eminence, and he suggested that a highly intelligent group of people might be produced through carefully choosing the proper marriages for a number of generations.

Scientists studying genetics are still unsure exactly how much of the variation in many polygenic characteristics are inherited and how much is due to environmental influences (this is the well-known nature-nurture debate). It is estimated that at least 25%–50% of the individual variation in intelligence is inherited. How much more than 50% is still being argued.

Unfortunately, most characteristics, such as intelligence, that eugenicists might like to encourage through selective reproduction are polygenic and may be greatly modified by the environment. This means that not only must scientists understand the contributions of various genes to a particular characteristic but they must also know what influence environmental factors may have had in its expression. The data derived from identical twin studies and studies of other closely related individuals indicate that there is an inherited component even in those characteristics strongly affected by the environment.

Aftereffects in Sociology

There is an interesting element of sociology that evolved from these genetics-oriented sociologists. As it became more difficult to demonstrate most of the genetic arguments put forth by social Darwinists and eugenicists at a scientific level, sociologists moved on. Many of these sociologists, such as William Ogburn, who was a student of Franklin Giddings, for much of his career, while disregarding the genetic influence on human behavior, did keep the laissez-faire philosophy. During the 1920s and 1930s, sociology became dominated by sociologists who did not believe sociology should focus on trying to solve problems (see LoConto, 2011). Instead, the goal was to collect data and then provide that to political leaders who would then take the data and use that information to make educated policy changes. They called this "scientism." Few of the original sociologists were alive or, if alive, were willing to stand up to Ogburn and many of the younger sociologists. Charles Ellwood and Pitirim Sorokin, however, tried to counter scientism, but few others joined in. Inevitably, due to the destruction that was caused by the Depression and the developing war, Ogburn and others eventually changed their views to see sociology as a potential means for making the world a better place. By the end of World War II, and with the evidence of the Holocaust, any remaining sociologists who were laissez-faire or who still followed social Darwinism or eugenics changed their views. Since World War II, rarely do or have sociologists advocated these theories, though sociobiology has a small following within the discipline. They do not, however, advocate the superiority of some groups over others.

Summary

When looking at the views of social Darwinists from the perspective of 21st-century life, much of it seems odd. However, we see elements around us. When advocates say we need smaller government, its origins come from people who believed that natural laws should dictate outcomes. Ironically, these same theorists did not believe that laws instituted by natural beings (i.e., humans) were reflective of natural law. Therefore, laws were viewed as largely restrictive in the evolutionary process. We see Spencer being far more consistent with biology in his views of human nature, trying to utilize ideas he interpreted of Darwin's to explain the development of humanity.

His use of these ideas in explaining human aggregates pushed him into an area where it was a logical rationale that if our understanding of nature was complete and if humans were part of nature, that humans would follow these same laws.

When looking at Sumner, he brought more economics (consistent with his training) into his discussion of human behavior, being concerned about the middle class and how governments should or should not make policies that could negatively impact the middle class. Sumner felt that unnecessary policies would put the most pressure on the middle class, as this economic class was the strength of any civilization. Giving money to the lower class would negatively impact the middle class more than the upper class, as the middle class has less disposable income. Likewise, wars would adversely impact the middle class, as monies taken for the war effort would come at the expense of jobs involved in everyday life. Likewise, to conquer a civilization through war would not allow for a laissez-faire governing, as there would need to be a heavy-handedness involved, leading to an overreliance on government restrictions, negating natural laws.

Gumplowicz, on the other hand, saw conflict as part of the process of natural laws wherein peoples would compete against each other in attempting to provide stability. The end result was that leaders would not necessarily have to be ethical in their behaviors, as they are attempting to circumvent overthrow and ensure that stability remains. The key element for Gumplowicz, however, involved his inclusion of socialization as a key element in society. Though conflict is assumed among peoples, socialization would inevitably be used as a means of gaining stability, as people would culturally assimilate, learning the various attitudes, values, and norms of the dominant society. Eventually, through intermarriage and time, people would be viewed as part of the whole.

What we see with social Darwinists is an attempt to try to explain and understand human behavior by utilizing the known or recognized beliefs of the day, just as we do now. So much of the research and social thought of the late 19th century involved a focus on genetics; therefore, it is no surprise that social thinkers would want to follow suit. And while there was virtually no valid evidence to support the claims of genetic influence on behavior or human organization, many social thinkers created a rational explanation of how we operate. Most of the ideas have been rejected, but there are remnants that still remain.

Comprehension Questions

1. What are the key differences between Galton and his ideas of eugenics compared to the ideas of Spencer, Sumner, and Gumplowicz?

2. What are the key ideas of Spencer, Sumner, and Gumplowicz as they relate to the stability of societies? Where do they overlap, and where do they differ?

3. In Sumner's writings, who is the forgotten man? How does he reach that conclusion? What would Spencer say about the forgotten man?

4. How were the ideas of social Darwinists used in United States immigration policies?

5. What are the views of Spencer, Sumner, and Gumplowicz on the role of education in society?

6. How does cultural assimilation in the ideas of Gumplowicz compare with Spencer's views on increasing complexities of civilizations?

7. What are Spencer's ideas on the relationship of the biological organism with the social or societal organism? Why did Spencer need to have symmetry in this comparison?

Critical Thinking Questions

1. Explain the concept of laissez-faire and the consequences of it in creating a civilization.

2. What role does socialization play if we believe in natural laws shaping human behavior?

3. How is the lower class viewed by social Darwinists? What would be national policies developed in societies that advocated the views of Spencer, Sumner, and Gumplowicz?

4. What are policies in the United States today that demonstrate a belief in what social Darwinists and eugenicists advocated?

5. What are social issues that exist today that reflect long-standing cultural beliefs in the validity of the views found within social Darwinism and eugenics?

6. Explain how Sumner's concerns regarding imperialism are evident or not evident in the economic and global policies of the United States, either currently or historically.

Additional Recommended Reading

Barnes, H. E. (1948). *An introduction to the history of sociology*. The University of Chicago Press.

Bogardus, E. S. (1940). *The development of social thought*. Longmans, Green and Company.

Ellwood, C. A. (1939). *A history of social philosophy*. Prentice Hall.

Gumplowicz, L. (2015). *The outlines of sociology*. Sagwan Press.

Hofstadter, R. (1992). *Social Darwinism in American thought*. Beacon Press. (Original work published 1944)

Spencer, H. (2017). *First principles*. CreateSpace Independent Publishing Platform. (Original work published in 1897)

Sumner, W. G. (1883). *What social classes owe each other*. Harper and Brothers.

Sumner, W. G. (1906). *Folkways: A study of the sociological importance of usages, manners, customs, mores, and morals*. Ginn and Company.

Sumner, W. G. (1963). *Social Darwinism: Selected essays of William Graham Sumner* (S. Persons, Ed.). Prentice Hall.

References

Allport, F. H. (1922). A physiological-genetic theory of feeling and emotion. *Psychological Review, 29*, 132–139.

Baldwin, J. M. (1896). Heredity and instinct I. *Science NS III*, 438–441.

Barnes, H. E. (1948). *An introduction to the history of sociology*. The University of Chicago Press.

Bogardus, E. S. (1940). *The development of social thought*. Longmans, Green and Co.

Davis, L. J. (1997). *The disability studies reader*. Routledge.

Ellwood, C. A. (1938). *A history of social philosophy*. Prentice-Hall.

Faris, E. (1937). *The nature of human nature*. The University of Chicago Press.

Gould, S. J. (1996). *The mismeasure of man*. Norton.

Gumplowicz, L. (2001). *La lutte des races: Recherches sociologiques*. Adamant Media Corporation. (Original work published 1893)

Hofstadter, R. 1992. *Social Darwinism in American thought*. Beacon Press. (Original work published 1944)

LoConto, D. G. (2004). Discrimination against and adaptation of Italians in the coal counties of Oklahoma. *Great Plains Quarterly, 24*(4), 249–261.

LoConto, D. G. (2011). Charles A. Ellwood and the end of sociology. *The American Sociologist, 42*(1), 112–128.

LoConto, D. G., & Jones-Pruett D. (2006). The influence of Charles A. Ellwood on Herbert Blumer and symbolic interactionism. *The Journal of Classical Sociology, 6*(1), 75–99.

McDougall, W. (1924). Can sociology and social psychology dispense with instincts? *Journal of Abnormal and Social Psychology*, 19(1), 13–41.

Park, R., & Burgess, E. (1967). *The city*. University of Chicago Press.

Small, A. (1916). Fifty years of sociology in the United States (1865–1915). *American Journal of Sociology, 21*(6), 721–864.

Sorokin, P. (1956). *Fads and foibles in modern sociology and related sciences*. Henry Regnery Company.

Spencer, H. (2017). *First principles*. CreateSpace Independent Publishing Platform. (Original work published in 1897)

Sumner, W. G. (1906). *Folkways*. Ginn and Company.

Sumner, W. G. (1963). *Social Darwinism: Selected essays of William Graham Sumner*. Prentice-Hall.

Sumner, W. G. (1995). *What social classes owe to each other*. The Caxton Printers. (Original work published 1883)

Thomas, W. I. (1901). The gaming instinct. *American Journal of Sociology, 6*(6), 750–763.

Turner, S. (1990). Delusions of empire. *The American Sociologist, 21*(3), 290–293.

Yerkes, R. M. (1910). Psychology in its relation to biology. *Journal of Philosophy, Psychology, and Scientific Method, 7*, 113–124.

Chapter 3: Building Consensus

The Need for Socialization

Consensus building is typically needed to get buy-in from citizens. If we agree that laws are needed and what those laws should be, then having and building a civilization is much easier. In addition, having the same or similar values takes time as well. But the process to consensus can be arduous. That is where socialization is essential. As mentioned in the previous chapter, Ludwig Gumplowicz was instrumental in highlighting socialization. As a sociologist in the 21st century, the concept of socialization is a cornerstone of what we observe in the world around us. *Socialization* **is the lifelong process where people learn the values, norms, and attitudes of a given society**. Though most assume that socialization begins at birth, some have suggested the process begins in the womb (Smith, 2005). To be successful in the culture or subculture in which people live, people must learn the rules and expectations, as well as the reasons for those rules and expectations. In going through this process, people inevitably learn the values, norms, and attitudes necessary to support the rules and expectations. In many ways, we learn the answer to the question of why we do what we do. For instance, here in the United States, most people now believe that they have to have a cell phone of some kind, specifically a smart phone. We learn that cereal, bacon, and eggs are breakfast foods and that sandwiches are appropriate for lunch. We find out that some people do work that is defined as highly valued, such as medical doctors, while those that collect trash are not held in esteem, even though imagine what life would be like if we did not have trash collectors! People learn that particular countries and people are friends and others are not. Women learn to smile when they are tense and also to cry at good news as a release of tension. Men learn that they should not cry at all and even withhold emotion as best they can. Much of what we, sociologists, attribute to the world is due to socialization.

Sociologists are interested in socialization because by studying how people learn the rules and expectations of society, we understand what people will think and how they will act in various situations. If we understand this, we are able to predict behavior in various situations. For sociologists, the civil unrest that occurred in the summer of 2020 after numerous reports of police violence toward African Americans went national was obvious and expected. When you have a population that has experienced discrimination for hundreds of years yet live in a society that proclaims equal opportunity, civil unrest is likely to happen.

But sociology does not have to be only for studying people at an academic level. Imagine someone with a sociology degree working for a marketing firm. Someone in marketing could and does use their sociological skills to ascertain what kind of products people will purchase. They could and do suggest the best ways to market to specific populations. This is all based on a knowledge of how people are socialized.

Research on infants who were comparatively isolated from human contact has shown that a lack of social interaction can have very serious consequences. The Spitz research (1945; 1946) is a classic study on the effects of socialization. In 1945 and 1946, Rene Spitz published work he had done in the late 1930s and early 1940s. He observed children who had apparently been healthy when they were born and who had been living in an orphanage for about 2 years. Nutrition, clothing, bedding, and room temperatures in the home were suitable, and every child was seen by a physician at least once a day. A small staff of nurses took care of the physical needs of the children, but other interaction was very limited.

Despite their excellent physical care, 34% of the 91 children in the home died within 2 years of the study, and 21 other children (23%) showed slow physical and social development. They were small, and some could not walk or even sit up. Those who could talk could say only a few words, and some could not talk at all.

Spitz compared these children with infants brought up in another institution where their mothers were being held for delinquency. Physical care was the same as in the orphanage, but their mothers who had little else to occupy them enjoyed playing with their children for hours. The infants received a great deal of social stimulation, and their development was normal. Spitz concluded that the difference between the orphanage and the home for delinquent mothers was the amount of attention the children received. This served to prove the necessity for human interaction for child development. The development of many of these innocent children were destroyed. Though the study seems rather barbaric by our standards today, it is a testament to the effects we have on each other. Imagine if we all became responsible for each other. Imagine if we took the time to befriend those around us. People have an immense impact on those around them. Community research has found that health outcomes improve for adults if they live in a community where there is a close bond.

All of this is fascinating, to see how we really do influence each other. But how does this apply to social theory and social theorists? All of the sociologists discussed in this section focused on not only the importance of socialization but also the structures that facilitate that socialization.

Guiding Questions

1. How is socialization made possible?

2. What factors/structures/institutions are involved in the socialization process?

3. What are the consequences of socialization?

4. What are the consequences of a lack of socialization?

5. What occurs when people are socialized differently?

Émile Durkheim

Émile Durkheim (1858–1917) was a French sociologist who rose to prominence in the late 19th and early 20th centuries. He is typically thought of as one of the founders of the discipline of sociology. Like many sociologists of his day, Durkheim believed that if orchestrated correctly, sociology could be used to not only make the world a better place but to form a utopia. Durkheim viewed society as a *sui generis reality*, **or a reality unique to itself and irreducible to its parts.** Societies get created when people interact and complement each other to create something that is greater than the sum of its parts. Take, for example, a university. It is far more than classes being taught by professors with support from staff and administration. A reputation builds. Power and influence develop. It becomes an institution. This happens through the process of socialization over time.

When Durkheim began his career, sociology was not recognized as an independent field of study in much of the world. As part of the campaign to change this, he went to great lengths to separate sociology from all other disciplines to demonstrate its uniqueness. For instance, Durkheim maintained that sociology and philosophy were in many ways complementary, going so far as to say that sociology had an advantage over philosophy by using research methods to address philosophical questions empirically rather than theoretically. As a result, Durkheim often used sociology to approach topics that were traditionally reserved for philosophical thought.

Durkheim is the forerunner of *functionalism*, **which is a school of thought within sociology that is based on the premise that all aspects of a society (i.e., institutions, roles, norms, etc.) serve a purpose and that all are indispensable for the long-term survival of that society.** He came from a conservative tradition; that is, he was against the Enlightenment emphasis of individualism that was influencing society. His concern was on the maintenance of social order and what promotes integration, solidarity, and group cohesion. Hence, you can see the need for effective socialization. The more people are socialized to fit into society, the smoother the running of that society will be.

Durkheim wanted to know what creates integration and solidarity in a society (hence the use of socialization as a key factor in his ideas). Two key assumptions of Durkheim are (a) social phenomena are real and exert an influence on an individual's consciousness and behavior distinct from biology and psychology; and (b) social phenomena are facts that can be studied with empirical methods, thus allowing for a science of society to emerge. Regarding the first assumption is the realization of how life impacts us. With the COVID-19 pandemic, as I am writing this people are talking about COVID fatigue or pandemic fatigue. The pandemic shapes how we interact with others. Some people have gone into almost total lockdown. I spoke with a friend recently, and she said she had not touched a human being in 8 months. Still others live in areas where COVID was portrayed as a hoax. I was just reading an article where a nurse was talking about how some COVID patients lay dying, yet they still hold that COVID is not real. The social phenomena we are exposed to is not uniform. Depending on what part of the country we live in or the news sources we use will dictate what information we learn. It will dictate how we are socialized, and that socialization will and does impact how we experience and perceive the world around us.

Likewise, social facts are not reducible but instead have an independent level of existence. *Social facts* are things such as institutions, norms, and values that exist external to the individual. There are three characteristics of social facts. First, they are external to the individual, impacting people from the outside. Second, social facts offer a constraint over the individual. There is a multiplicity of types of constraint, such as roles, law, gossip, social control, structural constraints, mobs, peer pressure, or fashion—to name just a few. We experience all the time doing or not doing something simply because we are concerned about the appearance of what we do and what our friends, family members, or colleagues might say or think. If socialization is complete, internalization will make constraints seem natural. Socialization is seldom complete; therefore, from Durkheim's point of view, this allows for differences in behavior. And third, social facts are general and widespread throughout society, such as social rates and trends, marriage, divorce, and legal codes. Therefore, if we were to look at the social fact of being a university professor, there are expectations that come from the rest of society. One cannot be a university professor unless there is a university with students. The expectation is that the person is well educated and knows a great deal about certain topics. Yet the professor is also an employee and representative of a university. As part of the university "family," the professor has a responsibility as a representative of that university to act appropriately when interacting with people on campus or in the community. What is more, people understand generally throughout the population that a university professor is well respected. There become expectations not only as to how the professor should act but also how the professor should be treated. People grow up in a society, and social facts serve as pressures to conform to the existing structures. Then you throw in further social facts. Let us say the professor is married, has children, and attends church locally. All three (married, parent, and religious) are social facts that serve to frame how the person should behave and how that person should be treated. We juggle these social facts, and if a society is relatively stable, these social facts will function well together.

Similarly, when it comes to morality, Durkheim lurks around the situational ethics argument, though not quite. It is similar in some ways as Mead and Habermas, who are discussed in Chapters 4 and 5. Durkheim stipulates that moral facts are social facts. Acts or action cannot be defined as moral in the interest of one person or even a small group of people. For Durkheim, morality or morals are defined through the collective efforts of a society. That is, just like social facts that are independent of and outside the individual, so too are moral facts. They are developed collectively, become real, and exert a force, carrying all the characteristics of a social fact.

***Collective representations* encompass culture, language, beliefs, norms, and values (i.e., what is worth striving for).** Think of patriotism as a collective representation. What constitutes patriotism varies, but we see that even when singing the national anthem or saying the Pledge of Allegiance, we often place a hand over our hearts. Collective representations are symbols and images that have a common significance and functionally similar understanding and belief among the population. These symbols or images would represent ideas, values, or ideologies. When thinking about collective representations, nationally, one might think of the flag. Think of the way the Capitol Building was talked about on January 6, 2021, when people stormed the

Capitol. This portrayal of the Capitol Building would represent the Capitol as a collective representation. When President Reagan talked about the United States as the "city upon the hill," he elicited a collective representation feel about it. The United States is supposed to be this beacon of democracy that shines bright for the world to see. On a smaller scale, a wedding ring is particularly a collective representation. The family has often been viewed as a collective representation; that is, it has almost a sacred tone. Durkheim used the collective representations in *The Elementary Forms of Religious Life*, so we would want to think of collective representations largely as something almost sacred. The home at one time in America was viewed as a collective representation, but it probably is not anymore, as it coincided with the family. With the increased rate of divorce, it has been weakened. Perhaps things like life, liberty, freedom, and the pursuit of happiness are still viewed as collective representations. Understand that these are also social facts, though not all social facts are collective representations. Collective representations have power over people. This is typically orchestrated through values. Values, for Durkheim, are social facts. They are ideas created by people. Through the power of socialization (that is, through interacting with others), we decide what is of value. These values can be more important than life itself. Think of people giving their lives for their country or their family. Look at secret service officers as they defend and protect government officials. Things have varying degrees of value for us that we learn through socialization.

There is a tremendous amount of importance that Durkheim placed on the togetherness created through socialization and the agreement upon a value system. He used the term *social solidarity* to mean the relationships between individuals and groups that rest on shared morals and beliefs reinforced by common emotional experiences. To ensure a strong social solidarity, there would need to be a strong collective conscience. A **collective conscience is an emergent characteristic of a group or society arising from and supporting a unified mental and emotional response to the events of the world.** In other words, it is when people think alike and value the same things. Hence, with a strong collective conscience, it would be easier to maintain collective representations as well as *social currents*, which are nonmaterial social facts that have the same objectivity and the same ascendancy over the individual but without the crystallized form. These could be enthusiasm, pity, or indignation. They are less concrete but can carry us away if we let them. If one is at a political rally or a rock concert, the enthusiasm is contagious and carries us away often times to a place of bliss. But we are there with thousands of others.

In *The Division of Labor*, Durkheim (1893/2014) analyzed the effects/social functions that the increased complexity of the division of labor has on social structure and the resulting change in the major forms of social solidarity. **Division of labor refers to the degree of specialization found within the workforce.** A low degree of division of labor would suggest that people tend to be jacks of all trades. These individuals can do a diverse array of work. A high degree of specialization is when people do one form of job. Universities are predicated upon a high degree of division of labor with all the different disciplines. As a sociologist, I can teach some sociology courses but not all. However, I cannot go into an art class and begin teaching art. I do not have that expertise. Even, however, in a subject such as businesses, there are various positions where people have their specific work they do. They are only trained in those areas. The accountant does accounting, not marketing or product design. Everyone is specialized in their training. An increase in the division of labor promotes a shift from mechanical to organic solidarity. *Mechanical solidarity* **is a society based on a strong common collective conscience.** This refers to all beliefs or feelings common to the average citizen in the same society. People are alike and share normative behaviors, attitudes, and values. Individuality is not stressed—conformity is. *Organic solidarity* **emerges as the division of labor increases and rests on a high degree of interdependence.** Specialization of the division of labor means more complexity. This encourages the development of individual differences. The basis of social order is interdependence.

Table 3.1: Differences Between Mechanical and Organic Solidarity in Societies

Mechanical	Organic
Lower division of labor	Higher division of labor
Stronger collective conscience	Weaker collective conscience
Weaker individualism	Stronger individualism

Low interdependence	Higher interdependence
Homogeneity	Heterogeneity
Primitive or rural society	Urban or industrial society
Repressive laws	Restitutive laws

Repressive laws are very strong sanctioning. They define *crime* **as any behavior that violates or threatens the strong collective conscience**. They view this as an attack on society. The punishment expresses the moral outrage of the group. It is severe. Restitutive laws maintain and protect the system. They return things to a normal state and are more rational, less passionate, and less violent. Civil cases represent restitutive laws. If a person breaks the law, they pay a fine and move on with their lives.

Durkheim saw two sources of strain in a complex organic society. First is increasing heterogeneity. This could lead to weakening the common bonds that unite people. This would weaken the collective conscience. Individuals would identify with smaller groups within society and not the collective whole. If this goes too far and there is a loss of identification with the larger society, small groups will promote their own views and not those of the collective whole. Arguably, we saw this with the attack on the Capitol Building on January 6, 2021. We saw a splintering of the American populous to a degree where hundreds broke the law and even were advocating murder of public officials, including the vice president of the United States. Second, organic solidarity can be undermined by an excessive use of individualism. This would encourage people to be independent and unique. This can happen if (a) independence goes too far to the point where it can weaken social bonds that unite people to groups or society; and (b) there becomes a loss of an adequate social anchorage. For Durkheim, the individual is dependent upon society for meaning and purpose of life. If these things do not take place, we then find *anomie*, **which is a sense of normlessness or meaninglessness in which individuals feel disconnected from the rest of society**. This occurs at a structural level. There is uncertainty, and life has no purpose. This takes place on an affective, cognitive, emotional, and social bond level.

Suicide

Durkheim was passionate about the discipline of sociology when he first began. As mentioned above, Durkheim felt that sociology could be used to make the world a better place, a utopia. His work on suicide (1897/2007) was a method to legitimize sociology. He stressed social influences on people. That is, if you take the lessons learned from his ideas listed above regarding social solidarity, social facts, and the collective conscience, he applies these ideas and more to the study of suicide. He was writing against certain theoretical perspectives. First, psychology posited that suicide was an act of insanity. Durkheim obtained records of the those with mental illnesses. There were more women in hospitals, yet he found that more men committed suicide. He thought that if suicide was an act of insanity, wouldn't more women be committing suicide? The fact that men were committing suicide at a higher rate warranted caution to the existing cultural view that suicide was an act of insanity.

Second, and similarly, Durkheim found that Jewish people were more likely to experience mental illness yet committed suicide at a lower rate than Catholics and Protestants. Again, this was a similar argument that Durkheim used regarding gender and suicide. If the prominent view was correct, people who were Jewish should have been committing suicide at higher rates. Third was the view that suicide was imitation. Durkheim concluded that people do not just blindly imitate. We are not robots. We will imitate behavior that is highly valued and condoned. Therefore, if suicide was highly valued, there was an obvious problem with society. Taking one's life, according to Durkheim, should not be highly valued, and as far as he could tell, it was not. Therefore, imitation as a reason for suicide was a bad argument. Interestingly, today in the United States, when children commit suicide, it is rarely made known. There is still the belief that suicide is imitated, especially among the young, though there is little evidence to support that claim.

Durkheim (1897/2007) then took these results and began interpreting what he was finding. He concluded that socialization was a key factor in suicide rates. The more we were integrated with each other, the more at ease we felt and the less we commited suicide. Certainly, empirical studies have demonstrated that over the years. Therefore, as people become more fragmented in their associations, lacking integration, Durkheim concluded that suicide rates rose. The form of suicide that reflected this lack of integration he called egoistic. *Egoistic suicide* **is when there is excessive individualism without support or ties to the group.** Social order contains ideas that lead to individuals seeing themselves as being separate. Self-reliance will not have recourse to others in the society. These individuals will more than likely commit suicide because they are unable to use others in the community for support. Durkheim found that unmarried individuals tended to commit suicide at higher levels. This is still true today. Also, intellectuals and Protestants fit into this category when they committed suicide. Intellectuals feel disconnected from others often times because the depth of their knowledge on topics can lead them into isolation, as many others will not be able to "keep up" in a conversation. Durkheim's thoughts on Protestants were interesting. In other religions, there is more bureaucracy. In Catholicism, people will confess their sins to a priest. In Protestantism, people confess their sins directly to God. From Durkheim's point of view, this created more opportunity for isolation. Instead of going to church to interact with others to confess sins, Durkheim thought Protestants confessing their sins by themselves was more isolating, which could explain why Protestants committed suicide at higher rates.

Another form of suicide that Durkheim identified was anomic suicide. *Anomic suicide* **results from partial deregulation or change within peoples' goals or aspirations.** This is related to anomie. When regulative beliefs and norms break down, the effect is to remove the constraints over our desires. Our desires then explode or grow over any realistic degree of attainment and expectation, leading to anguish, despair, and distress wherein human wants/needs/desires become insatiable. They are controlled, regulated, and constrained by social norms. He showed that sudden change in society, such as acute economic crises or exaggerated prosperity, resulted in higher suicide rates. An easier way of addressing this is to think what would happen if the various systems of society ceased. We saw elements of this when restrictions began after COVID-19 was declared a pandemic. Some things shut down or changed drastically. People lost their jobs. Many felt out of touch with the world around them.

A third form of suicide he identified was altruistic. *Altruistic suicide* **is when there are excessively strong levels of integration**: Individuals are less important than the group. Actors find satisfaction in sacrificing for the larger good of the group. When you have a society that values altruistic suicide, there are (a) norms of the group that demand sacrifice; and (b) norms of the group may demand the performance of tasks that are so hard to achieve, individuals will experience failure, in spite of their heroic efforts. This experience of failure will result in severe demoralization. Suicide may be chosen instead of living with disgrace, shame, and worthlessness. Military officers who have suffered defeat would be an example of this. We saw this many times with the Japanese military in World War II, where Japanese officers would commit suicide after failure to win a battle. Durkheim suggested the study of suicide was not the only empirical study to demonstrate social change, solidarity, and social integration. He inevitably encouraged research on all aspects of life. What followed were sociologists taking Durkheim's advice. Sociologists study anything and everything now and demonstrate the validity of Durkheim's claims.

Maurice Halbwachs (1877–1945) was one of the more well-respected and well-read social thinkers in the first half of the 20th century. He was arrested by the Gestapo in Paris in July 1944 and died about 8 months later in the Buchenwald concentration camp. Halbwachs was born in Rheims. He studied under Henri Bergson, who influenced him greatly. Halbwachs's study *Les Causes Du Suicide* (1930) extends and refines Durkheim's classic work on Suicide. Halbwachs felt that the nature and importance of the religious factor vary with the social and psychological context and that this context, in turn, varies in different countries. This aspect of his research placed more focus on more directed, contextualized research and understanding, as opposed to the more sweeping statements made by Durkheim. This approach has continued to this day. Methodologically, Halbwachs's approach brought sociology into a better position to understand everyday life. He used this same approach when considering the influence of collective memory and tradition on beliefs. By situating collective memory and tradition, he was able to provide a better understanding of the fluidity of past and its impact on the present.

Religion

Later in life, Durkheim (1912/2008) began getting disillusioned with what was occurring in the world. Sociology was supposed to make the world a better place, yet life did not appear to be improving at a global level. Between 1890 and 1915, there were 17 wars worldwide. If sociology was to make a difference from when Durkheim began in the early 1890s, it had failed in its attempt to do so. He began to look more into religion as a possible explanation for what was occurring in the world. A sociological study of religion began with the interdependence between religion and society. He studied more so-called primitive societies with the thought in mind that it would be easier to make clear the interdependence. He looked at beliefs, organization, and class. Morality was a key factor for Durkheim as well. Moral action is always aimed at achieving social or societal ends and is never focused on purely individual wishes, goals, or desires. An orientation to collective ends, which is the hallmark of moral action, is developed through socialization and the creation of the social or moral part of people's dualistic nature. Furthermore, a society's health is directly related to how well the collective conscience is developed.

For Durkheim, religion has a *dynamogenic* quality; that is, it has the capacity not only to accommodate individuals but also to elevate them above their ordinary abilities and capacities. It is the ultimate nonmaterial social fact. **Religion is a unified system of beliefs and practices relative to sacred things. Sacredness is the most important aspect of religion.** It is something special people collectively believe. It is awe inspiring. He believed every society distinguished between the sacred and the profane. Profane is the ordinary, everyday world. It has value only to the individual (when used by the individual). It has no social value.

Durkheim was searching for the sacred. What in human experience creates or finds the sacred? He felt it was impossible for the sacred to be found in superstition. It has to be based in something real, phenomena grounded in human life. It emerges out of social interactions and group life. It represents the reality of the group in symbolic form.

Primitive totemic tribes identified themselves by the name of the totem. Totemic objects were believed to embody the sacred spiritual force (mana) that resides in the totem. Since they were related to the totem, they shared in the spiritual force. The feeling of the group to which one belongs is projected/represented/symbolized in this concrete form of spiritual animal/vegetable that serves as a totem. It transcends power beyond the individual. People create the group power of religion that reflects the beliefs of the group.

How do people become aware of such a power? Typically, they become aware when they come together in ceremonial ritual, a social experience in which the intensity of the group is keenly felt. Through intense interaction, while concentrating on the totem or generalization of it, you get a gradual emotional buildup that is reinforced by each person so that all the others are sharing the experience. Each individual contributes to a shared experience, but it transcends the experience in which people are swept up on an emotional high and feel they belong to something greater than themselves. Religious experiences are products of collective beliefs. Contemporary religions lack the vitality of primitive religions, but Durkheim believed this would change and give new forms of social solidarity and provide a sense of power, collective values, and norms.

Inevitably, the views of Durkheim became part of the foundation for sociology that exists today. His focus on the importance of social solidarity and people looking out for each other became the cornerstone of his views. In so many ways Durkheim is the idealist, encouraging people to work together but demonstrating what happens when we do not. It is sad in many ways that people continue to ignore his recommendations.

Max Weber

Max Weber (1864–1920) was born in Germany, the son of a wealthy German politician. He was trained in law and economics, receiving his doctorate from the University of Heidelberg at the age of 25. For the next several years, he taught economics, but he soon succumbed to a severe mental illness that kept him incapacitated and a recluse for much of his life. Despite this condition, Weber was a prolific writer. His best-known works in sociology include *The Protestant Ethic and the Spirit of Capitalism, Theory of Social and Economic Organization, and Methodology of the Social Sciences.* Though Weber is now recognized as a major player in the origins of sociology, his influence did not manifest itself until the 1930s. Talcott Parsons used his powers within sociological circles to translate and incorporate the ideas of Weber into his own social theory. In doing so, he shaped the dialogue within sociology wherein sociologists had to include the ideas of Max Weber.

Weber's mixed feelings toward authority, whether familial or political, are reflected in his writings on the topic of power and authority. Weber discussed why people claim authority and expect their wishes to be obeyed. His approach to sociology, however, has probably been as influential as his ideas. His predecessors considered societies in terms of their large social structures, social divisions, and social movements. In Weber's work, however, the subjective meanings (i.e., the personal beliefs, feelings, and perceptions) that humans attach to their interactions with other humans played a much greater role (Weber, 1930, 1946, 1958). Weber believed that sociologists must study not just social facts and social structures, as articulated by Durkheim, but also *social actions*, **or the external, objective behaviors as well as the internalized values, motives, and subjective meanings that individuals attach to their own behavior and to the behavior of others**. He also contended that social actions should be studied through qualitative, subjective methods as well as objective and quantitative techniques (Weber, 1946). The goal, Weber believed, was to achieve a sympathetic understanding of others. He called this approach *verstehen*, **meaning understanding human action by examining the subjective meanings that people attach to their own behavior and to the behavior of others**. Once values, motives, and intentions were identified, Weber (1946) contended, sociologists could treat them objectively and scientifically.

Action, Economic Class, and Power

Weber did not make assumptions about human nature other than to see people as utilitarian. He viewed human action as the product of seeking material and nonmaterial objects. Therefore, humans were actively engaged in attempting to maximize benefits while minimizing costs. Of course, where one was in society would influence or determine access to material and nonmaterial objects. In other words, people relied on their social relationships. His conception of society was a vast complex of social relationships in which individuals pursue certain ends. These ends would be defined by the state of affairs individuals and groups wanted to bring about. Weber identified three ends: (a) gain economically; (b) gain political power; and (c) gain a style of life. Any of these ends could be ultimate ends, such as becoming rich for the sake of being rich. But to get one of these ends, you may need to get at least one of the other two because they are all instrumentally important and are usually interconnected. All this takes place in an institutional framework—that is, systems of inequalities, politics, power, and social circles. These interrelationships of means and ends are very complex, so it cannot be just the desire to get money. There has to be a variety of institutions and relationships individuals would use to obtain these goals. Therefore, to obtain more money, one might have to become better educated, choose paths that have optimistic and lucrative futures, and network with others who have information to help achieve these ends. One must socialize and be aware of how the various systems work or operate.

Marcel Mauss was born in 1872 in Epinal, France, into an Orthodox Jewish family. He was the nephew of Émile Durkheim. Mauss entered the University of Bordeaux where Durkheim was a philosophy professor. He is best known for his pioneering work on reciprocity and gift exchange in primitive cultures. Mauss viewed gift giving as binding people together in a social relationship that went beyond the material value of the object involved. Thus, he recognized that the act of giving and receiving had an internal component that created a spiritual or metaphysical connection between human beings that transcended the immediate, physical interaction. This giving, however, was never free but instead resulted in some form of reciprocal exchange. He saw the gift as a total social fact, echoing Durkheim's concept. But because the gift had spiritual or metaphysical attributes, it engaged both the giver and receiver of the gift.

This became a critical element that became popular when Mauss visited the University of Chicago. It coincided with some of the theoretical development that was occurring there, as it situated social life as a process that transcended the physical and appropriated metaphysical connections, where actions socially facilitated not only meaning but instead also created a bond between people. Therefore, this could represent a total social fact in that it completed the circle in human interaction.

While visiting at the University of Chicago, Mauss was critical, however, of the lack of theory development as a whole. Sociology at the university focused mainly on the application of ideas to the real world and attempted to solve social problems. While Mauss appreciated the effort and goals, he lamented the lack of theory development that was so common in Europe.

As Weber elaborated on these ideas, he divided this process into three levels of stratification. First is economic stratification. Weber saw this as a crucial step in stratification, as the economic system is instrumental in capitalist systems. Economic class consists of all those who share similar life chances as far as their economic fate is concerned. For instance, a college professor who makes $100,000 a year would have the same or similar class interests as a plumber making the same amount of money, though they may have very little else in common. There are two factors that influence class standing (i.e., the possession of goods and opportunities for income). Classes rest on an objective basis in that their standing is identified in measurable terms. This does not guarantee a class interest, class struggle, or knowledge of their class interest. Because these individuals travel in different circles, there may be little to no interaction. A class struggle will only arise when it becomes crystal clear it is inevitable—that is, when they are stuck in a class or share class interests. Usually, this becomes apparent when being discussed at a national level where all members of the society would be privy to the information.

Second is *status*, **the social construction by which people are ranked based on honor/prestige as manifested in a shared lifestyle.** The result of this is the ordering of people into status groups. Status does not reflect economic class as clearly as it does shared interests in lifestyles. Take, for instance, eight of my friends. Professionally, we are comprised of a sociologist, an engineer, an attorney, a tutor, a television writer, a high school math teacher, a seamstress, a photographer, and a storage peddler. The annual salaries among us are anywhere between $10,000 a year to over $250,000. Yet we share a common love and lifestyle when it comes to Star Trek. We have more things in common with each other in regard to lifestyle than economic class. We do not identify ourselves based on our careers when interacting with each other but instead on our shared enthusiasm for the Star Trek franchise. For Weber, by doing this, the inevitable result of this is the ordering of people into status groups (in this case, Trekkies or Trekkers). Status does not just reflect economic rank. Analytically, it is distinct from economic stratification. People seek status in and of itself, beyond economics. Weber also identified *prestige structure*, **that is, cultural refinement (a person who has high status is more cultured, worthy, and worthwhile).** Prestige is expressed by peoples' qualities of behavior, such as manners, habits, language, sports, body language, or how they dress. These dynamics can be used on other groups or classes.

An important connection that Weber identified, as mentioned above, was *status groups*, **which rest on a subjective bond, an awareness among people that they are bound by a shared lifestyle, shared values, and customs and feelings of social distance from other status groups.** They recognize one another as "our kind of people." They strive to maintain superiority over those outside their social circle when it comes to the subject matter at hand. Let's take, for example, a person who became wealthy through new technologies or platforms, such as someone like Mark Zuckerberg with Facebook. He became a billionaire before he was 30 years of age. He had new wealth. While he may have been respected, he did not have the old wealth of a high-prestige family. His money alone was not sufficient to become part of the status group of "old money." Other things are important to be considered old money, such as family background and generational wealth. Related to status groups are *adjustment mechanisms*, **where sometimes groups will adapt new ranking systems to raise their level, such as lower class religious groups or sects.** They see themselves as morally superior. Today, sociologists have noticed there are all kinds of indicators of status in society, such as education, income, occupation, race, ethnicity, residence, and lifestyle, to name a few.

Third is political power. Weber identified this as "party." Party is likely not as important as it was when Weber wrote his paper "Class, Status and Party"; however, it is likely that he was referring more to the concept of power associated with party. He died before he finished the section on party. ***Power* is the ability to impose one's will on another, despite the resistance of others**. People may strive to obtain political power for its own sake or to enhance their class or status. The political party is the type of organization that has power. This is clearest at the societal level. It is independent of itself. Processes in society involve competition between individuals and between groups to achieve economic gain, status, and power. Out of this process, inequalities may result. These inequalities can be correlated across all three strata, but not necessarily so; therefore, the three need not go together. Economics need not be the determining factor, though in a capitalist system it remains very important. Nevertheless, if we were to talk about power as it relates to political party, we could see people networking and gaining favor with others. In smaller settings this is easier to do. Whether it be a university or a small town, when networking, you can gain access and work your way up the ladder politically to have more say in the running of things. The process, however, still works at larger levels.

Associated, however, with political power is socialization. People have to buy in to the structure of society. People need to obey rules. Socialization is the vehicle to get people there. Weber identified five characteristics of the system of political domination: First, there are people who issue orders. Second, there are people who receive those orders. Third, there is the existence of a belief that those giving orders have a right to do so and that those receiving the orders have an obligation to obey. There is a legitimacy of authority. Fourth, there is an existence of a staff to execute commands to ensure the orders are communicated and that they are obeyed. Lastly, there is a belief that rulers or those in power have the right to use physical force.

The crucial factor for analysis and comparative purposes has to do with the third point: the structure of legitimating belief. What is the belief that people have? Weber felt this is important. Rulers are usually in the minority. Force alone will not work. This is why beliefs are important. Consider Nazi Germany. People nowadays portray Hitler as a monster and madman. However, there were 80 million people living in Germany when he took power. Why did people not stop him? How come some Jewish people were loading other Jewish people onto trains that were taking them to death camps? People follow rules if they believe the authority is legitimate. Getting people to comply is the basic problem every political system faces. That is why governments are concerned with how people perceive them. Nevertheless, through socialization people develop beliefs of how things should run. Once the beliefs develop, it is difficult to have them swayed. Beliefs tend to exist in a manner similar to Durkheim's social facts, and in Durkheim's views, beliefs are social facts. Beliefs inevitably serve as a force against and with people.

Related to this is the belief in *authority*, **the probability that a person will be obeyed based on a belief and the legitimacy of the right to exercise influence**. This is consistent with what socialization provides. We grow up learning to obey authority. According to Weber, there are three kinds of authority, which are ideal types. An ***ideal type* is a kind, category, class, or group of objects, things, or persons with particular characteristics that represent something**. The first is *traditional authority*, **which is a belief in the sanctity of immemorial, traditions, and customs**. These are traditional rules and time-honored customs. One important reason for obeying the custom is that it has always existed, or it feels as though it has always existed. The tradition says you should obey. And what is obeyed is the personal authority, not the office or position. Rebellion is against the person, not the system. The pope could fit with traditional authority. There are good popes and bad popes. There have been rebellions over various popes, but the tradition continues.

Second is *charismatic authority*, **which is where the leader is believed to have extraordinary or supernatural qualities or power**. Here there is a devotion to the specific and exceptional sanctity of an extraordinary person or persons and the normative order revealed by them. They have a mission, plan, vision, or project. It could be social or economic. People perceive these individuals collectively and believe in their mission. This confirms legitimation. Charismatic leaders arise against the powers that be, not oriented to a long-lasting stable routine. This calls for a break from tradition. Charismatic movements are unstable and fluid. The group is organized around an emotional form of communal relationship. Disciples would be the administrative staff. They arise to the call of the leader and have very intense relationships with the leader. There can be a lot of self-sacrifice. Their movements fail to endure after the death of the leader. However, there can be times where there develops a *routinization of charisma* **where the leader becomes structured, such as the case with the pope**.

Third is *rational legal authority*, **which rests on the beliefs in the legality of existing rules**. The belief is that the rules were established according to proper procedures. There is a belief that those elevated to authority have the right to issue those commands. Subordinates obey because the rules say so. Rules belong to positions and not to individuals. They have a right to issue commands from office. There are certain features of rational legal authority: (a) Functions are bound by rules, duties, and tasks; (b) people have a limited sphere of competence, expertise, and specialization; (c) there is a hierarchical organization—that is, a clear-cut ladder of authority; (d) there is a separation of administrators from the means of administration and staff; and (e) the office is not personally appropriated or owned. The person fits the office. These features exist for one basic reason: to get orders from the ruler to the ruled as quickly and undistorted as possible. This is bureaucracy. They are paid salaries.

Bureaucracies are the dominant type of organization in the modern world and reflect this rational legal authority. They are very efficient. They have legal restrictions and make no personal distinction, no discrimination, no favoritism, and no personal privilege, ideally. Office holders are accountable for their actions due to the rules.

Bureaucracy

A *bureaucracy* **is a formal organizational structure that directs and coordinates the efforts of the people involved in various organizational tasks**. It is a hierarchical arrangement of an organization's parts based on the division of labor and authority. A hierarchical structure is like a pyramid where the people at each level have authority over the larger number of people at the level below them. The authority resides in the office, position, or status, not in a particular individual. In other words, the responsibilities and authority associated with a particular job in the hierarchy remain the same, regardless of the person occupying the position. Weber believed bureaucracies were part of major modernization of the world. There is a growth of rationality, using our head and not our heart. Judgment, reason, calculation, evidence, and logic are used as the basis for understanding each other and reality. You can see this everywhere with contractual lifestyles, schools, military, marriages, occupations, communities, and in the field of medicine. He did not say this was good. This did not necessarily lead to personal happiness.

Weber's ideas on bureaucracy began with bureaucracy as an ideal type. Weber did not concern himself with describing a specific bureaucracy; rather, he wanted to identify the general principles that govern how they operate. An ideal type of bureaucracy, then, is not to be thought of as a perfect entity in the usual sense of the word "ideal." Bureaucracies are often far from perfect. Weber identified six characteristics of a bureaucracy. Below is a typology of bureaucracy from Weber:

- Division of labor: The staff and activities of an organization are divided into units. Each unit has carefully described responsibilities, and each job is designed to meet a specific need.
- Hierarchy of authority: Organizations are run by a chain of command—a hierarchy of bosses and workers who are, in turn, the bosses of other workers. All officials are accountable to those at a higher level for their own responsibilities and for those of subordinates.
- Rules and regulations: The operation of the organization is governed by a consistent set of rules that define the responsibilities of various positions, assure the coordination of tasks, and encourage the uniform treatment of clients. These rules are stable and comprehensive.
- Impersonal relationships: Employees play roles. They occupy positions. When they leave that position, they are replaced by someone else to play that position. So bureaucracies are comprised of people playing positions. They are not unique individuals. Therefore, relationships are not necessarily close.
- Career ladders: Employees typically understand that there is a structure in place that allows for specific promotions. They understand they will not get hired immediately as CEO but instead may have to begin at the bottom.

- Efficiency: Though the word "bureaucracy" is often used to describe lots of paperwork and slow processes within business, bureaucracies are able to move mass amounts of information and complete a great amount of work effectively and efficiently.

McDonaldization

Related to Weber's work on bureaucracies is George Ritzer's work on McDonaldization. ***McDonaldization* is the process by which a society takes on the characteristics of a fast-food restaurant** (Basirico et al., 2010). McDonaldization is a reconceptualization of the work of Max Weber and his ideas on bureaucracy and rationalization. Where Max Weber used the model of the bureaucracy to represent the direction of this changing society, Ritzer sees the fast-food industry as having become a more representative example. Ritzer provided four characteristics of McDonaldization.

The first is efficiency, which is another way of saying the optimal method for accomplishing a task. Ritzer equates this with the fastest way to get from Point A to Point B. In the example of McDonald's customers, it is the fastest way to get from being hungry to being full. Efficiency in McDonaldization means that every aspect of the organization is geared toward the minimization of time. I went to an Applebee's restaurant for lunch one day. They placed stopwatches on dining tables at lunch time, telling the customers that if their food did not arrive in 15 minutes, the meals were free. Likewise, other aspects of efficiency can be seen with carpool lanes, express lanes, ATMs, and the drive-thrus. According to Ritzer, societies are increasingly becoming more McDonaldized.

Second is calculability—that is, the objective should be quantifiable. McDonaldization says that quantity equals quality and that a large amount of product delivered to the customer in a short amount of time is the same as a high-quality product. This allows people to quantify how much they are getting versus how much they are paying. Organizations want customers to believe that they are getting a large amount of product for a small amount of money. This is seen throughout fast-food restaurants with their value meals. Research over the past 3 decades has demonstrated that Americans will buy more products if they believe they are getting a deal. For workers, they are judged by how fast they are instead of the quality of work they do.

Third is predictability, which means that no matter where a person goes, they will receive the same service and receive the same product every time when interacting with the organization. This also applies to the workers in those organizations. The tasks of workers are highly repetitive, highly routine, and predictable. When I travel around the United States, the various strip malls have the same chain stores selling the same products, as well as being surrounded by the same restaurants.

Lastly, control refers to the concept of employees and the operation of the businesses. More and more control can be seen when employees are either being replaced by machines or, more importantly, that the machine is doing the work the employee used to do. We can see this with pizza ovens. The uncooked pizza is placed at one end of the oven, and it moves through the oven, emerging on the other side. When it comes out, the pizza is done. The cook is no longer required to watch over the pizza in the oven. The computerization of many of our duties becomes obvious when the "system" goes down and many workers do not know what to do.

While McDonaldization is prevalent, there is a slow-food movement that began with Carlo Petrini in 1986 in Italy. McDonaldization is viewed as the Americanization of the world. People want to maintain their customs and traditions to ward off this Americanization. The slow-food movement emphasizes a slower lifestyle, stressing community over the individual. People are encouraged to take their time and work with their environment instead of stripping it, as is often the case with modernization. People are not considered customers or consumers but are viewed as working *with* the product being produced. Good food, good taste, and nutrition are at the heart of the slow-food movement. Therefore, homemade meals with fresh vegetables, fruits, and nuts are incorporated into the meals. Wine is also part of meals. Sitting down at the dinner table, taking one's time, and talking with each other is part of the experience. The goal is to savor each moment.

While this may seem strange for many Americans, at one time this was the way of life. Prior to the invention of microwaves, box dinners, and cable or satellite television, the norm in the United States was to sit and enjoy a family dinner. Encouraged by those technological innovations, as well as cell phones, the internet, and many other technological developments, Americans have found themselves more and more isolated from each other. Americans are rushed and preoccupied. Contact with each other has increasingly been through Facebook, Twitter, and texting. The human element of contact is going the way of the dinosaur. A concern for Robert Putnam was that if democracy was to endure, there needs to be social trust. But he found that without social connectedness, there is no trust. So as Americans increasingly isolate themselves with less and less social contact, democracy appears on the wane. It will be interesting to see if this trend continues in the United States.

Religion

In his book *Protestantism and the Spirit of Capitalism*, Weber (1930) studied the ethical system of Protestantism and the way it exerted an economic influence and promoted the growth of the modern capitalistic system. He studied various individuals and schools of thought: Luther, Calvin, Pietism, Puritanism, Methodists, and Baptists. His thesis for this book was that ideal interests could create an impetus for social change. Weber referred to this process as the Protestant work ethic. For Weber, the Protestant work ethic is an inner-worldly ascetic religious orientation more fully developed than in any other religion in the world. Inner-worldly asceticism is a commitment to deny oneself or limit severely the opportunity for the indulgence of physical and sensual desires or the enjoyment of materialistic pleasures to pursue a higher or spiritual goal, and this goal is to be achieved through systematic and diligent commitment to the task to be performed in this world. This resulted from genuine beliefs regarding the role of the church in mediating between the person and God. According to Weber, it was through this inner-worldly asceticism that led people to work hard, save money, invest, and inevitably build a strong economic system.

In Catholicism, the church was the link. Catholicism was more otherworldly. They downgraded the importance of earthly life. In the marketplace, profit did not exist. There was a just price, a price that enabled the seller to maintain their traditional social status. There was no usury—that is, making money on interest (lending money produces money). For Weber there was a stark difference between Protestants and Catholics in terms of their contributions to the capitalist system.

During the Protestant Reformation, according to Weber (1930), leaders were not aspiring capitalists. They were religious leaders, and their concern was to restore the true faith. They attacked the sacramental system where God's grace was governed by the priests. The reformers believed an individual could come to God personally. God's grace was available to everyone; therefore, there was no need for sacraments, as was found in Catholicism. With this shift in emphasis, these reformers downgraded the status of the church officials. Everyone would be equal before God. With this came equal opportunity to serve God in all vocations. Secular occupations took on a sacred calling. There was a duty to serve God, and you did so by doing your job as best you could. Religious obligation was extended to occupation as being part of the "walk" of every person. Work became part of the sacred quality of everyday life. Weber said that work became the highest form that the moral activity of people could assume. This stressed a lifestyle where behavior was controlled and regulated. People became devoted to their work as a religious duty.

Adoption of this lifestyle would have no bearing on life after death. They believed they were born in sin. Salvation was God's choice. People concerned with salvation see these issues as important. As Christians, they cannot be indifferent to their eternal fate. They suffer from anxiety, stress, and uncertainty. They needed a sign that indicated they were of the elect and would be able to enter heaven. With secular occupations seen as religious duty, it became natural that these individuals would see prosperity in their occupation as a sign of their salvation. What resulted was a motivational pattern: (a) devotion to occupational duties; (b) a strong achievement drive; and (c) a limitation on consumption. This inevitably fit with capitalism or a move directly toward capitalism. There then began a drive to seek profitability, to live a frugal lifestyle, and to ensure all the profit would go toward investment. In an age where motivation was religious and noneconomic, there became a change in attitude on usury; it became a positive quality. Capital accumulation developed through credit. According to

Weber, Protestantism represented a major break in tradition, from traditional to rationalism. This was not limited to economics. Robert Merton (1938), when speaking of Weber's ideas, said that Protestantism's growing rationalization led to (a) an increasingly disproportionate number of scientists because they were investigating the mysteries of God; (b) equality of all people being expressed in the growth of democratic institutions; and (c) providing an early stimulus for new universal education. However, secular activities began to undermine religious beliefs. Secularized attitudes influenced society. The Protestant ethic led to materialistic success, and people eventually began to enjoy this. This led to eroded beliefs and the move away from the ascetic lifestyle. Consumption became the informal rule of behavior that exists to this day. This was a gradual process, and certainly, socialization played a key role in the formation of attitudes, values, and norms that developed.

The impact of Protestantism, however, would not be permanent. It stimulated the formation of capitalism, but it did not mean capitalism should need a religious stimulation. It became autonomous, self-sustaining. The major point of all this is that an idea can play a role, regardless of the material conditions. The stereotypical bourgeois capitalist did not emerge anywhere in the absence of inner-worldly asceticism. You will see later how social thinkers like Theodor Adorno and Max Horkheimer used this change in how people thought of work and money to their criticism of the culture industry. It is an extension of Weber's ideas, integrating also the ideas of Karl Marx.

When looking at the work of Max Weber, one sees a tremendous amount of influence on modern sociology. His works, which are extensive, far beyond the scope of this text, have served to create the foundation for sociology and how to be a sociologist. None of this would have occurred if it was not for the work and influence of Talcott Parsons.

Talcott Parsons

Talcott Parsons (1902–1979) influenced the intellectual bases of several disciplines of modern sociology. His work was concerned with a general theoretical system for the analysis of society rather than with narrower empirical studies. He is credited with having introduced the work of Max Weber and Vilfredo Pareto to American sociology.

After receiving his bachelor's degree from Amherst College in 1924, Parsons studied at the London School of Economics and at the University of Heidelberg, where he received his PhD in 1927. He joined the faculty of Harvard University as an instructor in economics and began teaching sociology in 1931. In 1944 he became a full professor, and in 1946 he was appointed chairman of the new Department of Social Relations, a post Parsons held until 1956. He remained at Harvard until his retirement in 1973. Parsons also served as president of the American Sociological Society in 1949.

Parsons is typically viewed as the founder of structural functionalism, which integrated much of the work of Max Weber—that is, his rationalism with the general ideas of functionalism. Structural functionalism has its roots in the work of early sociologists, especially Durkheim and Weber. Among contemporary scholars, it is most closely associated with the work of Parsons and Robert Merton. Structural functionalism was the dominant American social theory of the mid-20th century. It fell out of favor during the civil rights and counterculture movements of the late 1950s and 1960s, yet their legacy remains a large part of sociology.

The terms "structure" and "function" refer to two separate but closely related concepts. ***Structure* refers to the complex and stable framework of society that influences all individuals or groups through the relationship between institutions (i.e., economy, politics, religion) and social practices (i.e., behaviors, norms, and values).** ***Function* refers to the purpose and action of these said structures.** Structures can be compared to the organs or parts of the body of an animal, and functions can be compared with the purposes of these structures. The stomach is a structure; digestion is its function. In the same way, health care organizations and the military are social structures (or social systems), and caring for the sick and defending governmental interests are their functions. Like a biological structure, a social system is composed of many interrelated and interdependent parts or structures.

Social structures include any component, or part, of society: clubs, families, nations, groups, and so forth. Central to an understanding of social structures are the concepts of status and role. Simply defined, a *status* is a socially defined position (e.g., woman, student, lawyer, Catholic, etc.). Some of these are **ascribed statuses— that is, given to us at birth (e.g., age, sex, race)**—whereas others are **achieved statuses (e.g., college graduate, father, teacher) where people work and earn their position**. Sets of interrelated statuses or positions are social systems. The interrelated statuses of mother, father, and children, for example, constitute a family system. The interrelated statuses of teachers, students, and school administrators constitute an educational system.

Each social system performs specific functions that make it possible for society and the people who comprise that society to exist. Each serves a function that leads to the maintenance or stability of the larger society. The educational system is intended to provide literary and technical skills; the religious system is intended to provide emotional support and to answer questions about the unknown; families are intended to socialize infants and children; and so on. The functionalist perspective assumes that these social systems have an underlying tendency to be in equilibrium, or balance. Any system that fails to fulfill its functions will result in disequilibrium, or an imbalance. In extreme cases, the entire system can break down when a change or failure in any one part of the system affects its interrelated parts. Parsons's ideas were to create a general theory that could be used by anyone to explain what was occurring in society. While socialization played a part in his theories, he tended to try and explain behavior through various systems of analyses, creating categories through which human behavior could be explained. One of the more general theories that he addressed was his systems theory where every society is comprised of four systems: The first is the *cultural system*, **which is the meaning and symbolic system of society**. These include the values and goals of the people in the system. Second is the *social system*, **which are the rules and norms telling people how to behave or interact, such as role, status, and position**. Third is the *personality system*, **and here is where we would find the identity or psychology of the individual persons and their motivation and self-gratification**. Last is the *behavioral organism*, **which are the biological dimensions or the physical aspect of people, such as the body or the brain.**

All four systems are involved in shaping peoples' behavior and thought. People interpret society through all four systems at once. All dimensions are real and interact together. While one can take a snapshot of what is occurring in society and focus on one system, in process, they are all interacting together—hence Parsons's fixation early in his career on action. He goes beyond Durkheim in terms of an analytical approach. Parsons is much more specific in his analyzation of what is occurring in the world.

What really put Parsons on the map among sociologists was his general theory of action. This is something that is still used to some degree within sociology. In the general theory of action, there are four elements: (a) an individual or collective; (b) goals; (c) situations or contexts; and (d) normative standards. In the process of using these four elements, researchers recognize that people are inspired by goals; therefore, researchers identify the goals of the individual or collective. They would identify the context where the individual or collective are acting, as well as the tools, facilities, conditions, and resources the individual or collective can use. Lastly, researchers would focus on the normative standards—that is, the expectations based on the first three areas of the action theory. Most people are inspired by the goals. People follow the rules every day. This takes place continually. Parsons emphasized these parts of life. He focused on the cultural system and the social system, mainly, which are the source of the goals and norms regulated.

He identified five pairs of patterned variables (Parsons, 1951; Parsons & Shils, 1951). These show that individual's behaviors are not uncertain. We do have expectations. A pattern variable is a dichotomy, one side of which must be chosen by an actor before a meaning of the situation is determinant for actors and then before they can act with respect to that situation. It is a kind of problem for actors who need to solve problems before acting. They are structured because of boundaries. Socialization gives rules on how to act. Therefore, when people are moving throughout the day, while they are making decisions on how to act, this becomes so natural that people do not acknowledge the judgments they are making in the moment unless they are extreme.

Parsons broke the patterned variables up as such:

- Ascription versus achievement: *Ascription* refers to qualities of individuals, often inborn qualities, such as sex, ethnicity, race, age, and family status. Typically, these will dictate a life course or life opportunites for people. These are things they are born into. *Achievement*, on the other hand, refers to performances of individuals and emphasizes what people achieve in life. For example, we might say that someone has achieved a prestigious position even though their ascribed status was that of poverty and disadvantage. We act toward people based on these perceived traits, or we actually even act accordingly based on those traits we have.

- Diffuseness versus specificity: Diffuseness and specificity deal with the range of obligations involved. These refer to the nature of social contacts and how extensive or how narrow the obligations are in any interaction. In everyday life, we rely on friendships and family relationships to meet our needs. These individuals in our lives wear many hats; therefore, the relationships are more diffuse. We rely on friends for a broad range of types of support, including conversation, support, accommodation, and intimate relationships. The diffuse relationships associated with everyday life have the potential of dealing with almost any set of interests and problems. Just think about how the amount of diversity exists in terms of conversations you have with friends and family. It is quite diffuse. In the workplace, however, social relationships are very specific, where we meet with or contact someone for some very particular reason associated with their status and position. In a university, we have specializations in areas of study where we are the experts in that field. Not only am I a sociologist but also within that field I specialize further in social psychology, disability, and race/ethnicity.

- Affectivity versus affective neutrality: This set of concepts refers to the amount of emotion (affectivity) that is appropriate or expected in any social interaction. The role one is playing or the context in which the interaction occurs will influence the amount, if any, of emotion acted out or felt. Therefore, at a funeral, there probably will be more emotion felt and acted out among those who were friends or family of the deceased, while in the business world, a bureaucracy may be devoid of emotion and characterized by affective neutrality. Affective neutrality may refer to self-discipline and the deferment of gratification.

- Particularism versus universalism: This pair refers to the range of people that an individual must consider when involved in social action. The issue here is whether to react or act toward people based on a specific relationship, such as that with a loved one where you have a connection that is particular and specific to that individual or in the workplace where people are expected to follow general rules.

- Collectivity versus self-orientation. This pair emphasizes the extent of collective or shared interest as opposed to self-interest that is associated with social action. Each social action is carried out in a social context and in various types of collectivities. Where individuals pursue a collective form of action, the interests of the collectivity may take precedence over that of the individual.

Even with this organization, according to Parsons and Shils (1951), the pattern variables do not have to happen exactly like this. Sometimes, people choose or are influenced by both patterned variables. Regardless, patterned variables can be used to analyze large macro structures, as well as the values of society at the cultural level. Classifying is just the first step in analysis. He then came up with the functional imperatives of adaptation, goal attainment, integration, and latency (AGIL). He wanted to build a framework to describe all interactions. This again is a general and systematic model, like all of Parsons's work. The survival and maintenance of a system required the solving of these four basic problems:

- *Adaptation*: The problem of securing or acquiring resources from the environment, then distributing them for survival throughout the system (e.g., economic institutions, food, machinery, oil, transportation, etc.).
- *Goal attainment*: Creating or making shared goals, and achieving those goals, such as political institutions.
- *Integration*: Interrelatedness of the parts of society and the need for solidarity if the system is to function effectively. This ensures the rules of the system are followed. Key examples are legal institutions. They uphold the norms of society.

- *Latency* (latent patterned maintenance): The need for actors to play parts they are motivated to play. This keeps the value system intact. This involves conforming to the values and ensuring the values are transmitted/learned through schools, family, and religion.

The key point here is that these are prerequisites of the social equilibrium and the survival of society. This is secured by two processes: (a) socialization and (b) social control. If socialization is successful, all or most of society will be committed to shared values; that is, people will have similar choices. This is a matching of role expectations and need dispositions. Socialization creates complementary expectations. This means all parties involved in an interaction have learned and shared values, norms, and beliefs so that each person knows what is expected of them and what to expect of others. People are motivated to the demands of societal expectations. The basic motivation will be to meet the demands of others.

The above theory of action was dominant in terms of analyzing human behavior in the 1950s and 1960s. As mentioned earlier, it began to crumble in terms of analyses during the civil rights and counterculture movements of the late 1950s and 1960s. The mass amount of change, the questioning of authority, undermined the stability and consensus on which Parsons tended to focus.

Dennis Wrong was one of many of the critics of Parsons. Wrong (1961) felt that Parsons represented what would be considered an oversocialization of humans. He suggested this gives Parsons the illusion in which he underrates other parts of social life, such as power and the unconscious. In addition, Wrong suggested that Parsons had no theory of change, that Parsons focused much of his career on seeing societies as evolutionary and comparative. When looking at Parsons's work on change, we do see this evolutionary process. In one of his last major works, *Societies: Evolutionary and Comparative Perspectives*, Parsons (1966) identified four basic processes of change. First was differentiation, where the division of a unit or of a system is divided into two or more units or systems. This led to increased specialization or a higher division of labor. Second was adaptive upgrading, which is increased control or dominance of the environment. This is where people become more adept at what they are doing. This resulted in increased efficiency and productivity, made possible by specialization and differentiation. Third was inclusion, where integration and keeping all parts connected were made possible. This involved such things as organizing society on a democratic basis, or the right to vote and participate. In organization structures, this is team building. Because this is a theory of change, inclusion was part of the process wherein previously excluded groups were allowed to contribute. We can see this as the ending of apartheid, or the end of segregation. Lastly was value generalization—that is, the tendency of shared values to become more general and abstract as differentiation increases. For a civilization to become stable, the overwhelming majority of the population has to share in common values and attitudes. Partially shared values in a society will not work. This is like Durkheim's collective conscience in that people would eventually buy into the values and attitudes of the whole. If value generalization does not occur, differentiation can lead to divisions or civil war. We have seen elements of this occurring culturally in the United States, where the collective conscience or value generalization has weakened.

Parsons had various concepts that fit into various aspects of his systems of analysis. One of these concepts was ***institutionalized rationalization*, or that societies would have a value system in place that would facilitate change**. An example of this is that Americans tend to value science and technology, and therefore, the roll out of new ideas through technology is an acceptable reason for changing behavior, whether it be through new phones, computers, or other forms of technology. Overthrowing a government is typically not viewed as a rational choice to facilitate change.

The structured nature of society is also found in how Parsons discussed the more micro leanings of social analysis. Everything was relatively structured. Take, for instance, the concept of role. The position or the situation that a person occupies in society is called "status." As a result of that status and position, people are expected to discharge certain functions. These functions are known as "roles." In life, people have a great variety of roles, such as father, mother, firefighter, clerk, consumer, bus driver, teacher, voter, politician, and so on. These roles are an integral part of group behavior, but they also reflect how a society needs to function properly. If people act out the appropriate roles, society functions smoothly. If not, chaos can develop. Think of how a class would spiral out of control if students in the class did not play the role of student but instead played the role of angry customer.

An example of a role would be the sick role. The *sick role* **is a concept that concerns the social aspects of becoming ill and the privileges and obligations that come with it**. Parsons (1975) believed that someone who gets sick is not a productive member of society and therefore gets policed by the medical profession. Hence, you should be able to recognize how people behaving appropriately allows for other roles to be acted out, functioning together. The general idea was that the individual who had fallen ill is not only physically sick but also now adheres to the specifically patterned social role of being sick. What are people supposed to do when sick? Do they stay home from work and school? Go see the doctor? Others will stay in bed and drink plenty of clear fluids. These behaviors are all developed and become part of the structure of a society. People become socialized to know how to act these out.

Ultimately, Parsons was a larger-than-life figure and dominated sociology for decades. His contributions to sociology involve the mass amounts of concepts that are now commonplace within the discipline. His focus on being more analytical in evaluating social life also has been instrumental in making sociology conduct itself in a more scientific manner. Ultimately, like so many sociologists, once Parsons fell out of favor, he was largely forgotten. Few textbooks mention Parsons any longer, and still fewer sociologists take the time to read his works.

Robert Merton

Robert King Merton (1910–2003) was a student of Talcott Parsons at Harvard, and his interests were varied and reflect the continual changes that occur within the discipline. After receiving a PhD from Harvard in 1936, Merton joined the school's faculty. In his first work in the sociology of science, following a similar path as Weber did with the *Protestant Work Ethic*, *Science, Technology and Society in Seventeenth Century England* (1938), he studied the relationship between Puritan thought and the rise of science. He next served on the faculty of Tulane University (1939–1941) and then accepted an appointment at Columbia University (1941), where he became a full professor in 1947 and was named Giddings Professor of Sociology in 1963. He served as associate director of the university's Bureau of Applied Social Research (1942–1971).

One difference between Parsons and Merton is that Merton believed that there should be theories of the middle range. These theories look at specific parts of society, or at specific problems, typically associated with mesolevel analysis, connecting the micro with the macro. This way, it provided a fuller picture of what was occurring. Merton stressed actions that impact the survival of the social systems. He was not concerned with the subjective expectations or orientations of people. He was concerned with the objective social consequences of the situations. That is, Merton was concerned with outcomes in that he was not so much interested in peoples' motives or their perceptions but instead how their actions impacted outcomes. For instance, some people did not like former president Trump yet liked many of his policies; therefore, they voted for him. For those who own stocks, the market did well during his presidency. This is consistent with Merton's social theory and analysis. The focus is on the outcome. Therefore, those that did not like President Trump yet supported him looked at how the outcomes during his presidency impacted them personally. It is a very utilitarian perspective. Merton insisted on maintaining a strong distinction between subjective motives and objective consequences. It was not peoples' intentions as much as it was how things turned out.

Merton inevitably translated this approach into functions that are manifest and latent. This is something that is typically in every introduction to sociology textbook. *Manifest functions* **are consequences that you expect, that are obvious**. For example, you come to college to gain an education or a degree. The manifest functions of going to college are part of the brochures and other propaganda associated with that school. *Latent functions* **are consequences that are not intended or recognized**. They are more hidden. Latent functions are the source of sociological explanation. For instance, there is a good chance you will meet your future spouse or partner while attending college. You may experiment with different drugs or behaviors that many would deem deviant or bad. These are not part of the advertising found in college materials. Yet they serve as latent functions that open other doors for students.

Parsons's work tended to imply that all existing institutions are inherently good or used as a function. Merton did not believe this. In his view, some practices are *dysfunctional*; **that is, some practices or institutions can have negative consequences for society**. It is going to lessen adjustment or integration and possibly increase strain in the system. The consequences vary depending on who you are talking about. For instance, people who break the law and end up in prison may learn how to be better criminals. Therefore, when they are released from prison, they may have gained better criminal contacts that help them succeed in breaking the law. Or, more simply, they could have been isolated from society for so long that when they return, they lack the social skills to integrate back into society. In essence, potentially, for some, prison serves as a dysfunction because it influences inmates to be less successful in life after they are released.

Likewise, is poverty functional or dysfunctional? This distinction can be brought out by using manifest and latent functional analyses. Poverty is also functional or dysfunctional depending on whom you ask or what point of view you take. Poverty certainly provides jobs for those who inevitably work in social services. Their jobs are to assist those who are disadvantaged. In the United States, we also place more police officers in these areas, operating under the assumption that more laws will be broken. However, poverty is also a drain on resources for a society. The lack of income means less tax revenue. This lack of tax revenue impacts the quality of the schools children attend. The maintenance of those areas of cities or communities are also underfunded, lending to less upkeep, thereby making the areas look more rundown and lowering morale. Inevitably, what we know is that people born into poverty are also more likely to die in poverty.

The dysfunctional aspect of various structures and their functions can inevitably lead to deviance and deviant behavior as people attempt to adjust and adapt to their surroundings.

From Merton's point of view, deviant behavior is not due to an abnormal personality but stems from problems with the social structure. Therefore, if the economic system is constructed poorly or is negatively affected by outside forces, which leads to unemployment of citizens, what are the consequences of that phenomena? We typically see suicide levels increase and more negative health outcomes due to stress, children potentially having to "hustle" to help with raising money for the family, and adolescent children potentially delaying college because of lack of funds. Do these same children take on debt via student loans? Do some individuals turn to deviant behavior? Merton (1938a) said that deviant behavior results from strains in the social structure. These strains arise from a lack of fit between two key elements in society—that is, goals and means, otherwise known as values and norms.

Values are culturally defined goals; they legitimate our objectives. *Norms* are culturally approved means of reaching our goals. Rules and regulations describe how we are supposed to seek goals and the avenues through which we reach them. Merton came up with what he referred to as "anomie theory." Some now call it "strain theory." *Anomie/strain theory* posits that when the two (that is, values and norms) fit or match, society runs smoothly. There is equilibrium. When the two do not fit, deviance occurs.

This takes place in four steps:

1. There develops a disjunction between goals and means.

2. Social stress occurs when people cannot attain the means to reach their goals.

3. Anomie develops as the rules of society fail to influence people.

4. Deviance occurs.

Merton reasoned that in American society, it is encouraged that all people should strive for success, and that entails income and wealth. Two core values of American society are success and equality. It is reasonable to expect that the means to achieve these values and goals would be readily available to everyone. This is not the case, however. For different groups, the means are different. This creates a disjunction. The greater the disjunction, the greater the chance of deviance. Merton developed a scale that describes alternative modes of adaptation to stress and the fundamental ways deviance will develop.

Table 3.2: Merton's Anomie Theory Typology

Modes	Goals	Means
Conformity	+	+
Innovation	+	-
Ritualism	-	+
Retreatism	-	-
Rebellion	+,-	+,-

As seen in the table above, Merton listed five ways in which people adapt to the goals of a culture and the institutionalized means of achieving them. Only conformity to both the goals and the means is considered nondeviant. With conformity, people buy into the goals and the means to achieve those goals. They are successfully socialized to follow the accepted path to success whether they achieve that success or not. The other four methods of adaptations are all varieties of deviant behavior, including Merton's second mode of adaptation: innovation. Innovators accept social goals but reject the normatively prescribed means of achieving them. Students who want to get good grades are adhering to widely held values, but if they cheat, they are violating a norm for achieving that goal. Therefore, cheating is an innovation to achieve the goal of a good grade. When computers and the internet became the common mode used by school administrators, some students would hack into university systems and change their grades or gain access to exams. This allowed them to have the grades they needed, but they broke the law to achieve them. At one university I worked at, the residence halls were across the street from my office. One night the FBI showed up on campus and surrounded one of the residence halls because one of the students was hacking into the systems.

A third mode of adaptation is ritualism. *Ritualists* follow rules rigidly without regard for the ends for which they are designed. Office managers who spend all their time making sure employees come to work on time, do not drink coffee at their desks, and do not make personal phone calls are ritualists. By focusing on petty rules, they lose sight of the real goal of the office. Ritualists conform to traditions and never take chances. Merton said that lower middle-class Americans are likely to be ritualists because parents in this group pressure their children to compulsively abide by the moral mandates and mores of society. This form of adaptation is not generally considered a serious form of deviant behavior. People cling to safe routines and institutional norms, thereby avoiding dangers and frustrations that they feel are inherent in the competition for major cultural goals. If you have ever heard people saying something like "Things have always been this way and will always be this way," it is safe to assume they probably have ritualist leanings.

Retreatism is a more drastic mode of adaptation. *Retreatists* reject both the cultural goals and the institutional means. These individuals are truly aliens: They are in the society but not of it. They are members of their society only in that they live in the same place. Merton spoke of retreatists as potentially being vagrants and vagabonds, as he was writing during The Great Depression. However, today we might think of individuals who join cults who physically and socially isolate themselves fitting this adaptation. Retreatism is probably the least common form of adaptation, and it is heartily condemned by conventional representatives of society. Retreatist deviants are widely regarded as a social liability.

The fifth and final mode of adaptation is rebellion. Rebels, such as members of revolutionary movements, withdraw their allegiance to a society they feel is unjust and seek to bring into being a new, greatly modified social structure. Most social movements, such as the gay rights or women's liberation movements, fall short of what Merton considered rebellion because these activists do not reject most societal goals. These movements do advocate substituting new values in some parts of society, however. Merton said that it is typically members of a rising class rather than the most oppressed who organize the resentful and the rebellious into a revolutionary group.

Merton's theory has been criticized on a number of different grounds (Thio, 1988). Some critics argue that it erroneously assumes that a single system of cultural goals is shared by the entire society. It has also been faulted for failing to explain why some people choose one response, while others choose a different one. Other critics argue that Merton's theory ignores the influence of societal reactions in the shaping of deviance and the fact that much perceived deviance involves collective rather than individual action. Finally, much criticism has been leveled at Merton's underlying assumption that deviance is disproportionately concentrated in the lower socioeconomic levels.

Anomie/strain theory does have some strengths, however. It provides a framework for examining a wide range of social behavior, it has stimulated many research studies, and it has raised the social consciousness of deviance analysts. This last-mentioned point is particularly true of some members of the new generation of sociologists. These theorists have devised conflict theories of deviance that emphasize the widespread social oppression and basic contradictions found at the heart of our socioeconomic system. Merton views deviance as something wrong with society, that there is something out of whack. Deviance is a sign of disequilibrium and dysfunction in the system. Repair work is reform or revision of the system. This could occur by developing a new agency to deal with the deviance.

Robert Merton was a highly influential sociologist of his time, though due to the changes that were occurring, gradually lagged behind in development after the 1960s. His work on the sociology of knowledge (1972) is still used as a means of explaining the process by which groups of people fail to work together and understand each other. He focuses on the polarization of knowledge and how diverse groups seek to not only acquire truth but to also possess it. This inevitably leads to an us-versus-them mentality among the populous.

Summary

Inevitably, what we see through the above theorists is the interplay between large-scale structures and individuals. We see how people are socialized to fit into a society. More importantly, we see the grasp that society has on individuals and how people are shaped by it. We learn to recognize right and wrong, and we stand up and want retribution when people do not follow rules. Rules and regulations become so ingrained in society that we learn to accept them as normal and obvious. Inevitably, we come together, recognizing our place. Beyond that, however, we also learned from theorists like Émile Durkheim that humans need each other. We look out for each other. One element that is necessary for humanity is that human connection. Durkheim as well as Merton identified how critical it is for humans to be there for each other. That social support is a critical element of the development and maintenance of human societies and humanity in general. Weber and Parsons gave us a more critical eye for analysis, searching for analytical tools to evaluate social phenomena. What we found with the above theorists is a structure for understanding people and societies.

Comprehension Questions

1. What are social facts? What are three characteristics of social facts? List and explain five social facts that are part of the college student life.

2. Late in his career, Parsons became interested in evolutionary theory. He developed a four-part theory that outlined the four basic processes of change. Explain this system of change.

3. According to Talcott Parsons, what are the four systems that every society is made of? Explain how they assist in doing evaluative research in American society. What is the strength of this approach?

4. What is Weber's thesis for the Protestant ethic and the spirit of capitalism?

5. What are the three things that Robert Merton said Protestantism's growing rationalization led to? Explain how these things are either positive or negative.

6. Explain what a status group is. How is an ethnic group an example of a status group?

Critical Thinking Questions

1. What are the similarities and differences between the views of Durkheim and Weber on religion? Which view better explains the role of religion today, and why?

2. Some have suggested that in the United States, individualism is the only thing that is sacred, if we used Durkheim's use of the term "sacred." Explain what sacred and profane are, but also provide an argument that would support the idea that individualism is the only thing sacred in the United States.

3. How does dehumanization occur in Weber's views of bureaucracy? How is that consistent with Durkheim's views on organic solidarity? During the time of COVID, has this been amplified, stayed the same, or shrunk? Please explain and support your answer.

4. Explain how Parsons's action theory would approach and explain the behavior of a college student on an average day.

5. How would Merton's anomie theory address how people are adjusting to life after COVID?

Additional Recommended Reading

Durkheim, E. (2007). *On suicide*. Penguin Classics. (Originally published in 1897).

Durkheim, E. (2008). *The elementary forms of the religious life*. Oxford University Press. (Originally published in 1912).

Durkheim, E. (2014). *The division of labor in society*. Free Press. (Originally published in 1893).

Merton, R. K. (1968). *Social theory and social structure*. Free Press.

Parsons, T. (1951). *The social system*. Free Press.

Parsons, T. (1966). *Societies: Evolutionary and comparative perspectives*. Prentice Hall.

Parsons, T. (1967). *The structure of social action*. Free Press.

Parsons, T., & Shils, E. A. (Eds.). (1951). *Toward a general theory of action*. Harper and Row.

Weber, M. (1930). *The Protestant ethic and the spirit of capitalism* (T. Parsons, Trans.). Scribner's.

Weber, M. (1946). *From Max Weber: Essays in sociology* (H. Gerth & C. Wright Mills, Trans. and Eds.). Oxford University Press.

Weber, M. (1958). *The city*. Free Press.

References

Basirico, L. A., Cashion, B. G., Eshleman, J. R., & LoConto, D. G. (2010). *Understanding sociology* (5th ed.). Horizon Textbook Publishing.

Durkheim, E. (2007). *On suicide*. Penguin Classics. (Originally published in 1897).

Durkheim, E. (2008). *The elementary forms of the religious life*. Oxford University Press. (Originally published in 1912).

Durkheim, E. (2014). *The division of labor in society*. Free Press. (Originally published in 1893).

Merton, R. K. (1938). *Science, technology and society in seventeenth century England.* The University of Chicago Press.

Merton, R. K. (1938a). Social structure and anomie. *American Sociological Review*, 3, 672-682.

Merton, R. K. (1972). Insiders and outsiders: A chapter in the sociology of knowledge. *American Journal of Sociology*, *78*, 9–47.

Parsons, T. (1951). *The social system.* Free Press.

Parsons, T. (1966). *Societies: Evolutionary and comparative perspectives.* Prentice Hall.

Parsons, T. (1975). The sick role and the role of the physician reconsidered. *The Milbank Memorial Fund Quarterly. Health and Society*, 53, 257-278.

Parsons, T., & Shils, E. A. (Eds.). (1951). *Toward a general theory of action.* Harper and Row.

Smith, K. (2005). Prebirth gender talk: A case study in prenatal socialization. *Women and Language*, *28*(1), 49–53.

Spitz, R. A. (1945). Hospitalism. *The Psychoanalytic Study of the Child*, *1*, 53–72.

Spitz, R. A. (1946). Hospitalism: A follow-up report. *The Psychoanalytic Study of the Child*, *2*, 113–117.

Thio, A. (1988). *Deviant behavior.* Houghton Mifflin.

Weber, M. (1930). *The Protestant ethic and the spirit of capitalism* (T. Parsons, Trans.). Scribner's.

Weber, M. (1946). *From Max Weber: Essays in sociology* (H. Gerth & C. Wright Mills, Trans. and Eds.). Oxford University Press.

Weber, M. (1958). *The city.* Free Press.

Wrong, D. H. (1961). The oversocialized conception of man in modern sociology. *American Sociological Review*, 26, 183-93.

Chapter 4: The Process of Interaction

The Pragmatists

The counter to social Darwinism in the late 1800s and early 1900s was found in the pragmatism of Charles Sanders Peirce. More liberal in its approach, parts of this philosophy were accepted or integrated into many aspects of the social sciences and humanities over the past century. Pragmatism had its origins within the Metaphysical Club at Harvard in the 1870s where people such as Charles Sanders Peirce, William James, Oliver Wendell Holmes, and others would gather in Cambridge to discuss, among other things, the philosophical doctrines of Hume, Kant, Aristotle, and many others (Menand, 2001). The assemblage included scientists, thinkers, and laymen who provided the context for a powerful collection of ideas born of a wide range of interests of those in the club. This odd assortment of individuals created a way of thinking that would change the face of the disciplines of philosophy, psychology, and sociology.

Determined on disproving Cartesian dualism (part of this philosophy suggested a separation of the human mind from the material world and therefore did not abide by the same laws of nature), Peirce's ideas found a home at the University of Chicago through the works of many of the behavioral and social scientists and philosophers there. Although most were in agreement regarding the nature of reality, it was John Dewey, James Angell, and George Herbert Mead who paved the way philosophically and theoretically for the others. Unlike social constructionist ideas in sociology today, Dewey, Angell, and Mead adamantly argued for a foundation. They agreed with Charles Sanders Peirce, who felt that anything unknowable was nothing more than heresay, dismissing the idea that experience is all people know. He suggested something more profound than the simplistic explanations of experience. Peirce referred to something more complex that would later become identified as a stratified nature of reality, allowing for diverse forms of possibilities.

For this form of pragmatism, one would acknowledge that there is a reality, and it is "real" and knowable. On the concept of *pragmatism,* **Peirce (1934) said, "Consider what effects, which might conceivably have practical bearings, we conceive the object of our conception to have. Then the whole of our conception of those effects is the whole of our conception of the object"** (p. 1). This is a holistic, thorough definition of understanding and goes beyond simple experience. The solution to a problem must take into account "a real fact and not a mere state of mind" (Peirce, 1934, p. 18). Dewey and Mead bought into Peirce's realist pragmatism and argued against the nominalist pragmatism of William James. As scientists, philosophers, and theorists, Peirce (1934) said we must "open our mental eyes and look well at the phenomenon and say what are the characteristics that are never wanting in it, whether that phenomenon be something that outward experience forces upon our attention, or whether it be the most abstract and general of the conclusions of science" (p. 29). In other words, "the entire intellectual purport of any symbol consists in the total of all general modes of rational conduct which, conditionally upon all possible different circumstances and desires, would ensue upon the acceptance of the symbol" (Peirce, 1934, p. 293). This is consistent with both Dewey and Mead. Dewey (1929), seeing a connection between knowledge and truth, stated, "There is complete correspondence between knowledge in its true meaning and what is real" (p. 21). Likewise, Mead (1926) said, "When there was but one recognized order of nature, possibility had no other place than in the mental constructions of the future or the incompletely known past" (p. 84). However, "it is important to recognize that this world is not made up out of these individual experiences. They lie within this world. If it were made up of such individual experiences it would lose all its reality" (Mead, 1931, p. 101).

Gradually, into the 1920s, the works of Dewey and Mead, specifically, began to incorporate more physics and quantum physics into their writings. Integrating empirical research and theory from physics, both

Dewey and Mead were able to provide a convincing argument against Cartesian dualism, as well as address issues of human development, morals, and ethics. Their ideas, however, were complicated and were coming at a time when academic disciplines were still trying to identify their purpose. As mentioned in Chapter 2, in the 1920s and 1930s, there developed a movement within sociology against theory and philosophy, preferring to focus solely on statistics and for sociologists to not make any attempts at improving the world. Within a decade, many of the ideas of the pragmatists were largely forgotten, misinterpreted, or simply ignored.

Guiding Questions

1. What is the self?

2. How is knowledge possible?

3. How is group behavior similar and dissimilar to individual behavior?

4. What role does emotion play in everyday life?

5. How is reality created?

George Herbert Mead

George Herbert Mead (1863–1931) was an American philosopher who contributed to the development of both social psychology and pragmatism and used his skills to assist in the creation of the lab school at the University of Chicago, studying how people learn and addressing many phenomena associated with humanity. He had studied physiological psychology in Germany and had earlier worked under William James and Josiah Royce at

Harvard. Between 1891 and 1894, he was an instructor in philosophy and psychology at the University of Michigan. In 1894 he joined the Department of Philosophy at the University of Chicago at the request of the department head, his close friend John Dewey. Mead remained there until his death.

From Mead's perspective, all animals interact, but we humans are thought to be unique in our ability to create societies, cultures, and social institutions. The influence of pragmatist philosophers such as John Dewey and George Herbert Mead at the University of Chicago was paramount in creating a direction sociology and philosophy students would take their work. Dewey and Mead, and particularly Mead (1934), demonstrated that the unique feature of humanity is its capacity to use symbols. He discussed how human development proceeds because of this ability. Language is a symbol system. The words in a language have meaning, and when we know the meanings of words, we can communicate with others who share the same or similar language.

People use language when they think or talk to themselves and others. When people see another person, they do not simply react to the person instinctively. They interpret the situation by giving meaning to the other person's behavior. How the person acts will inform them on their own place in the potential interaction. Does the person smile? Frown? Ignore them? These gestures all serve as cues. People then respond in what they deem to be the appropriate manner. And so the dance begins.

Mead used the term **"role-taking" to describe the process of figuring out how others will think and act in a situation**. This can take place in the moment of an interaction or ahead of schedule, in preparation for the interaction. The ability to take a role is extremely important to children. In fact, play is a way of practicing role-taking. Children often play house, taking the role of significant others. A *significant other* **is any person or persons with a strong influence on someone's self-concept or development**. By taking the role of these significant others, children can better understand their own roles as children, students, sons, or daughters. By practicing the roles of others in play, they learn to understand what others expect of them and how to behave to meet those expectations in everyday life. As adults, when people take roles, they figure out what others are thinking and how others will act. At that point they can adapt and adjust and then act accordingly.

The key element here is how the self develops. Mead identified a two-stage, or phase, process: (1) play and (2) game. *Play* is where young people, toddlers, and even babies take on the role of significant others, family members, and important friends as a means of understanding the world they occupy directly. The game stage is when people start to blend the generalities that are needed to participate in larger groups and, eventually, society as a whole.

Mead's (1934) famous example to illustrate the game stage is that of a baseball team. When people play team sports, such as baseball, all players are acting in unison, knowing what everyone else is expected to do. In the case of baseball, depending on who the batter is, the opposing team will adapt and adjust, move around together as a team. Probably a better example would be football. The various motion offenses keep defenses continually adjusting to what is occurring, working in unison. If the defenses are not able to do that, more than likely the offense scores a touchdown. These generalized expectations are what we do in everyday life. We learn the roles and expectations of others around us, and we adapt and adjust accordingly. Mead referred to this as the *generalized other*, **which are the expected behavior, norms, and values considered the standard in one's community or society**. Without being able to take the role of the generalized other, according to Mead, we would struggle to fit in. Imagine going someplace where you do not understand what is expected of you. You experience that regularly when you are meeting new groups of people. On college campuses, everyone is surrounded by people from many countries who may speak different languages or have different customs, values, and attitudes. Coming to a college campus can be intimidating, especially if people are unsure what is expected of them. Quickly, though, they learn. They are able to take the role of the generalized other associated with the college they are attending. If people were not able to take this role across all aspects of life, they would lose all social cohesion. There would no longer be a society.

The I and the Me

One of Mead's contributions to social psychology is his distinction between the "I" and the "me." These are phases of the self; that is, they reflect how people learn the appropriate identity to act out in any given situation. Mead (1934) more typically uses the word "self" or "elementary self" to refer to the "me." The self that arises in relationship to a generalized other is referred to as the "me." This is how it all works: First, it is important to understand that there is only one "I" but literally billions of "Me's" a person will have by the end of their lives. The *me* is the identity or self that a person is in any given situation. Therefore, when you walk into a classroom, your "I" reflects on which "me" it should be. Let's take the example of a student. You, the student, knows how to act in the classroom. You, as the student, sit down in the appropriate place and proceed to take out your materials to prepare for the class. Another student sits down next to you, and when you look at that person, you realize that person is a friend. Your "I" reflects on the "me" associated with that person as a friend, and that inevitably is what your identity or self is at that moment. As soon as you face forward to turn toward the professor, the "me" associated with being a student that is acted out by the "I" returns.

Now imagine all the caveats that are associated with this in any particular day as you walk around a college campus. This process is occurring in some manner every time you interact with a person. If you are in a situation where there is no "me" affiliated with the situation, that generalized other comes into play and you try to make something work until you find or "create" a new "me" to fit that situation. As we move or change over time, our relationships change, our age changes, and so forth. We adapt and adjust, creating more "me's" to fit where we are and what we are doing. The more experiences we have, the easier it becomes for us to adapt and adjust to any situation we may encounter.

Time

In "The Nature of the Past" (1929a) and *The Philosophy of the Present* (1931), Mead discussed three issues that may be important areas regarding time: (a) The past provides direction (Maines et al., 1983; Mead, 1931); (b) the past provides continuity (Maines et al., 1983; Mead, 1931, 1938, 1964; Strauss, 1991); and (c) humans feel a necessity to complete acts (Mead, 1929a). The past provides direction, as human experience has meaning and therefore involves more than mere passage. Mead (1929a) said, "The order within which things happen and appear conditions that which will happen and appear" (p. 237). The past also provides the direction in the present. Without this, events would signify little more than disappearance and would negate the strength the past brings to consistency in the present. Consistency of action explains through activity the conditions, sets the limits, and structures what is likely to occur in the future (Maines et al., 1983).

Continuity through rationalization of the past helps make sense in the present (Mead, 1931, 1938, 1964; Strauss, 1991). This issue is similar to Maines et al.'s (1983) idea of a symbolically reconstructed past. Each present must reconstruct its past to allow for understanding of the present. The past or history gives individuals the room to cope with the ever-changing stream of reality (Maines et al., 1983; Mead, 1929a; Strauss, 1991). Reality would be entropy without individuals remembering and rationalizing. Humans would rely on instinct, unable to make sense of the present. Therefore, the restructuring of the past is a necessary process that provides continuity from past to present, constructing a foundation for coping with the present (Maines et al., 1983; Mead, 1929a).

The necessity to complete acts or something that is lacking is another issue Mead addressed. The past provides direction and continuity and manifests itself through action and the completion of acts. Humans feel the necessity to complete acts or find closure, and this feeling or need is greater than the ability to stop it (Albert, 1984; Mead, 1929a). Individuals define a situation and act accordingly, defining goals, whether they are immediate or distant (Charon, 1992; McCall & Simmons, 1978). Each goal ends by being achieved, altered, or forgotten (Charon, 1992). For example, in a popular-culture class, a student can plan on writing a term paper addressing the relationship of identity to cosplay. They may, in fact, complete that term paper (achieved). They may change the term paper topic to how hip-hop music is used in teaching science (altered). Or maybe the student got so overwhelmed with their other classes that they forgot they had a term paper due (forgotten). This process is continual, with all action overlapping.

Communication and Mind

As mentioned above, Mead (1934, 1964) described how the individual mind and the self arises out of the social process. He analyzed experience through communication as essential to the social order. The focus in terms of research and explanation should always focus on the social processes.

Mind, according to Mead (1934, 1964), arises within the social process of communication and cannot be understood apart from that process and involves two phases: (1) the conversation of gestures and (2) language, or the conversation of significant gestures. Both phases presuppose a social context within which two or more individuals are in interaction with one another.

For Mead, the development of the self is intimately tied to the development of language. An example of this would be when a person sees someone and waves. The other person waves back; in essence, they are greeting each other. They are using physical gestures to say "hello." For Mead, this means that the gestures involved were significant. For a gesture to have significance, it must call out or mean in the second person a response that is functionally similar to the meaning that the original person anticipates. In other words, for a gesture to be significant, it must mean more or less the same thing to both people. This meaning involves the capacity to consciously anticipate how others will respond to symbols or gestures. This is where the voice comes into play. Mead calls this the "conversation of gestures." It is a dance, so to speak. The same process is involved in speaking. Language is simply another symbol. Language represents. When people talk, they try to convey meanings to others. If they understand, the conversation proceeds unimpeded. If in this process the meaning is not the same or similar to the other person, it does not mean there is no meaning; it simply means the meaning is different. Potentially, the meaning achieved in the interaction is confusion. The people involved then proceed in the interaction until the meaning they want is achieved, or they move on to other things. For instance, the other day a friend of mine was texting me. For whatever reason, his grammar was awful. Words were missing as well from what he wrote. What he was trying to convey to me left me confused. The meaning from the interaction was that I did not understand what he was trying to communicate. That particular meaning of confusion was understood by both of us. Then he began over again. At that point I was able to understand what he was trying to communicate, and we were on the same page.

Mead describes the communication process as a social act since it requires at least two individuals in interaction with one another (though, eventually, we can see this same process involved in self-talk). Meaning arises during the act. The act of communication has a triadic structure consisting of the following components: (a) an initiating gesture on the part of an individual (e.g., a person waves their hand at me); (2) a response to that gesture by a second individual (e.g., I wave my hand back); and (3) the result of the action initiated by the first gesture (e.g., we said hello to each other). There is no meaning independent of the interactive participation of two or more individuals in the act of communication.

People can and will anticipate the responses of others, consciously and intentionally making gestures that will bring out appropriate responses in others. A gesture, then, is an action that implies a reaction. The reaction is the meaning of the gesture and points toward the result of the action initiated by the gesture. The conversation of significant symbols is the foundation of Mead's theory of mind. Without this "conversation," if you will, the mind cannot exist. The mind, for Mead, is consciousness. Consciousness requires thought (i.e., the ability to process language and other gestures). This process signifies how the mind exists. Without the ability or having these processes, people would not be able to think; therefore, they would have no mind. The mind, however, is simply part of the process. Like "the self," it is not tangible. You cannot do an X-ray and see the human mind. The emergence of mind is contingent upon interaction between the human and its social environment; it is through participation in the social act of communication that the individual realizes their potential for thought.

The mind arises out of the social act of communication. Mead's concept of the social act is relevant, not only to his theory of mind but to all facets of his social philosophy.

There are two models of the act in Mead's general philosophy: (a) the model of the act-as-such and (b) the model of the social act. Mead (1938) speaks of the act as determining "the relation between the individual and the environment" (p. 364). Reality, according to Mead, is a field of situations. In these situations, we find people going through four stages to facilitate an act: (1) the stage of impulse upon which the person responds to some natural disruption; (2) the stage of perception upon which the individual defines and analyzes what is occurring; (3) the stage of manipulation upon which action is taken with reference to the individual's perceptual appraisal of the situation; and (4) the stage of consummation upon which the encountered situation is completed and the continuity of life continues. For instance, suppose I decide to go for a walk. While walking, (1) it begins to rain (impulse); (2) I realize that if I do not do something that I will get soaked and maybe get sick (perception); (3) I quickly begin to run for cover toward an awning (manipulation); and (4) I manage to get cover under the awning and barely get wet at all (consummation). The process is complete. The time factor involved in these processes are layered, so we are participating in multiple acts simultaneously. Some acts may be completed in 15 weeks, like getting through a sociology course, while others, such as taking a bite out of a taco, can take just a few seconds.

What is of interest in this description is that individuals are not merely passive recipients of external, environmental influences but are instead capable of taking action with reference to such influences; people reconstruct their relationship with their environment through selective perception and through the use or manipulation of the objects selected in perception. Reality is not simply out there, independent of the person, but is the outcome of the relationship of humans and their environment. Perception, according to Mead (1938), is a relation between the person and object. Perception is not, then, something that occurs in the person but is an objective relation between the person and their environment. And the perceptual object is not an entity out there, independent of the person, but is one pole of the interactive perceptual process.

The Social Act

While the social act is analogous to the act-as-such, it is important to remember that people are members of social groups and that their actions must be viewed in the context of social acts that involve other individuals. They are truly social. The social act is a complex organic process within which the individual is situated, and it is within this situation that individual acts are possible and have meaning.

Mead defines the social act in relation to social objects. The ***social act* is a collective act involving the participation of two or more individuals**; and the ***social object* is a collective object that has a common meaning for each participant in the act**. There are many kinds of social acts: some very simple, some very complex. These range from the (relatively) simple interaction of two individuals (e.g., dancing, making love, tennis, etc.), to rather more complex acts involving more than two individuals (e.g., a play, a religious ritual, playing softball, etc.), to still more complex acts carried on in the form of social organizations and institutions (e.g., law enforcement, education, economic exchange, etc.). The life of a society consists in such social acts.

Communication through significant symbols is what renders the intelligent organization of social acts possible. ***Significant communication* involves the comprehension of meaning— that is, the taking of the attitude of others toward one's own gestures**. Significant communication among individuals creates a world of symbolic meanings within which further and deliberate social acts are possible. The specifically human social act, in other words, is rooted in the act of significant communication and is, in fact, ordered by the conversation of significant symbols.

Morality

Like many philosophers, Mead addressed morality. Consistent with his views as a pragmatist, morals and morality were continuous with how meaning developed. Specifically, Mead (1908) did not believe that specific morals existed prior to social action. Instead, he situated everything within the environment in which things happened. This is where things can be tricky. Mead still considered this view of morality and ethics to be consistent with realism (that is, that something has independent existence from human consciousness). The method, or way, that he gets there is simple; that is, the process is framed within the nature of reality. Therefore, the process by which morality is gleaned fits with realism.

With that said, morality, according to Mead (1908), is that "the moral interpretation of our experience must be found within the experience itself" (p. 315). But this experience that Mead reflects upon is not individual experience. Instead, it is found within the environment, much like most of what Mead addresses. Therefore, this process is that in order for it to be moral when humans act, they have to take into account the public good, but not by itself. That would mean it is coming solely from outside the individual. No, what Mead (1908) means is that

> the necessity of uprightness in public affairs does not rest upon a transcendental ideal of perfection of the self, nor upon the attainment of the possible sum of human happiness, but upon the economy and effectiveness, and consistency demanded in the industrial, commercial, social, and aesthetic activities of those that make up the community. To push reform is to give expression to all these impulses and present them in their consequences over against those of all the other social impulses out of which an organism of personalities arises. (p. 317)

By that, Mead means that when entering any action, people must be aware of all the consequences of their actions. In understanding that, it can then be deemed that moral behavior has been achieved. For instance, if a person says they are fighting for America yet in the process are creating policies that create an atmosphere of hate and weaken our position around the world, that is not moral behavior. For behavior to be moral, in its truest sense, people have to be aware of the consequences of actions. This will be addressed by critical theorists in Chapter 5.

This is a philosophy that is consistent with pragmatism. The situatedness of the moral behavior is framed within the whole. Therefore, it is not situational ethics in the sense that killing someone because you want to join a gang is not moral behavior even though it might be expected within the gang. When looking at the bigger picture, murdering someone is taking a life, which is not good for the whole.

Later, Mead (1929b) wrote about war and in the process reflected the view that he presented in 1908. That is, he advocated international-mindedness. Mead wanted people to think of the whole. He lamented the fact that people will often unite and do amazing things while in the heat of battle or in the process of war and yet, at the same time, that people who prior to war would not cross the street to help a specific person, in time of war would be willing to give their life for that same person. Mead believed that if we recognized that we were part of a whole—that is, every person on the planet—and recognized that same fervor that exists during time of war, people could accomplish almost anything. Indeed, we see in various science-fiction stories where utopias exist, people think of the whole instead of the country or the person. The process for Mead is consistent with pragmatism and what he sees as natural laws.

The overall picture for Mead is that if people took the time to be more thorough in their understanding of the consequences of their actions, moral behavior would occur. Instead, because we are shortsighted, often crouched in our filter bubbles and echo chambers, lacking in-depth knowledge, we act in ways that do not benefit the whole. In the classroom, I often ask students how their behavior would change if they took responsibility for everyone. Most students acknowledge their behavior would change dramatically. This is what Mead is talking about with moral behavior. In this process, people are interacting with others, having honest dialogue, listening and contributing. Ultimately, what Mead saw would happen is that moral behavior would emerge.

Inevitably, Mead had a huge influence on sociology, though he was a philosopher. Yet most of his ideas have largely been ignored. Sociologists, specifically Charles Ellwood and Herbert Blumer, both former students of Mead, took bits and pieces of his ideas and fit his ideas into their own theories. Yet Mead is still looked upon, though incompletely, as one of the founders of sociological thought.

Charles Ellwood

Charles Ellwood (1873–1946) was the son of a preacher. Initially, Ellwood studied sociology as an undergraduate at Cornell University under Edward Alsworth Ross (Jensen, 1946; Thompson, 1947), a major contributor to early sociology and sociological social psychology (Small, 1916). Ellwood went to graduate school at the University of Chicago in 1896 where he was taken under the wing of Albion Small and John Dewey. Like many sociologists from the University of Chicago during this time, Ellwood (1902, 1916, 1925, 1927a, 1933) preferred qualitative methodologies as a means to understanding human action and behavior, while he downplayed the methodologies of the physical sciences. His dissertation (with Dewey as chair and also included Mead as a member) was published in four parts in the *American Journal of Sociology* between 1899 and 1900. His dissertation resonated with the themes that would continue to present themselves throughout his career: (a) similarities in group and individual behavior; (b) qualitative methods as a means to understanding human behavior; (c) utilizing the social sciences as a means to helping others; and (d) a focus on communication as a means of creating reality through human interaction. This focus on creating reality through human interaction was instrumental to his student Herbert Blumer who went on to coin the term "symbolic interaction."

During his tenure as a sociologist first at the University of Missouri and then at Duke University, Ellwood was a pioneer in social psychology and, specifically, what he referred to as "psychical interactionism" (LoConto & Pruitt, 2006). The overlap with what eventually became symbolic interactionism within sociology should be obvious. There are four general areas of Ellwood's ideas: (a) interaction, (b) methodology, (c) emotions, and (d) group behavior.

Interaction

In the mid-1930s, Floyd House (1936) stated that Ellwood was the leader, or head, of sociological social psychology. Ellwood did this by giving a sociological slant to the functional psychology and pragmatism of John Dewey. One of those areas involved the concept of interaction and its importance. He tended to lean toward being able to not only observe the social process of interaction but also identify its importance. Ellwood believed that the process of interaction, or of ***interadjustment* (the process of two or more people interacting together adapting and adjusting to each other),** among its members can be studied accurately through observation. He felt that sociologists could then compare theory with observable facts. It would be easy to identify how people act out cooperation and conflict as different aspects of the process of social adjustment. Ellwood (1927b) said, "We have culture only when individuals learn to modify their conduct through what is communicated to them by other individuals. Culture, therefore, depends upon the interchange of experience, and so upon language in some form, though verbal language is itself the primary form of culture" (p. 4).

This interaction, according to Ellwood (1899, 1925), would be one where people interacting would be exchanging their experiences through communication, or as he referenced it, "inter" communication. The key usage of Ellwood and the prefix "inter" indicates the process of the exchange of information leading to the communication of ideas and experiences. By using "inter" he was acknowledging the process of action between two or more people. He saw this as a form of interstimulation and response, consistent with Mead's ideas of interaction using gestures. ***Interstimulation* is the process where people facilitate or encourage communication with each other by creating a common subject matter to address.** People enable each other toward common meanings, common values, and common attitudes, which is another way of saying "socialization," as utilized by those like Durkheim and Weber. Therefore, this interaction, stimulating intercommunication, provides the foundation for a society to develop. Elwood (1927a) stated, "Culture is nothing more than a series of mental patterns passed along from individual to individual in a group by means of the process of intercommunication" (p. 35).

Methodology

Another key area for Ellwood involved methodology. Ellwood addressed four areas concerning methodology: (a) studying human behavior in contexts; (b) a disdain for the physical-science method; (c) using inductive approaches; and (d) the avoidance of hypotheses. First, Ellwood used the term "case study" in the sense of studying things in their context, whether that be watching two people on a date or people watching a football game. It is a context. The context serves as framing the meanings in the moment. Therefore, I can lecture in a classroom, and students will sit and take notes. My same behavior in Aisle 5 at a Walmart would completely change the meaning of my behavior. Therefore, context for Ellwood is critical in understanding the intercommunication occurring. In this sense, then, Ellwood favors more qualitative methods (e.g., participant observation, unobtrusive observation, in-depth interviews, etc.) to study the context. His view was that since sociologists should be studying group behavior and the communication process that is found between and within groups, it is best warranted to study this behavior addressing the social, historical, and biological background of these groups (Ellwood, 1899). This required the sociologist to get out into the field or the environment of people to study human behavior

John Dewey (1859–1952) was one of American pragmatism's early founders, along with Charles Sanders Peirce, William James, and George Herbert Mead. Arguably, Dewey is the most prominent American intellectual for the first half of the 20th century. His educational theories shaped American education for over a century. His psychological theories (e.g., functionalism) had an influence not only in psychology but also in philosophy and sociology. His writing about democratic theory and practice provided discussions of what was the appropriate path for the Western world (Dewey, 1927). In addition, Dewey developed extensive and often systematic views in ethics, epistemology, logic, metaphysics, aesthetics, and philosophy of religion.

The union between theory and application began with Dewey's development of a laboratory school at the University of Chicago in 1896 and the publication of "The Reflex Arc Concept in Psychology" (1896), which attacked the philosophy of atomism, a theoretical approach that regards something as interpretable through analysis into distinct, separable, and independent elementary components. Dewey also stood against the concept of elementarism, which likewise was the procedure of explaining a complex phenomenon by reducing it to simple elemental units. He also stood against the behavioral theory of stimulus and response that was so popular at the time. As such, he theorized that everyone is interconnected in various ways and that thought was or could be objective. The lab school inevitably used Dewey's and others' ideas to facilitate better teaching methods so children would learn more efficiently. The central focus for Dewey, as suggested above, was *epistemology*, or the theory of knowledge. In his view, epistemology had largely made too great a distinction between thought and fact, specifically tangible objects, such as things or behavior. He was critical of Cartesian dualism, which suggested that the human soul or spirit was different than nature and therefore operated under different laws. This belief in Cartesian dualism led to the field of psychiatry, which does not often use measurable observations to draw conclusions. Dewey was able to demonstrate how thought and action or thought and fact operated under the same laws of physics, making everything or nearly everything real, observable, and measurable in some manner. It would take until his publications in the 1920s for much of this came to fruition, as proven through the works of quantum physicists Werner Heisenberg and Niels Bohr.

Second, Ellwood's ideas of methods countered those of the physical sciences. The focus of the argument was that the excessive variables involved in studying human activity would render the scientific method ineffective in the understanding of humanity. As Ellwood (1925) himself stated regarding physical science methodologies:

> The physical sciences have become bodies of accurate, tested knowledge largely through the method of experimentation. ... While this method is not absolutely closed to the social sciences, it seems to have such limited possibilities in the field of social phenomena. ... Quantitative measurements are desirable in every science for the sake of exactness; but the social sciences for a long time will probably have to content themselves with the critical qualitative analysis, comparison, and correlation of social phenomena. While they may not become exact quantitative statements, the social sciences may become bodies of critically established, and therefore, of trustworthy knowledge. (pp. 2–4)

Third, philosophically, Ellwood advocated the use of inductive approaches. Ellwood heralded Aristotle to begin a discussion on the importance of inductive methods in the social sciences. He wrote:

> He [Aristotle] started with the facts in human society as they presented themselves to him, and sought for their explanation in the nature of man, without any metaphysical assumption as to the relation of man to his physical environment. In thus explaining human society primarily in terms of man rather than in terms of the physical universe. (Ellwood, 1902, p. 5)

According to Ellwood, Aristotle achieved this through realistic and inductive approaches. Only when these approaches were put into practice could a researcher then develop a theory that generalizes the behavior. This is a recurrent theme for Ellwood and one he spent his entire career following. He argued tirelessly against the use of physical science methods and deductive approaches within the social sciences.

Fourth, Ellwood admitted a function for hypotheses yet was hesitant about their use in the social sciences. In Ellwood's (1933) view, hypotheses can serve a positive function, but he made a distinction between a hypothesis and a pet hypothesis, which he deemed wishful thinking. In Ellwood's eyes, hypotheses were only utilizable when used within their context. Multiple working hypotheses were useful in understanding human behavior, as they provided the framework for examination. They allow the researcher to study a fuller range of social phenomena. An isolated hypothesis is not functional for human behavior, because it avoids this full range of social phenomena, lending itself to the wishful-thinking category of which Ellwood was critical. Herbert Blumer (1969) was in agreement with Ellwood regarding the idea of wishful thinking, questioning whether or not "the hypothesis genuinely epitomizes the model or the theory from which it is deduced" (p. 29). Blumer was concerned with the narrow focus of hypothesis testing, which is Ellwood's main point when talking about hypotheses and wishful thinking. "Nothing gives rise to narrow views than narrow methods" (Ellwood, 1933, p. 5). Ellwood is in search of multiple working hypotheses where the researcher can test or find a multiple of information "out there." To solely rely on a hypothesis limits and badly taints any information gathered. Sociologists would be left with no more than a fragmented understanding of human behavior. By both Ellwood's and Blumer's standards, using a more diverse or triangulated approach enables the researcher to observe and understand the depth of human experience.

Emotions

An interesting aspect of Ellwood's work had to do with emotion and interaction. He stated that "all our social life and social behavior are not only embedded in feeling, but largely guided and controlled by feeling" (Ellwood, 1925, p. 365). In 1925, Ellwood devoted an entire chapter of his book to emotions and their relationship to motivation. He believed other behavior that required consciousness also required emotions of some manner within them. He took Charles Horton Cooley's (1927) position that "sentiment lies deeper than thought" (p. 177), and feelings or emotions tend to inhibit or facilitate action (Ellwood, 1925). He saw them as existing deep within an individual, therefore acting as a guide at an unconscious level until the feelings become evident and unavoidable. In Ellwood's eyes, feelings or emotions were a foundation for action; however, he believed conscious action took place through ideas. Thus, to persuade individuals, ideas alone can be used, but for complete success, an appeal must be made to the feelings and emotions of individuals.

Group Behavior

Lastly, Ellwood applied Dewey's functional psychology to the study of groups. Functional psychology focused its analysis on the individual. To apply this to sociology, Ellwood treated society as a "superindividual" (Lewis & Smith, 1980). Ellwood (1900) stated, "Social psychology, then, in regarding the social groups as functional unities, necessarily regards them as individualities or individuals" (p. 35). This demonstrates a key feature of Ellwood's views on collective behavior and social organization. Ellwood (1927a) believed that changes in the group could be explained in the same manner as changes within the individual:

> The continuity of the group, again can be explained in terms of the process of intercommunication between its members and the resulting growth of tradition and custom. The changes within the group can be explained by the same process of intercommunication, functioning with reference to new situations, so that by a learning process new values and attitudes become diffused throughout all members of the group. (p. 37)

Like many of the early sociologists, Ellwood's ideas often were translated into different terms and then became part of the canon of sociology. His overall influence in the field of sociology appears to have been through the work of one of his former students, Herbert Blumer (LoConto & Pruitt, 2006). However, when reading sociology textbooks today, he is largely absent. By the time of his death in 1946, he felt he had failed. The last article he published in 1945 largely was Ellwood lamenting about how he had failed to make sociology a discipline that focused on real-world issues and attempted to make the world a better place (LoConto, 2011). Though he published and sold the most books of any American sociologist pre–World War II and was arguably the most published of American sociologists of his era, within 10 years of his death, he was largely removed from all sociological textbooks.

Herbert Blumer

Herbert George Blumer (1900–1987) was an American sociologist who is best known for developing the theory of symbolic interactionism and for his ideas regarding methods of social research. Believing that individuals create social reality through collective and individual action, he took certain elements of Mead's and Ellwood's works and made them more palatable to his own ideas (LoConto, 2011; LoConto & Pruitt, 2006). Blumer was the one who coined the term "symbolic interactionism," which eventually became a school of thought within sociology (see Blumer, 1936).

Blumer earned his bachelor's and master's degrees at the University of Missouri, where he was fortunate enough to work with Charles Ellwood and psychologist Max Meyer. In 1925, he relocated to the University of Chicago, where he spent time as a graduate assistant for both Mead and sociologist Robert Park. Upon completing his doctorate in 1928, he accepted a teaching position at the University of Chicago where he remained until 1952 before leaving for Berkeley.

Symbolic Interactionism

Though he published occasionally, certainly not as much as either Mead or Ellwood, Blumer's ideas were best represented by the students he had at both the University of Chicago and the University of California, Berkeley. Sociologists like Howard Becker, Anselm Strauss, Tomatsu Shibutani, Erving Goffman, Stanford Lyman, and many others brought forth his ideas and made them real, studying everyday life. Nevertheless, Blumer (1969) presented his articles on symbolic interactionism in a single volume in which he conceptualized symbolic interaction into three main points: (a) Humans act towards things on the basis of the meanings they have for them; (b) the meaning of things arises out of the social interactions one has with one's fellows; and (c) meanings are seen as a series of interpretive actions by the actor.

Charles Horton Cooley (1864–1929), was an American sociologist who employed a social psychological approach to the understanding of society. He earned his PhD at the University of Michigan in 1894. He had been teaching at the university in 1892 and became a full professor of sociology in 1907. Cooley remained there until the end of his life.

Cooley believed that social reality was qualitatively different from physical reality. This inevitably made him contest the alleged scientific methods of the physical sciences, suggesting sociologists should focus more on inductive, qualitative work. Because of this, at a time when inductive, qualitative research was not as well accepted, he spent more time writing theory than conducting research. His *Human Nature and the Social Order* (1902) discussed the determination of the self through interaction with others. Cooley theorized that the sense of self is formed in two ways: (a) by the experiences of people and (b) by what people imagine others' ideas of themselves to be. As every introduction to sociology textbook states, this is known as the "looking-glass self." This dual conception contributed to Cooley's theory that the mind is social and that society is a mental construct. He reached these conclusions by trying to address fractures within the intellectual community about the nature of humanity and its societies. He focused on what he thought was the necessity to create an understanding of societal phenomena that highlighted the subjective processes of people yet realized that these subjective processes were effects and causes of society's processes, seemingly a tautology. He also focused on the development of a conception of society that portrayed states of chaos as natural occurrences that could provide opportunities for adaptive innovation. And he examined the need to manifest publics that were capable of exerting some form of informed moral control over current problems and future directions. Cooley's ideas inevitably became part of the canon of symbolic interactionism, which focuses on how meanings develop through people interacting with each other. Ontologically, Mead (1926, 1930) disagreed with Cooley's conceptions of society, feeling that relying on subjectivity to explain the world and the social phenomena within it would make everything incomprehensible.

Blumer believed that what creates society itself is people engaging in social interaction continuously. If people stopped interacting with each other, society would cease to be. It follows then that social reality only exists in the context of human experience. Something is real because people come together and, through interaction, agree upon what is occurring. Therefore, if people come together and agree that climate change caused by human activity is not real, they will act accordingly, regardless of whether scientists all over the planet say climate change caused by humans is indeed factual. The same is true for the university or college you attend. If all students decide not to attend, the university or college would close down.

According to Blumer (1969), interaction between individuals is voluntary and is based on the subjective meanings people attribute to social objects and/or symbols. Thus, individual actors regulate their behavior based on the meaning they attribute to objects and symbols in their situation. Blumer, much like Ellwood, theorized that assigning objects meaning is an ongoing, two-fold process. First is the identification of the objects that have situational meaning. Second is the process of internal communication to decide which meaningful objects to which to respond. This is much more individualistic than either Mead or Ellwood but carries with it the "psychical" and subjectivity that Ellwood emphasized. Acknowledging that others are equally autonomous, individuals use their subjectively derived interpretations of others to predict the outcome of certain behaviors and use such predictive insight to make decisions about their own behavior in the hopes of reaching their goal. Thus, when there is consensus among people through social coordination, or intercommunication as Ellwood stated, individual people create the meaning of the objects that make up their situation, and social coordination ensues. Social structures are determined as much by the action of individual actors as they determine the action of those individuals. That is, people create and re-create social structures or institutions, but in turn, those social structures or institutions influence people. Based on this, Blumer sees things only occurring in the moment of the interaction. Stability ensues when people gather and create and re-create reality or realities continually. As mentioned above, the university or college you are attending only exists because there are students who continually attend. That allows for this institution to hire people to maintain and facilitate the university or college. If students chose to not attend your university or college, it would cease to be. The process of creation would not happen; therefore, it would vanish.

This complex interaction between meanings, objects, and behaviors, Blumer reiterated, is a human process because it requires behaviors based on the interpretation of symbols. Because social life is a fluid and a negotiated process, humans must engage in symbolic interaction in order to understand each other. Blumer criticized the contemporary social science of his day because, instead of using symbolic interactionism, they made false conclusions about humans by reducing human decisions to social pressures like social positions and roles. Blumer was more invested in the psychical interactionism of Ellwood that holds that the meanings of symbols are not universal but rather are subjective and are attached to the symbols and the receiver depending on how they choose to interpret them.

Objects

The importance of thinking to symbolic interactionists is shown through their views on objects. Blumer (1969) defined *objects* as the things "out there" in the world. The significance of objects is how they are defined by the people using them. In other words, different objects have different meanings depending on the individuals using them. Physical objects are tangible items that lack *agency*—**that is, the ability to independently act on their own (e.g., desk or clothing)**. *Social objects* are entities that humans act out but are given meaning within the community, such as student, mother, or friend. Lastly, there are *abstract objects*, which are ideas or moral principles. The key with social objects is that people name them and act toward them based on those names or meanings. They sit down and study at a desk. People do not wear a desk. Similarly, Americans and those from other countries have strong feelings for a mom, and because of this, Moms are treated differently than someone who is known as a student. And the feeling of love motivates people far more than the abstract notion of apathy. All of these are objects, and according to Blumer, humans operate everyday moving around, interacting with others, and creating meanings and then acting toward those things based on the meanings they give to them. These meanings and symbols provide the basis for distinctive human action and interaction. Modification of meanings and symbols occurs through the interpretation of situations. Humans' capability of modification is due to their ability to interact with themselves. The intertwining of interaction and action make up groups and societies.

Methods

According to Blumer, the most valid and desirable social research is conducted through qualitative ethnographic methodology. He critiqued the idea that the only form of valid knowledge is derived through an objective perspective—that is, through quantitative methods. Blumer believed that theoretical and methodological approaches to studying human behavior must acknowledge human beings as thinking, acting, and interacting individuals. They also must use theories and methods that represent the humanly known, socially created, and experienced world. This flies in direct opposition to the standard view on using quantitative methods, which typically represent scientific research (LoConto, 2011).

Blumer believed that when quantitative methods were applied to social research, they created results that were ignorant to the empirical realities of the social world. Because people act toward the world based on the subjective meanings they attribute to different objects, consistency in those meanings remain elusive. Therefore, quantitative methods are intrinsically subjugated to the researcher's own social reality, only documents the researcher's own personal assumptions about social interaction, and ultimately yields biased findings. For a researcher to truly understand sociological phenomena, Blumer asserted, they must understand their subject's subjective interpretations of reality.

Following this logic, Blumer discounted social research that blindly applies methods that have been traditionally used in the natural sciences. Such quantitative, objective analyses do not acknowledge that humans have the ability to consciously entertain opinions and to apply meanings to objects, which enables humans to take an active role in shaping their world. Because society is composed of interactions between individuals, the only empirical reality is that which stems from human interaction. Therefore, contextual understanding of human action is necessary for valid social research.

Thus, Blumer advocated for sociological research that sympathetically and subjectively incorporated the viewpoints of the subject, therefore pushing for a microsociological approach. Concluding that there is little validity in research that attempted to understand the social world objectively, Blumer felt that objective interpretations of society were biased to the social location of the researchers and thus had little empirical value. To uncover the social realities of others, observers must be mindful of their framework and be open to different understandings of social reality. That is, the researcher must see the world from the perspective of the people being studied.

Macro Versus Micro

Blumer believed that society is not made up of macrostructures but rather microstructures, specifically in people and their actions. These microstructures are not isolated but consist of collective action, giving rise to the concept of joint action. Joint action is not just the sum of individual actions but takes on a character of its own. Blumer did not reject the idea of macrostructures but instead focused on the concept of emergence. What he meant was that larger social structures emerge from the smaller. It is cumulative. That is, as stated earlier with the example of a university or college, any macrostructure is literally the result of people coming together and socially interacting with each other. Whereas his mentor Charles Ellwood saw macrostructures as existing and acting much like humans do, Blumer wanted to focus on the people creating those macrostructures. Blumer admitted that macrostructures were important but asserted that they have an extremely limited role in symbolic interactionism.

Overall, Herbert Blumer was successful in pushing symbolic interactionism to the fore at a time when much of the sociology world was focusing on macrostructures. His charisma, not his publication record, was notable, as Blumer was able to motivate his students to push into new areas, reshaping sociology in the latter half of the 20th century. For nearly 50 years until his death in 1986, Blumer was able to largely control the direction of symbolic interactionist research.

Erving Goffman

Erving Goffman (1922–1981) was born in Mannville, Alberta, Canada. After 3 years of high school in Winnipeg, he became a student at the University of Manitoba, majoring in chemistry. It was during this time that he met Dennis Wrong who was a renowned North American sociologist at the time. This meeting worked as a motivation to leave Manitoba and enroll at the University of Toronto, where he graduated with a BA in sociology and anthropology in 1945. Afterward, he went to the University of Chicago and earned his MA and PhD for sociology, in 1949 and 1953, respectively. He taught at the University of Chicago, then moved on to the University of California, Berkeley, with Herbert Blumer, and then finished his career at the University of Pennsylvania.

Goffman (1959, 1961, 1967) compared interaction with people playing dramaturgical roles. People have roles, scripts, props, and what not. ***Roles* are the parts people play in a given context or setting**. Am I a professor, husband, or researcher? It will depend upon the context or setting in which I find myself. The ***scripts* are the accepted discourse for the role and context being acted out**. We have expectations of behavior associated with roles. As a professor I find myself using the appropriate language if I am playing the role of Dr. LoConto. But hanging with friends from high school, it is a different role for me and different scripts. Therefore, too, the ***props*, or tangible tools that accent interaction, come into play**. As a college student, you use computers, notebooks, pencils, and pens to play that role. Clothing also is a needed prop in American society. The audience also is a critical part found in dramaturgy. In interaction, the ***audience*—that is, those one is interacting or attempting to interact with—have to buy in or accept your behavior and actions**. Without that, the interaction tends to flounder.

Every interaction, Goffman believed, began with a presentation of self. The way people present themselves gives other people cues about the type of interaction to expect. In formal situations, people usually greet friends with a handshake or a remark, whereas in informal situations, they may greet friends with a hug or a kiss. If people are with friends, they talk and laugh, but on a bus or in an elevator, people, specifically Americans, do not speak to strangers. And they keep a social distance even when space is crowded. People give cues about themselves in the way they present and use their bodies in interaction.

As mentioned above, in an attempt to analyze how interaction takes place, Goffman compared social interaction to a drama on stage, a comparison known as the dramaturgy. Whenever people interact, they prepare themselves backstage and then present themselves as if onstage according to what they have learned in the socialization process. Goffman believed that all behavior, even the most routine, is neither instinctual nor habitual; it is a presentation. Most Americans prepare to present themselves by showering, washing their hair, and using deodorant. In American society, cleanliness and a lack of body odor are important. Complexions must be smooth, so men shave, women put on makeup, and adolescents use cosmetics to cover up acne. Suitable clothing is selected so that people can present themselves formally in formal situations and casually in casual situations. A formal setting, such as a church, a more informal setting, such as a classroom, and a casual setting, such as a basketball arena, require very different presentations. In some settings, one can race for a front-row seat, talk loudly, wave to friends, and eat and drink. In other settings, these behaviors would be quite inappropriate.

Maintaining the Self

Once people have presented themselves in a particular role and have begun to interact, they must maintain their presentation. In class, students cannot tell jokes with fellow students, wander around the room, or write on the board. It would not only disrupt the class but it would also spoil the presentation of these students who would be considered disruptive, strange, or worse. If students or others want to maintain the definitions others have of them, they must maintain a performance in accord with the definition agreed upon for the situation.

Sometimes, we inadvertently do not maintain our performance, so we try to account for our behavior. An *account* is a **"linguistic device employed whenever an action is subjected to valuative inquiry"** (Scott & Lyman, 1968, p. 46). In other words, when someone asks you if someone did something, the response is an account. If we miss class and want to avoid giving the impression that we are bad students, we make excuses or justifications. An *excuse* is an **account that suggests the person has or claims no responsibility regarding their action**. An excuse would be something such as "I missed class because I was sick." A *justification* is an **account of behavior where people admit they did the act but deny any wrongdoing associated with the act**. A justification would be "I missed class because I already knew the material we would cover today."

People also try to maintain their presentations by *disclaimers*—that is, **disclaiming a role even while we are acting in that role**. "I usually don't drink, but this punch is so good" disclaims the role of drinker. "I'm not prejudiced, but …" followed by a racist remark or "I'm no expert, but …" followed by a remark only an expert could make are phrases that tell the audience that the person is not what they appear to be. We find these kinds of statements given when people are trying to reduce the gravity of the situation yet still make the claim.

Often, the audience accepts a person's accounts or disclaimers, and the interaction proceeds smoothly, but sometimes, the drama does not work out so well. People may present themselves in the role of someone who knows how to act in social situations but does not live up to those claims. Someone may fall down a flight of stairs as they make their grand entrance. Another may stand up at a meeting to give a report and claim to be an expert, but their trembling hands and factual errors will not support this claim. The speaker and those in the audience may attempt to ignore the errors, but at some point, the speaker may get too flustered to continue the pretense of living up to the role or may become embarrassed and laugh, cry, faint, or blush. When a group can no longer support the claims made by an individual, the whole group may become embarrassed or angry.

Implicit in interactions is the assumption that presentations will be maintained. Each person agrees to maintain the self and to support the presentations of others. If the presentations are not supported by the people themselves or by others, they may be followed by an emotional response. For example, in some situations, I may become embarrassed, and if my presentation is ridiculed, I may get angry. In another situation, if someone seems to fill your image of the ideal romantic love, you may fall in love with that individual; if the person then is cruel, unfaithful, or behaves in some other way that tarnishes your image of them, you may grow angry and eventually fall out of love.

Not only do people learn behavior in the process of socialization and interaction but people also learn appropriate feelings about themselves and others. People learn self-esteem by understanding how others evaluate them; they learn when to be embarrassed, when to be angry, and both when to fall in love and with what type of person. If people are angry at someone who deserves respect, they feel guilty about their feelings. If they love someone whom others define as entirely inappropriate, they become confused. Again, people have expectations about maintaining these performances of self and then respond emotionally when these expectations are not met. This happens in all roles and in whatever groups in which people act.

Goffman was also instrumental in conceiving the concept of frames in his book *Frame Analysis*. Goffman was trying to explain how conceptual frames structure people's perception of the society; therefore, frame analysis was about organization of experiences rather than organization of society. **Frames organize the experiences and guide action for the individual and/or for everyone. *Frame analysis*, then, is the study of organization of social experiences.** One example that Goffman used to help people better understand the concept is associating the frame with the concept of a picture frame. He used the picture frame concept to illustrate how people use the frame (which represents structure) to hold together their picture (which represents the context) of what they are experiencing in their life. The most basic frames are called primary frameworks. ***Primary frameworks* take an experience or an aspect of a scene of an individual that would originally be meaningless and turn it into something meaningful**. One type of primary framework is a ***natural framework*, which identifies situations that happened in the natural world and is completely physical, with no human influences**. The other type of framework is a *social framework*, **which explains events and connects it to humans**. An example of a natural framework would be the weather, and an example of social framework would be the meteorologist who reports to people the weather forecast. Goffman concentrated more on the frameworks and tried to construct a general statement regarding the structure, or form, of experiences individuals have at any moment of their social life.

Inevitably, Goffman has been instrumental in sociology, demonstrating to researchers how to orchestrate research and what forms of behaviors on which to focus. Nevertheless, his initial writings from early in his career that focused on theater metaphor have been the most popular on college campuses. Arguably, his analysis or recommendations for analyses of human behavior have been far more detailed than sociologists appear to be willing to pursue. Instead, sociologists take elements of Goffman's writings and integrate them into their research.

Summary

What emerged in the late 1800s through today were theories about social life that focused on more social psychological processes. The difference, though, between George Herbert Mead and the others listed here are quite stark in one sense, similar on another. Mead was a realist who believed in natural laws, objective reality, deductive research, and the importance of movement. Because of this, he focused much of his work on addressing the consequences of his ideas—that is, how people learn, grow, and develop. The use of taking roles, learning, and melding general expectations of others provided a beginning. At the same time, he focused on how people experience the world around them, including the sense of time. He demonstrated how people develop consciousness. Inevitably, these ideas provided a foundation for understanding the world around us.

When we reach two of his students, Charles Ellwood and Herbert Blumer, they translated his works into more sociological discussions but also eliminated elements of the realism to which Mead adhered. Instead, they focused more on subjectivity and the need to do more inductive, qualitative work. By doing this, researchers would gain a better understanding of the people they studied and, in turn, gain a better understanding of the world in which they live. Ellwood purposely focused on group behavior, concluding that groups operate and function much like an individual does, seeing groups as larger forms of an individual. In approaching groups this way, he remained consistent with the ideas of Mead and Dewey in their approaches to understanding, by recognizing natural laws. Blumer focused more and more of his time on human experience and how that shaped perception, relying heavily on Mead's ideas on consciousness and action.

Goffman, who studied under Blumer, assumed most of the ideas accentuated by Mead, Ellwood, and Blumer, or at least the ideas they agreed upon, and took things in a slightly different direction. In a never-ending struggle to observe and understand human behavior, Goffman took it upon himself to identify the details of human life, addressing how or what a researcher might do to frame human behavior. What he left us with were the parameters for detailed analysis that no one has integrated completely. It is still there to be seen.

Overall, the theorists and their respective schools of thought are still active in sociology today. The legacies of each of these individuals have taken very odd turns. Much of the work of Mead and Ellwood is largely forgotten. What exists of Mead in sociology today is interpreted from a Blumerian perspective, thereby changing what Mead wrote in some manner. Nevertheless, the enduring qualities are the methodologies that force us to examine in detail the very humans we wish to understand. That, decades later, is the legacy they leave us.

Comprehension Questions

1. What are Charles Ellwood's ideas on the self and group identity?

2. What are the similarities and differences between Ellwood and Blumer when it comes to research methodologies?

3. Explain Darwin's role in providing the context for processual theories.

4. What is the "act-as-such" and the "social act"? Please give examples of how each would function.

5. Explain the importance of the "other" as it applies to social consciousness from the perspective of George Herbert Mead.

Critical Thinking Questions

1. Explain Mead's ideas on the two-phase process of the "I" and "me." How would this be used to explain Goffman's dramaturgy?

2. What is Mead's views on the concept of time? Is this consistent or inconsistent with symbolic interactionism's premise on meaning? Please explain your answer.

3. What are significant gestures? How might the concept of significant gestures work with "habit"?

4. Explain how the generalized other might be consistent with Durkheim's ideas on a strong collective conscience.

5. What does it mean to take the role of the other, or role-taking? How would this phenomena play itself out on a first date?

Additional Recommended Reading

Blumer, H. (1969). *Symbolic interactionism: Perspective and method.* University of California Press.

Ellwood, C. A. (1925). *The psychology of human society.* D. Appleton.

Ellwood, C. A. (1927). *Cultural evolution*. Century.

Ellwood, C. A. (1933). *Methods in sociology: A critical study*. Duke University Press.

Goffman, E. (1959). *The presentation of self in everyday life*. Anchor Publishing.

Goffman, E. (1974). *Frame analysis: An essay on the organization of experience*. Northeastern University Press.

Mead, G. H. (1964). *Selected writings*. University of Chicago Press.

References

Albert, S. (1984). The sense of closure. In K. J. Gergen & M. M. Gergen (Eds.), *Historical social psychology* (pp. 159–172). Lawrence Erlbaum Associates.

Blumer, H. (1936). Social attitudes and nonsymbolic interaction. *The Journal of Educational Sociology, 9*(9), 515–523.

Blumer, H. (1969). *Symbolic interactionism: Perspective and method*. University of California Press.

Cooley, C. H. (1927). *Social organization*. Charles Scribner's Sons.

Dewey, J. (1896). The reflex arc concept in psychology. *Psychological Review, 3*, 357–370.

Dewey, J. (1927). *The public and its problems*. Henry Holt and Co.

Dewey, J. (1929). *The quest for certainty: A study of the relation of knowledge and action*. Minton, Balch & Company.

Ellwood, C. A. (1899). Prolegomena to social psychology: The need of the study of social psychology. *American Journal of Sociology, 4*(5), 656–665.

Ellwood, C. A. (1902). Aristotle as a sociologist. *Annals of the American Academy of Political Science, 19*, 1–5.

Ellwood, C. A. (1916). Objectivism in sociology. *American Journal of Sociology, 22*(3), 289–305.

Ellwood, C. A. (1925). *The psychology of human society*. D. Appleton and Company.

Ellwood, C. A. (1927a). Recent developments in sociology." In E. C. Hayes (Ed.), *Recent Developments in the Social Sciences* (pp. 1–49). J. B. Lippencott Company.

Ellwood, C. A. (1927b). *Cultural evolution*. The Century Co.

Ellwood, C. A. (1933). The uses and limitations of the statistical method in the social sciences. *The Scientific Monthly, 37*(4), 353–357.

House, F. N. (1936). *The development of sociology*. McGraw-Hill.

Jensen, H. E. (1947). Charles Abram Ellwood, 1873–1946. *American Journal of Sociology, 52*(4), 362.

Lewis, J. D., & Smith, R. L. (1980). *American sociology and pragmatism: Mead, Chicago sociology, and symbolic interaction*. The University of Chicago Press.

LoConto, D. G. (2011). Charles A. Ellwood and the end of sociology. *The American Sociologist, 42*(1),112–128.

LoConto, D. G., & Jones-Pruett, D. (2006). The influence of Charles A. Ellwood on Herbert Blumer and symbolic interactionism. *The Journal of Classical Sociology*, *6*(1), 75–99.

Maines, D. R., Sugrue, N. M., & Katovich, M. A. (1983). The sociological import of G. H. Mead's theory of the past. *American Sociological Review*, *48*(2), 161–173.

Mead, G. H. (1908). The philosophical basis for ethics. *International Journal of Ethics*, 18, 311-323.

Mead, G. H. (1926). The objective reality of perspectives. In E. S. Brightman (Ed.), *Proceedings of the sixth International Congress of Philosophy* (pp. 75–85). Unknown Publisher.

Mead, G. H. (1929a). The nature of the past. In John Coss (Ed.), *Essays in honor of John Dewey* (pp. 235–242). Henry Holt & Co.

Mead, G. H. (1929b). National-mindedness and international-mindedness. *International Journal of Ethics*, *39*(4), 385–407.

Mead, G. H. (1931). *The philosophy of the present*. The University of Chicago Press.

Mead, G. H. (1934). *Mind, self, and society*. The University of Chicago Press.

Mead, G. H. (1938). *The philosophy of the act*. The University of Chicago Press.

Mead, G. H. (1964). *Selected writings*. University of Chicago Press.

Menand, L. (2001). *The metaphysical club*. Farrar, Straus & Giroux.

Peirce, C. S. (1934). *Collected papers: Vol. 5, Pragmatism and pragmaticism*. The Belknap Press of Harvard University Press.

Scott, M. B., & Lyman, S. M. (1968). Accounts. *American Sociological Review*, *33*(1), 46–62.

Small, A. (1916). Fifty years of sociology in the United States (1865–1915). *American Journal of Sociology* *21*(6), 721–864.

Strauss, A. (1991). Mead's multiple conceptions of time and evolution: Their contexts and their consequences for theory. *International Sociology*, *6*(4), 411–426.

Thompson, E. T. (1946). Charles Abram Ellwood, 1873–1946. *American Sociological Review*, *11*, 753–754.

Chapter 5: Power and Oppression

Utopia and the Dreams of the 19th Century

In the 1800s, with the advent and acceptance of science and the Enlightenment, there increasingly became the belief that humanity was moving toward a *utopia*, a perfect society in which people work well with each other and are happy, with perfect laws, government, and social conditions. This was consistent with how many interpreted the works of Darwin, that people were evolving and continually improving life and existence. Given the technological changes that were occurring in the late 1800s, it did not seem far-fetched for people to believe that.

However, not all social thinkers were in agreement with that ideology. Some social thinkers were concerned that those in power would continue to manipulate and oppress the masses, taking advantage of these new technologies. The explosion of wealth during this time was extraordinary. The wealth of people like John D. Rockefeller, Cornelius Vanderbilt, Henry Ford, and Andrew Carnegie would by today's standards be measured in the hundreds of billions of dollars, far more than tech giants like Elon Musk, Bill Gates, Mark Zuckerberg, and even Jeff Bezos, the wealthiest individual in the world as of 2021. For instance, John D. Rockefeller's wealth in today's dollars would be approximately 400 billion dollars. Jeff Bezos at the time of this writing has an estimated wealth of just under 200 billion dollars. And that is after the expansion of his wealth during the COVID-19 pandemic.

Big business boomed, with technology such as typewriters, cash registers, and adding machines helping to transform how people worked. And the economic explosion included not only industrial growth but also a growth in agricultural technology, such as mechanical reapers. In a time of such great expansion and fewer regulations surrounding wealth and business practices, circumstances were perfect for the rise of a class of extremely wealthy individuals who made up a very small percentage of society. They had the power and means to create opportunities and jobs for the masses. Unfortunately, with less social prioritization on workers' rights, issues like discrimination, exploitation, and low wages were characteristics of the era. For some social thinkers, this increase in wealth of the most wealthy at a time when so many were still struggling to literally survive gave rise to caution.

In this chapter, the various theorists and theories focus on inequalities of power. With power comes the ability to manipulate others. We see this today in the world where we are manipulated by individuals and companies to think the way they want us to.

Guiding Questions

1. Generally, how do those in power use their wealth to manipulate the masses?

2. How do those in power shape how the masses think in terms of attitudes, values, and desires?

3. How do those in power shape the economy?

4. How do categories or labels placed upon people influence or determine their opportunities?

Ultimately what you will find here is that these theorists are suspect of the *status quo*—**that is, the existing state of affairs**. Their desire was and is to find ways to facilitate freedom and equality for everyone.

Karl Marx

Karl Marx (1818–1883) was born in Germany. His father, a lawyer, and his mother were both descended from long lines of rabbis. Marx attended college, planning to practice law, but after becoming involved with a radical antireligious group, he decided to devote his life to philosophy. Unable to get a university position, he became a writer for a radical publication and wrote a series of articles on various inhumane social conditions that were common in the western world. His articles attracted the attention of government officials who opposed his views. Subsequently, he lost his job. Shortly thereafter, he moved to Paris and met the leading intellectuals of the radical movements of Europe, completing his conversion to *socialism,* **a political and economic theory of social organization that advocates that the means of production, distribution, and exchange should be owned or regulated by a strong central government or the community as a whole**. During this time, he began his lifelong friendship with Friedrich Engels, with whom he wrote several articles and books, including the now-famous *Communist Manifesto* (1847/2014). Having joined the Communist League in Brussels, he returned to Germany. He was again pressured to leave the country for his activities. He moved to London where, with his friend Engels, he continued to promote his views until his death in 1883.

The theme common to all the writings of Marx and Engels was a sense of moral outrage at the misery produced in the lower classes by the new industrial social order. They concluded that a political and violent revolution was necessary in the evolutionary process of society and that it was the only means by which the improvement of social conditions could be achieved. This was a consistent view for Marx throughout his life and is also why his ideas were feared by those in power.

Marx believed that social conflict, struggle, and strife were at the core of society, the source of all social change. This was made clear through the book *The German Ideology* (Marx & Engels, 1844/1998). Marx asserted that all history was influenced by this struggle of people over scarce resources. He believed that all change, social conditions, and even society itself were based on economic factors and that economic inequality resulted in class struggles between the *bourgeoisie* **(the owners and rulers of the means of production) and the** *proletariat* **(the workers)**. These conflicts between the rich and the poor, the owners and the workers, lead to feelings of *alienation* **among the proletariat, a feeling of frustration and disconnection from work and life**. The recognition among workers that society is stratified and that they share the same plight is known as *class consciousness*—**that is, awareness of one's place in a system of social classes, especially (in Marxist terms) as it relates to the class struggle, which, according to Marx, would lead to a revolution**. It was Marx's belief that conflict, revolution, and the overthrow of capitalism were inevitable.

This process was consistent with his view of dialectic materialism, the dialectic as proposed by German philosopher Georg Wilhelm Friedrich Hegel. Hegel used the dialectic as a means of an intellectual exercise in which someone would begin with an intellectual proposition (i.e., a thesis). The antithesis would follow, negating the thesis—that is, a reaction to the proposition. Lastly, there would be synthesis that solves the conflict between the thesis and antithesis. This would begin a new intellectual proposition. While Hegel used this much in the same way Mead saw the act-as-such, Hegel saw this more as through thinking, not in social action. Marx, however, as they say, turned Hegel on his head by seeing this process in material terms. Hence, things in terms of thesis, antithesis, to synthesis. That is, there is the class situation, then the revolution abolishing the class system, and finally there would develop a new system that would stabilize. Marx referred to this as "socialism," which will be addressed later. However, the dialectic is also a form of a part of an analysis of progress in all forms, including philosophical thought and history. The ideal of this is that it demonstrates a process of how problems potentially get worked out. In this sense, then, Marx was following suit with most of the 1800s in that there was this evolution of humanity. The major difference was that Marx felt those that did not have power would need to stand up to correct the wrong. This was part of that process.

Today, regardless of whether they agree or disagree with Marx's ideas, few sociologists deny the importance of the contributions he made. Sociologists are still trying to understand the influence of the economy, social conflict, social structure, social class, and social change on society. Students in the United States often think of Karl Marx as an atheist and a bad person. Nothing could be further from the truth. Marx never denied the existence of God. He was born into a Jewish family and as an adult became a Lutheran. His concern was how the wealthy were using the concept of God and religion to further their own selfish desires. Marx's goal was to create a society where people worked together to further the goals of everyone. He wanted to see people become less selfish and be united, not just at a community or state level but globally.

Karl Marx believed the driving force of history is the unfolding of ideas whereby the spirit of reason gradually unfolds. Marx rejected Hegel's idealism but accepted history as a continued unfolding of different states or stages, eventually being replaced by new ones (hence, dialectic materialism). Marx was a *materialist*, **which is to say he believed that material factors influence events**.

Marx made various assumptions about the model of a human being. First, humans are natural beings; that is, they are part of nature. They are real. This may sound strange, but at the time, many philosophers, theologians, and social thinkers bought into Cartesian dualism and considered humans as separate and different from the rest of nature. This was definitely influenced and supported by Christianity. Nevertheless, there were others, like Marx, who believed that while there may be something unique about humans, people also were part of creation and were bound by natural laws.

Second, Marx recognized that humans have innate needs, such as hunger, sex, survival, food, and so much more. This becomes important because for a civilization to exist and thrive, these innate needs have to be accommodated. Otherwise, the civilization would cease to be, potentially falling into the abyss of conflict and disarray.

Third, humans also have capacities or potentials to create—that is, *self-actualization*, **meaning to create self-beauty, pleasure, enjoyment, and intellectual enticement**. We see this not only in museums all over the world but also in the creation through architecture, clothing, makeup, sports, games, music, and so much more. Many of us have been drawn to tears of appreciation and joy when visiting a museum, listening to music, or watching a movie. This reflects self-actualization and demonstrates humans' capacity to create.

Fourth, Marx believed that humans' needs are plastic; that is, they are conditioned by the physical and social environment. Of course, this becomes critical from a sociological point of view. It does not take much imagination to see the differences found among people around the world. The foods we eat and our religions, values, and attitudes are shaped by where we were raised. In the United States, we see politically red states and blue states. Various ethnic groups settled in different parts of the country and brought with them preexisting views. They helped establish these geographical areas. All phenomena get filtered through these preexisting views. They become subcultures that makes up the entire country. We get shaped by the social and physical environment around us.

Fifth, Marx believed that humans are social beings. People need people. People influence and shape each other. This is consistent with humans being plastic. We all recognize how we are shaped by others (e.g., friends, family, people in authority). We all use them as references to identify how we want to be. Sometimes, social pressures in the groups we belong to force us to act a certain way. It can be uncomfortable but only because we value those individuals or groups.

Sixth, humans are also producers. Objects have to be made, such as food, shelter, and material conditions. This production assists in establishing institutions and structures that facilitate the values and attitudes of the people. Therefore, it helps in maintaining the status quo. Human survival depends on productive activity in which people transform the natural environment. That is why labor becomes so important for Marx. It is part of human essence. This is the way our human energies or potential can be expressed. By doing this, people expand their capacities.

Marx suggested that while this is the nature of human life, sometimes the objects and products of people's labor become alienated from the producer. As mentioned above with regard to alienation, this is when products are external to the producer, and products do not expand our capacities. This is both at the structural and individual level. Workers become estranged from the objects, and they are beyond their control. Objects take on a force of their own, and people have to adapt to them (the world of objects), and that limits our capacities of being. Instead of facilitation, it has the obverse effects. People become trapped by the material and social conditions around them. You may have seen that with your own family members who claim that things have always been this way and will continue to be this way. Yet every day they go to work and go through the motions of everyday life. People are stuck with limits as to where they can go and what they can achieve. How many times do people overspend on clothing, shoes, or cars simply because they are trying to find a life that portrays a certain image? People who make these products typically cannot afford them or purchase them at the expense of needs.

Antonio Gramsci (1891–1937) was an intellectual and politician as well as a founder of the Italian Communist Party. In 1911 Gramsci attended the University of Turin, where he encountered the Socialist Youth Federation and joined the Socialist Party. During World War I he studied Marxist thought and became a leading theoretician. He formed a leftist group within the Socialist Party and founded the newspaper *L'Ordine Nuovo*.

Gramsci led a leftist walkout at the socialist congress at Livorno in 1921 to begin the Italian Communist Party and then spent 2 years in the Soviet Union. Back in Italy, he became head of his party in 1924 and was elected to the country's Chamber of Deputies. After his party was outlawed by Benito Mussolini, Gramsci was arrested and imprisoned in 1926. In prison, despite rigorous censorship, Gramsci carried out an extraordinary and wide-ranging historical and theoretical study of Italian society and possible strategies for change.

One of the key areas that Gramsci wrote about was hegemony. *Hegemony* **refers to the political, economic, or military predominance or control of one state over others**. Marx had predicted that socialist revolution was inevitable in capitalist societies. By the early 20th century, no such revolution had occurred in the most advanced nations. Rather, capitalism seemed stronger than ever. Capitalism, Gramsci suggested, maintained control not just through violence and political and economic coercion but also through ideology. The bourgeoisie developed a hegemonic culture, which propagated its own values and norms so that they became the obvious values of all. People identified their own good with the good of the bourgeoisie and helped to maintain the status quo rather than revolting.

During this process of alienation, people find themselves continually in a state of reification. *Reification* **is when the mental creations of people take on a reality of their own**. Peoples' ideas become a power against themselves. This is an idealist connotation. People become trapped by their own ideas. Think of all the money people spend because they believe they have to have a new phone every 2 years or those who have to have the new styles of clothing or new technologies for video games. People become trapped by this thinking and spend too much money in those endeavors. Also, however, at a more macro level, think of the political problems associated with being trapped by one's own ideas. If one believes that the only way for society to succeed is to have less government, what happens when there are economic catastrophes? We have seen in recent years how Republicans claiming to be conservative do not want to spend as much money to help the average citizen because that will allegedly cause dependence, though there is no significant evidence to support that. Yet because of a philosophical belief, aid does not arrive to help people, because that belief says in the long run it will even out. The belief is that this process will be more extreme but will remedy itself quicker.

Marx placed a great deal of emphasis on how the material world shaped people. The economy was a key feature. Though he was not an economic determinist, the economy, in Marx's eyes, influenced humans quite a bit. He identified what he referred to as the means of production. **The *means of production* are all the aspects of economic production, such as tools, technological structure, capital, and money**. All social institutions are built on that economic foundation, and they conform to a greater or lesser degree to the requirements of the economic system. Those who own the means of production hold a tremendous amount of sway in society. Those in power usually connect the means of production with the state and legal systems, as well as to education, religion, family, culture, morality, religious beliefs, and the media. Inevitably, according to Marx, the economic system becomes the foundation of society. The struggle mentioned above in terms of conflict and oppression then becomes a struggle in part to own or possess the means of production. From Marx's perspective, whomever controls that controls much of society.

Marx's Theory of Change

From Marx's perspective, if you look at any one time in history, there are only two classes who are paramount in society. This denotes the character of society; this denotes the struggles and antagonism: increasing effort to get power and increasing effort to keep power and achieve more. Class conflict is a permanent, ongoing feature of society. Since the means of production change over time, the nature of the class struggle also changes. ***Ideologies*, or a group of interrelated ideas that serve interests of a particular class and serve the vested interests of the powerful, are critical to Marxist philosophy**. This comes into play when talking about the theorists who come later in this chapter, such as Adorno, Horkheimer, and Habermas.

People have ideologies, but often they do not realize it. Ideologies provide illusions that compensate for deficiencies in life. These are distorted beliefs. The degree to which these beliefs become internalized influence how people are then unable to grasp what their true interests are. They fail to see the close connection between their position and the structure with which they are involved. This is referred to as *false consciousness*—**that is, not recognizing one's place in the social structure and thereby subscribing to beliefs nonbeneficial to them**. People do not understand they are in an alienated system. Religion is one way to create or maintain false consciousness. In the 21st century, however, it is those filter bubbles on the internet and social media. People keep getting fed the same information and assume that it must be true.

False consciousness inevitably leads to *class consciousness*, **which is a subjective awareness of objective class interests shared with others in similar positions in the productive system**. Marx and Engels (1844/1998) developed a theory or model of change that would lead toward *communism*, **a socioeconomic order structured upon the ideas of common ownership of the means of production and the absence of social classes, money, and the state**.

Marx and Engels (1844/1998) began with the view that property relations determine class. In other words, those who own the means of production are the ruling class. Marx and Engels divided classes up loosely as the ruling class (bourgeoisie) versus the oppressed class (proletariat). The ruling class is the dominant force and controls property, which is the means of production, and of course the many other institutions or social structures that shape society. This in turn influences class structure.

For class consciousness to emerge, specific things need to happen. Marx and Engels (1844/1998) said that there are certain factors that will contribute to class consciousness. First, there would be increasing concentrations of workers in urban industrial areas. As cities developed due to increased industrialization, more people began moving to these developing cities. The areas of exploitation became more concentrated in these areas as opposed to farmland. Workers would live closer together and in doing so would begin sharing stories of their common plight. At that time, a shared consciousness would emerge.

That is not enough, however, as there is always the concern that many people would not fight against the system if they have a job. This is often why most who demonstrate tend to be younger people. They have less to lose. Therefore, the oppressed conditions would become worse. Living conditions would make it so it would be harder and harder for people, specifically the proletariat, to survive. This is literally a life and death situation. At the same time, the gap between the rich and the poor would become larger. As mentioned in Chapter 2, this did in fact happen, and we have seen it also during the time of COVID where between March of 2020 and January of 2021, of the 660 billionaires in the United States, their net wealth increased 40%, or 1.1 trillion dollars (Collins, 2021).

As this phenomenon occurred, the proletariat would find it harder and harder to sustain their illusions. I suppose it is similar to those who originally believed COVID-19 was a hoax but then had friends or family get hospitalized or die because of it. These kinds of events happening is what makes it hard to sustain illusions or lies. For Marx and Engels (1844/1998), they saw the proletariat in living conditions with a lot of disease and death. Illusion can take you only so far. It is at this point that they begin to organize. But the problem with their organization is that they do not have the knowledge to know how to proceed. Therefore, the organization is a step, but a small step. They would still be manipulated by those in power.

At this point, the ***intellectuals*, the intermediate class of citizens who support the system by teaching and producing ideas that support the system**, collectively have a change of heart. They switch sides and join the proletariat organizations. They take a leadership role in these organizations and help the proletariat make their move. By this time, a change would take place in the stratification system in which there would be a polarization of the two major classes, the bourgeoisie and the proletariat.

The violent revolution then would begin where the proletariat must overthrow the bourgeoisie. The military who at that time was comprised mainly of proletariat then would defect as well and support the proletariat revolution. The bourgeoisie at this point would lose control of the situation, and eventually, the revolution works. At this point, a new government and economic system—that is, ***socialism* (people collectively own the means of production)**—is instituted and characterized by ownership of the means of production and all properties by the state. Some refer to this as the ***dictatorship of the proletariat*, meaning a central state that organizes, educates, and leads the masses toward communism and organizes defense against external capitalists**. All private property is abolished, and there would be a movement toward a classless society. The state would control everything, including education, teaching its citizens to be selfless and work for the benefit of the larger society. Altruism would become the strongest value of that society. Over a period of time, as people more and more adopt this philosophy, there would become less and less need for the government to be involved. Eventually, the government would fall away, and there would still be a civilization but with no government, no monetary system, and people would work together to provide for each other (i.e., communism).

This is definitely an idealistic view of what was going to happen, though tragic in the means to reach this end. This view though was consistent with the utopian views of the day. The difference was that Marx and Engels (1844/1998) felt it would happen only after a violent revolution, while others saw it happening gradually over time and evolving (see Bellamy, 1888). The role of Marx and his standing among social thinkers today is still strong. Oddly enough, his ideas frighten many Americans, and much propaganda has developed over the last 150 years that aims for the thought of his name or his ideas to be met with vitriol. How many times do we hear people suggest that liberal policies are socialist? Yet public schools are socialist, as are the maintenance of our roads. Social security, Medicare, the military, the police, and many other commonplace things in our society are all based on socialist principles.

The Frankfurt School

What became known as the Frankfurt School was originally a group of researchers associated with the Institute for Social Research in Frankfurt, Germany. The Institute was founded by Carl Grünberg in 1923. Like many who read Marx, the Frankfurt School promoted socialism and the overthrow of capitalism. It was responsible for the creation of what became known as critical theory. ***Critical theory* maintains that a primary goal of social thought, in general, is to understand and to help overcome the social structures (which facilitate capitalism) through which people are dominated and oppressed.** Believing that science, like other forms of knowledge, had been used as an instrument of oppression by those in power, those at the Frankfurt School warned against a blind faith in science and its accomplishments. Originally, they believed that scientific knowledge must not be pursued as an end in itself without acknowledging its impact on humanity.

Herbert Marcuse (1898–1979) was a critical theorist, sociologist, and member of the Frankfurt School. His theories and critique of capitalism earned him popularity among radicals and college students in the 1960s. His ideas in critical theory contributed to the extreme anticapitalist and antiestablishment sentiments within the counterculture movements of the time. Marcuse was born in Berlin in 1898 to a Jewish family. He served in the German army during the First World War. After the war, he attended the University of Freiburg, where he studied Marxism and joined the Social Democratic Party. He returned to Freiburg in 1929 and studied philosophy under Martin Heidegger. In addition to his Marxist leanings, he was greatly influenced by the existentialism of Heidegger. In 1933, Marcuse was invited to join the Frankfurt School. Soon after, he left Germany, following the other members of the institute to Geneva and Paris before finally settling in New York.

Marcuse was known for his critique of postwar capitalist society, ultimately being consistent with the work of Adorno and Horkheimer. Marcuse believed that the citizens of capitalist democracies were unwittingly enslaved and dehumanized by the economic and political system in a similar manner as the culture industry by Adorno and Horkheimer. In his classic work *One-Dimensional Man*, Marcuse describes these capitalist societies as places where citizens become victims by facilitating false needs that drive toward consumption and lack of interest in important issues in society. He sees citizens as being pacified in this process. Much like Marx, he sees those in middle and working classes being ignorant of the role Marx had believed they would turn. In essence, the system worked to ward off any form of revolution. Potentially due to his willingness to see hope from the existing system, where some people would lead a revolution, Habermas may have gained his "way out" for people in an oppressive system without a revolution. Unlike Adorno and Horkheimer, Marcuse still held to Marx's hopes that the people would rebel.

However, from 1930 onward, under the directorship of Max Horkheimer, the work of the Frankfurt School began to show significant deviations from orthodox Marxism. Principally, the Frankfurt School began to question the strict economic determinism orthodox Marxists focused on at the time. This coincided with a firm belief among the members of the Frankfurt School that social phenomena, such as culture, mass entertainment, education, and the family, played a direct role in initiating and maintaining oppression. Marxists prior to that time dismissed the importance of such phenomena on the grounds that these social phenomena were mere reflections of the underlying economic basis of the capitalist mode of production. An undue concern for such phenomena was generally thought of as a distraction from the real task of overthrowing capitalism. In contrast, the Frankfurt School argued that such phenomena were fundamentally important. The Frankfurt School's rejection of elements of Marxism and their focus on the various aspects of cultural oppression questioned whether capitalism would end anytime soon. The Frankfurt School rejected Marx's belief in the economic inevitability of capitalism experiencing cataclysmic economic crises. They believed that capitalism remained an oppressive system and increasingly viewed the system as far more adaptable and robust than Marxists had given it credit. The Frankfurt School came to portray capitalism as potentially capable of averting indefinitely its own demise. The final break with orthodox Marxism occurred with the Frankfurt School's condemning the leadership of the Soviet Union as a politically oppressive system. Politically, the Frankfurt School sought to distance itself from both Soviet socialism and capitalism.

Ultimately, the Frankfurt School focused on the problems of the Enlightenment. *The Enlightenment was a European intellectual movement of the late 17th and 18th centuries that emphasized reason and individualism rather than tradition.* This view covered most of the Western world and eventually the entire globe by 1900. People like Immanuel Kant felt that to avoid reason and individualism would lead to laziness and cowardice, that if people avoided reason and individualism they would be sheep, simply following the herd. The problem that Theodor Adorno and Max Horkheimer saw, however, was that people were not enlightened as much as originally thought. People were not in control of the world around them. Instead, Adorno and Horkheimer saw that humans were creating one disaster after another. They believed that rationality itself was becoming irrational. People were using bizarre or incorrect information to justify or encourage behavior. In doing so, people made bad choices and inevitably harmed each other. We could no longer *negate,* **or make ineffective, all the lies.**

Consider what was occurring at the time Adorno and Horkheimer were writing these things, the 1930s, 1940s, and 1950s. There was a world war that left over 55 million people dead. The United States, followed by the Soviet Union, developed the atomic bomb. And racist policies continued to dominate the United States and other parts of the globe. If people were so enlightened, Adorno and Horkheimer suggested, why were we so dominated by catastrophic events created by humans? Their response was that people became dominated by *subjective reason*—**that is, thinking in terms of means and ends and not addressing whether something was actually reasonable.** For example, if a company wanted to produce a product that would generate profit and jobs, they would go ahead and do so without thinking of long-term complications in making that product. But what if the production of that product damaged the environment (e.g., polluted the waterways)? Horkheimer advocated *objective reasoning*, **which is reasoning that would place value on the ends.** If the ends devastated the environment and in the long term caused irreparable damage, then the action should not be pursued. What Adorno and Horkheimer believed was that through short-term thinking generated by greed and selfishness, people were not enlightened but instead blinded by subjective reasoning, which led them down a destructive path.

The Culture Industry

This is no more true than in the critique of the culture industry. *Culture industry* **is the term used to describe the production and marketing of culture as a branch of the industry, covering a wide variety of industries, such as architecture, craft, film and television production, music, publication, and more.** Critical theorists took and take mass entertainment seriously. They were among the first social thinkers to recognize the potential social, political, and economic power of the entertainment industry. Adorno and Horkheimer (1979) saw the culture industry as constituting a principal source of domination within complex capitalist societies. They demonstrated that the very areas of life within which people believed they were genuinely free actually perpetuated domination by denying freedom and obstructing the development of a critical consciousness. Their discussions of the culture industry were a depiction of mass consumer societies as being based upon the systematic denial of genuine freedom.

They described the culture industry as a key integrative mechanism for binding individuals, as both consumers and producers, to modern capitalist societies. Where many sociologists have argued that complex capitalist societies are fragmented and heterogeneous in character, Adorno and Horkheimer (1979) insisted that the culture industry functions to maintain a uniform system, to which all usually conform or worse, obey. The culture industry facilitates a culture in which mass consumption becomes the ideal. The consumer no longer has freedom of choice. The goal of the culture industry is the production of goods that are profitable and consumable. It operates to ensure its own reproduction. To achieve that goal, consumers must be blinded to the thought of freedom of choice and instead socialized to think they must possess these products in some form. The culture industry is a global, multitrillion-dollar enterprise, driven primarily by the pursuit of profit. What the culture industry produces is a means to the generation of profit, like any commercial enterprise.

Adorno and Horkheimer (1979) believed that individuals' integration within the culture industry had the fundamental effect of restricting the development of a critical awareness of the social conditions that confront the world. The culture industry promotes domination of the masses by subverting the psychological development of people in complex capitalist societies. In other words, people are socialized to think that what is most important in life are products of the culture industry. Everyone becomes more concerned with celebrities. People focus more on clothing styles and the cars they drive. In the process of doing this, people forget or ignore the important things that are occurring in life. That is, those in power are blinding everyone, much like false consciousness, and influencing them to think and behave the way they want and in the process allow those in power to continue oppressing the populous.

Adorno and Horkheimer (1979) stated that cultural commodities are subject to the same instrumentally rationalized mechanical forces that serve to dominate individuals' working lives. ***Instrumental rationality, according to Max Weber, is a pursuit of any means necessary to achieve a specific end.*** Similar to Horkheimer's subjective reasoning, in this sense, then, those in power were pursuing profit and domination by making people believe these products of the culture industry were important. Through the veritably exponential increase in volume and scope of the commodities produced under the culture industry, individuals were increasingly subjected to the same underlying conditions through which the complex capitalist system was maintained and reproduced. As Adorno and Horkheimer (1979) asserted, "Amusement under late capitalism is the prolongation of work. It is sought after as an escape from the mechanized work process, and to recruit strength in order to be able to cope with it again. But at the same time mechanization has such a power over man's leisure and happiness, and so profoundly determines the manufacture of amusement goods, that his experiences are inevitably after-images of the work process itself" (p. 137). Accordingly, then, consistent exposure to the culture industry pacified its consumers. Consumers were presented as being denied any genuine opportunities to actively contribute to the production of the goods to which they are exposed. People simply buy.

For Adorno and Horkheimer (1979), this was a cumulative and critical mass of the economy that impacted consciousness and lives. When taken altogether, the assorted media of the culture industry created conditions where the capacity for critical reflection upon oneself and one's social conditions were obstructed. The form and content of the culture industry increasingly became misidentified as an expression of reality: Individuals come to perceive and conceive of reality through the predetermined form of the culture industry. The culture industry is understood by Adorno and Horkheimer to be an essential component of a reified form of second nature, which individuals come to accept as a prestructured social order to which they must conform and adapt. The commodities produced by the culture industry do not necessarily have to be good or bad, but their effects upon individuals become deadly serious.

Morality and Nihilism

Inevitably, this pursuit of understanding the effects of the culture industry led to Adorno and Horkheimer pursuing ideas on morality. They were particularly interested in Adorno and Horkheimer's work, as they were not only concerned with what constituted a moral life but were also concerned with the ability to identify of what exactly this moral life would be comprised. They believed that social life and societies no longer organized around a set of widely promoted moral truths, as Durkheim had hoped, and that modern societies lacked a moral foundation. What replaced morality as the foundation of social life became the enjoyment of the capitalist market. According to Adorno and Horkheimer, modern capitalist societies are fundamentally *nihilistic*; **that is, they subscribe to the idea that life is inherently meaningless.** Within a nihilistic world, moral beliefs and moral reasoning are held to have no rational authority. Moral claims are conceived of as, at best, inherently subjective statements, expressing not an objective property of the world but peoples' own prejudices. Morality is presented as thereby lacking any objective, public basis. The promotion of specific moral beliefs is thus understood as an instrument for the assertion of one's own partial interests. Morality has been subsumed by instrumental rationality. Think of how Americans are so divided now with regard to what they believe to be true. Scientists, police, and journalists have become the enemies of many Americans. Tucker Carlson tells the American people categorically different stances on issues than Rachel Maddow. Who do we believe? But more importantly, why?

Adorno and Horkheimer's account of nihilism rests, in large part, on their understanding of reason and of how modern societies have come to conceive of legitimate knowledge. They argued that morality had fallen victim to the distinction drawn between objective and subjective knowledge. *Objective knowledge* **consists of empirically verifiable facts about material phenomena, whereas** *subjective knowledge* **consists of all that remains, including such things as evaluative and normative statements about the world.** Adorno and Horkheimer argued that moral beliefs and moral reasoning had been confined to the sphere of subjective knowledge. They argued that under the force of instrumental rationality or subjective reason, people had come to conceive of the only meaningfully existing entities as empirically verifiable facts—that is, statements on the structure and content of reality (though that is no longer true, as we see people in power presenting fiction as fact). Moral values and beliefs, in contrast, are denied such a status. Morality is thereby conceived of as inherently prejudicial in character so that, for example, there appears to be no way in which one can objectively and rationally resolve disputes between conflicting substantive moral beliefs and values. Under the condition of nihilism, one cannot distinguish between more or less valid moral beliefs and values since the criteria allowing for such evaluative distinctions have been excluded from the domain of subjective knowledge. Hence, we currently see Americans making value judgments based on the view that either liberalism or conservatism are inherently bad and are leading the country down a narrow, wicked path. Most Americans do not know what either philosophy states. Correspondingly, the same is true regarding politicians from both Democratic and Republican Parties. People blindly follow.

Adorno and Horkheimer argued that, under nihilistic conditions, morality had become a function or tool of those in power. The measure of the influence of any particular moral vision was an expression of the material interests that underlie it. They identified the effects of nihilism as extending to philosophical attempts to rationally defend morality and moral reasoning. Thus, in support of their argument, they did not rely upon merely pointing to the extent of moral diversity and conflict in modern societies. Nor did they rest their case upon those who, in the name of some radical account of individual freedom, positively propose nihilism.

Instead, they identified the effects of nihilism within moral philosophy itself, paying particular attention to the moral theory of Immanuel Kant. Adorn and Horkheimer criticized Kant, arguing that the moral law offered by Kant demonstrated the extent to which morality had been reduced to the status of subjective knowledge. Ultimately, Kant was condemned for proposing an account of moral reasoning that was every bit as formal and devoid of any substantively moral constituents as instrumental reasoning. The thrust of their criticism of Kant was not so much that Kant developed such an account of morality, since this was, according to Adorno and Horkheimer, to a large extent prefigured by the material conditions of Kant's time and place, but that he both failed to identify the effects of these conditions and, in so doing, failed to discern the extent to which his moral philosophy provided an affirmation, rather than a criticism, of such conditions. Kant, of all people, was condemned for not being sufficiently reflexive.

Unlike some other thinkers and philosophers of the time, Adorno and Horkheimer did not think that nihilism could be overcome by a mere act of will or by simply affirming some substantive moral vision of the "good life." They do not seek to philosophically circumnavigate the extent to which moral questions concerning the possible nature of the good life have become so profoundly problematic. For Adorno and Horkheimer, this process had been so thorough and complete that we could no longer identify the necessary elements of the good life since the philosophical means for doing so had been subverted by the domination of nature and the instrumentalization of reason. The role of the critical theorist is therefore not to positively promote some alternative, more just vision of a morally grounded social and political order. This would far exceed the bounds of the potential of reason. Rather, the critical theorist must fundamentally aim to retain and promote an awareness of such conditions and the extent to which such conditions are capable of being changed. Adorno and Horkheimer's somewhat dystopian account of morality in modern societies followed from their argument that such societies are charmed by instrumental reasoning and the prioritization of "objective facts." Nihilism served to fundamentally frustrate the ability of morality to impose authoritative limits upon the application of instrumental reason.

Jürgen Habermas

Jürgen Habermas (1929–) has produced a large body of work since the early 1970s. He represents the second generation of the Frankfurt School and critical theory. His work was part of a change in critical theory and a break from Adorno and Horkheimer. His early work was devoted to the *public sphere*, **which for Habermas was an area in social life where individuals could come together to freely discuss and identify societal problems and influence political action.** In essence, it is when people have true dialogues. The internet by itself does not qualify as the public sphere but elements on the internet can. Anywhere there is free access to information and the sharing of that information is considered the public sphere. Criticisms, however, regarding the public sphere focus on whether there can be a place free enough to not be spoiled by those in power. Adorno and Horkheimer might argue that the public sphere is rare or rarer than Habermas alludes. The public sphere itself is largely consistent with how Mead hoped people would interact with each other in his thoughts on international-mindedness.

Habermas (1990) as also critical of how earlier critical theorists addressed modernity. *Modernity* **was associated with individual subjectivity, scientific explanation and rationalization, a decline in emphasis on religious worldviews, the emergence of bureaucracy, rapid urbanization, the rise of nation-states, and accelerated financial exchange and communication.** Habermas felt that modernity was more than just a period, it was the social, political, cultural, institutional, and psychological conditions that arise from historical processes. He felt that to reverse modernization, as postmodernists did, would be futile (see Chapter 7). The goal for Habermas was to work with modernity, not against it. He then slowly began to articulate theories of rationality, meaning, and truth.

A contrast with early critical theory was that Habermas defended the unfinished emancipatory project of the Enlightenment against criticism. Remember that Adorno and Horkheimer felt that life in the 1930s through the 1950s shattered hopes that modernity's increased rationalization and technological innovation facilitated human emancipation. Instead, we were spiraling toward the abyss of consumption and an inability to negate problems occurring within the world. Habermas defended the Enlightenment rationality, stating that the problems identified by Adorno and Horkheimer only occurred if we combine and confuse instrumental rationality with rationality as such, if technical control is mistaken for the entirety of communication. Habermas focused on the lack of communication that was occurring. He subsequently developed an account of **communicative rationality oriented around achieving mutual understandings rather than simply success or authenticity**. This inevitably led to *intersubjectivity*, **which is when people interact together and agree upon a reality.** In essence, Habermas was and is far more optimistic about the potential of humanity and focuses more on what can occur.

Theory of Communicative Action

This optimism is found in Habermas's *The Theory of Communicative Action*. Habermas (1984) highlighted four kinds of action by people in society: (a) teleological action, (b) normatively regulated action, (c) dramaturgical action, and (d) communicative action. *Teleological action* **is when the individual or individuals make a "decision among alternative courses of action, with a view to the realization of an end, guided by maxims, and based on an interpretation of the situation"** (Habermas, 1984, p. 85). In many ways, this is similar to instrumental rationality. It is very utilitarian in nature. A key aspect is the acknowledgement that this is an interpretive exercise by individuals. They are interpreting their situation, making decisions, and acting on those decisions.

Normatively regulated action **is when people in a social group pursue common values or norms of the group, "fulfilling a generalized expectation of behavior"** (Habermas, 1984, p. 86). In many ways, this is similar to Mead's ideas on the generalized other in that people are being socialized to think and perceive things in a similar and functional manner. Therefore, people will pursue actions that are consistent with the expectations placed upon them by the group or larger society. And like so much of human behavior, many of these actions become habitual over time; therefore, people are not consciously acting out. They are doing what they are supposed to do and have done. Normatively regulated action "does not refer to the behavior of basically solitary actors who come upon other actors in their environment, but to members of a social group who orient their action to common values" (Habermas, 1984, p. 85). That potentially suggests that teleological action is by solitary actors, but the phrase refers not specifically to solitary behavior per se but to the formation of goals and values.

Dramaturgical action **is when people are neither solitary nor a member of a social group but are interacting with people who are "constituting a public for one another, before whom they present themselves. The actor evokes in his public a certain image, an impression of himself"** (Habermas, 1984, p. 86). People have privileged access to their own intentions and desires but can monitor or regulate public access to them. There is a presentation of self, as Goffman might say, that is not spontaneous but stylized, with a view to the audience. It is a form of impression management and an extension of the utilitarian style of teleological action.

Lastly, is the idea of *communicative action*. **Here, two or more people establish a relationship and "seek to reach an understanding about the action situation and their plans of action in order to coordinate their actions by way of agreement. The central concept of interpretation refers in the first instance to negotiating definitions of the situation which admit of consensus"** (Habermas, 1984, p. 86). While seemingly like Mead's work in terms of people working together, and especially Blumer in an ontological manner, what we see with Habermas is a clear delineation with teleological action in that communicative action is a more social (in its truest sense) act, where people inevitably work together to create that intersubjectivity on the one hand but work toward helping others on the other. This is consistent with Mead's work, as stated above, on international-mindedness, where people work together for the betterment of all peoples.

In addition, the lifeworld is an important concept in Habermas's work. The *lifeworld* **for Habermas is typically viewed as the background environment in which people live**. As part of communicative action, the lifeworld serves as foundational for types of interaction and reflects in part the language used. Habermas viewed language as not simply a tool to convey information but that in its most basic form is contextual, thereby promoting understanding. On such a view, when people are interacting with each other, not only do they use agreed-upon language and their meanings but they also use that to achieve mutual understanding—that is, the intersubjectivity mentioned above. This may not seem like that big of a deal, but when talking about something such as communicative action, it becomes important to recognize how people interact. When going out on a first date, typically what is attempted is to identify common ground from which two people will be able to successfully interact. As part of that process, the language people use helps them get there. Eventually, Habermas (2006) would use this and these concepts to identify what is going right and wrong in types of communication between people in power.

Habermas agrees that culture and socialization are important, but he contends that it works with and is underpinned by certain deep structures of communication itself. Therefore, what occurs is the lifeworld serves to assist in the framing of communicative action. We are socialized into the shared meanings found within any particular civilization. The lifeworld is a reservoir of taken-for-granted practices, roles, social meanings, and norms that constitute a shared understanding and possible interactions. This is made available through the social institutions of a culture or civilization, such as education, religion, and marriage, to name a few. The lifeworld sets out norms that structure our daily interactions. We do not usually talk about the norms we use to regulate our behavior. People simply assume they stand for good reasons and deploy them intuitively. This is similar to what Mead (1910) wrote about. People become socialized into a system, and that serves as normal for them. They usually only notice these things when they travel or are around others from outside their culture or subculture. In these situations, they identify or see that their own "normal" is not the norm. This could involve something as strong as political or religious views or even how people greet each other in everyday life.

Specifically, though, what happens when people purposefully choose to not go along? Or what happens if they act differently by accident? This calls for discourse to explain and repair the breach or alter the norm, much as Scott and Lyman (1968) used in their seminal work "Accounts." For instance, a simple example would be if a student decides to not study for the first exam. They do poorly, but when questioned about it, they say that they like to see the first exam and take it "cold." That way they can judge how much studying they really need to do for the rest of the semester. Something more complex, however, may involve making up an excuse for not doing something, such as the reason why you could not make it to a party was because you could not find a sitter for your child. The truth may have been instead that you did not want to go to the party because an "ex" was going to attend. You did not address that, as you did not want to look childish. Regardless of how serious the norm breach or breakdown is, once caught, we need to engage in discourse to repair, refine, and replenish shared norms that let us avoid conflict, stabilize expectations, and complement interests. Discourse is the legitimate modern mechanism to repair the lifeworld; it embodies communicative action.

As mentioned above, communicative action is a method for working together to not only create shared meanings (intersubjectivity) but is also the manner in which people work together to create the world or lifeworld. In later writings, Habermas distinguishes weak and strong communicative action. Weak communicative action is an exchange of reasons aimed at mutual understanding. The strong form is a practical attitude of engagement seeking fairly robust cooperation based in consensus about the substantive content of a shared enterprise. This allows solidarity to flourish. In either form, communicative action is distinct from *strategic action* **wherein socially interacting people aim to realize their own individual goals by using others like tools or instruments**. A key difference between strategic and communicative action is that in strategic action, people have a fixed, nonnegotiable objective in mind when entering dialogue. The point of their engagement is to compel others into complying with what they think it takes to bring their objective about (similar to Goffman's impression management, only more linear). In contrast, communicatively acting parties seek a mutual understanding that can serve as the basis for cooperation. In principle, this involves openness to an altered understanding of one's interests and aims in the face of better reasons and arguments.

The contrast between communicative and strategic action is linked to the distinction between communicative and purposive rationality. ***Purposive rationality* is when people adopt an orientation to the world focused on cognitive knowledge about it and use that knowledge to realize goals in the world.** Purposive rationality facilitates or is the foundation for teleological action. *Communicative action* is when people also account for their relation to one another within the norm-guided social world they inhabit and try to coordinate action in a conflict-free manner. On this model of communicative action, people not only care about their own goals or following the relevant norms others do but they also challenge and/or revise them on the basis of new and better reasons. Therefore, this paints a picture of humans in communicative action being more adaptive; they are willing to listen and have open discussion.

This approach becomes critical in understanding how Habermas addressed some of the problems associated with modernity. Habermas noted that many theorists start with rationality as a foundation, then move toward analyzing action based on that rationality. This creates a problem if the presupposition (the rationalization) is incorrect. For instance, what happens if someone operates under the assumption that all politicians are liars? Tuning them out becomes problematic, as that does not negate the existence of the politicians or their impact on society. Indeed, they can potentially proceed in their actions more easily because people are not engaged, as they do not trust politicians. This is the exact kind of thing that Habermas addresses. Weber framed Western rationalism in terms of mastery of the world, which was the foundation for Adorno and Horkheimer's critique of what went wrong with humanity. Because of this, the logical or rational conclusion is that people would succeed. That is, they would interact together and use purposive rationality to create a means to an end that would make the world a better place. Obviously, this was not the case, as Adorno and Horkheimer pointed out. As is apparent from Habermas's account of social learning, this is not the only way to understand the evolution of societies as a whole throughout history. By expanding rationality beyond purposive rationality, Habermas is able to resist the Weberian conclusion that modernity's increasing rationalization presented a world devoid of meaning, where people focused on control for their own individual ends, and that the spread of Enlightenment rationality went conceptually hand-and-glove with domination. Habermas feels the notion of rationality in his *The Theory of Communicative Action* resists such critiques.

As can be seen, the difference between communicative and strategic action mainly revolves around how an action is pursued (i.e., intent). However, goals can be both communicative and strategic. For instance, there could be a situation where a local neighborhood attempts to have a neighborhood watch, where two of the neighbors would walk about the neighborhood at night simulating a patrol as a means to keep an eye on the community. Instead, one of the individuals in the neighborhood decides they neither want to take the time to walk around the neighborhood nor do they particularly like their neighbors. They instead pay one of the high school students in the neighborhood to take their place. In this sense, then, the same outcome is achieved—that is, neighborhood watch occurs—but it takes a different form through a different intent from one of the neighbors. Strategic action is about eliciting, inducing, or compelling behavior by others to realize one's individual goals. This differs from communicative action, which is rooted in the give and take of reasons and the unforced force of the best argument justifying an action norm.

It should be noted that strategic action and purposive rationality are not always undesirable. There are many situations in which they are useful. Think about situations where communicative action is taxing. We have all been in situations where we do not feel like taking the time and energy to talk with someone or people to work out a plan to accomplish a task. For myself, when I was department head, there were times when I wanted something done within the department. To work with my colleagues, I would have had to inform them of the details of what was expected, let's say from the dean's office. I would then have to explain the situation and work with them to facilitate an action to complete a task. Instead, I often did not feel as though it was worth my time to engage in all that extra effort. I would simply do the action myself, alone. This is why Habermas thinks weak communicative action is likely sufficient for low-stakes domains. For Habermas, modern societies require systematically structured social domains that relax communicative demands yet still achieve a modicum of social integration.

Habermas thinks the lifeworld self-replenishes through communicative action. He felt that if people would reject inherited mutual understandings embedded in normative practices, people could use communicative action to revise norms or make new ones. Hence, this would ensure adapting and adjusting to the environment. Systems of integration depend on this lifeworld backdrop for their understanding as they achieve a degree of social integration. The trouble is that these systems have their own self-perpetuating logic that, if unchecked, will completely change (for the worse) the lifeworld. This is a main thesis in *The Theory of Communicative Action*; that is, strategic action embodied in domains of systems integration must be balanced by communicative action embodied in reflexive institutions of communicative action, such as democratic politics. If a society fails to strike this balance, systems integration will slowly encroach on the lifeworld, absorb its functions, and paint itself as necessary, immutable, and beyond human control, doing nothing but causing problems. Current market and state structures will take on an image of being natural, and those they govern will no longer have the shared normative resources with which they could arrive at mutual understandings about how they collectively want their institutions to look. According to Habermas, this will lead to problems at the micro level, including, but not limited to, anomie, alienation, lack of social bonds, an inability to take responsibility, and social instability.

In *The Theory of Communicative Action*, Habermas pins his hopes for resisting the colonization of the lifeworld by supporting new social movements at the grassroots level, as they can directly draw upon resources of the lifeworld. This model of democratic politics urges groups to shore up the boundaries of the public sphere and civil society against encroaching domains of systems integration, such as the market and administrative state.

Discourse Ethics

Like Mead, Durkheim, Adorno, and Horkheimer, Habermas also addressed morality. He referred to this as discourse ethics. *Discourse ethics* applies the framework of a pragmatic theory of meaning and communicative rationality to show how moral norms are justified in contemporary societies. It is also an attempt to provide a formal procedure for determining which norms are in fact morally right, wrong, and permissible. Discourse ethics takes the rightness and wrongness of obligations and actions to be universal and absolute. On such a view, the same moral norms apply to all agents equally. In this sense, then, Habermas takes the position of Mead and Dewey's pragmatism, as Habermas takes a realist view of morality. And like Mead, they strictly bind one to performing certain actions, prohibit others, and define the boundaries of permissibility.

There are three characteristics of discourse ethics that Habermas addresses: (a) cognitivism, (b) justice versus good, and (c) universalization. Regarding cognitivism, it is important to recognize that cognition refers to thought. Therefore, Habermas begins with the assumption that moral problems are capable of being solved in a rational and cognitive manner. Reason is not part of the argument here. The difference between rationality and reason is that *rational* or *rationality* refers to the process where people use logic to understand phenomena. *Reason*, on the other hand, focuses on the use of facts to make the determination if something is accurate. Therefore, it could be rational to think that if people come into the United States, they would be taking jobs away from existing citizens. However, a reasoned understanding would take into account that an entire economy was built based on people arriving in this country illegally. Therefore, the likelihood that jobs are being taken is inaccurate, with the reality being that this sub-economy, if you will, actually generates revenue for the United States and increases the amount of jobs. Therefore, in cognitivism, as it applies to morality, Habermas recognizes the weakness of this form of discourse ethics. The problem becomes one of validity. How can something be claimed to be the truth if it is based on cognitivism? This form of moral truths becomes more apparent in a larger, more diverse society. There ceases to be a single moral authority but instead a series of subauthorities to which people answer. This was seen in the United States during the Trump administration when the moral authority he brought with him was very different than what most Americans recognized. Within a short time, we saw Americans justifying "men being men" in their addressing of women; referring to African countries as "shit-hole" countries; and the acceptability of Americans not only charging the Capitol Building in Washington, DC, but also beating up law enforcement officers and damaging federal properties.

The second type of discourse ethic applies to the distinction of "justice" and "good." This is another piece of morality that can be applied to the Trump administration. We typically thought of presidents equated to justice and good. Presidents Nixon and Clinton were impeached, and the populous equated justice and good.

They were not good; therefore, they could not be trusted when it came to justice. Habermas does not do that. And this is something that many of those that supported Donald Trump actively followed suit. While they did not like President Trump and did not feel he was a good person, they felt that he was aiming for justice and attempting to right decades of wrongs, in essence, trying to make America great again. This is consistent with Habermas's views on justice and good. They are indeed separate and should be treated as such.

Lastly is *universalization*, which is the principle of discourse that falls back to Habermas's concept of communicative action and its relationship to intersubjectivity. In this process, which was discussed above, people are openly and honestly interacting with each other, facilitating a belief that impartiality is somewhat achieved or does occur (just as Mead advocated). Habermas insists on the principle of impartiality that first makes possible a formal framework for both different mores and acts of solidarity. Parallel to this, Habermas (1990) sees universalization as a norm being valid only if all affected can accept the consequences and the side effects its general observance can be anticipated to have for the satisfaction for everyone's interests. In this way, the principle of universalization formally determines those conditions that must be met if the claim of legitimacy the claim advanced is justified.

This principle is at the same time a principle for argumentation; that is, it summarizes the normative implications bound up with the situation of entering into an argument. These implications can be summarized as (a) equal participation of all who are affected; (b) the postulate of unlimitedness (i.e., the fundamental openness concerning time and persons); (c) the postulate of freedom from constraint (i.e., the freedom, in principle, of discourse from accidental and structural forms of power); and (4) the postulate of seriousness or authenticity (i.e., the absence of deception and even illusion in expressing intentions and in performing speech acts). We can see from these four postulates that Habermas is making the case that people can and do approach communicative action with a belief that fairness and equity is assumed.

For Habermas, the principle of universalization with these postulates should be applicable to the critical examination of practical, everyday norms only with the approval of those impacted. He sees institutionalized discourses that come closest to achieving the idea of justice, as formulated in the principles of universalization and discourse, as a connection between real resolutions and not when people come into the situation being dishonest. Ultimately, what Habermas is suggesting is that when people come together openly, honestly, and approaching matters in factual ways, truth and morality will emerge. Though appearing subjective, because Habermas allows for absolutes, much like Durkheim and Mead, he sees morality emerging and as being obvious when people take the necessary steps to open their eyes and see.

Habermas has been criticized for being Pollyannaish in his ideas. Unlike other critical theorists, and sociologists in general, Habermas is optimistic in seeing the potential that humans have when they place their energies and efforts together to achieve. This is consistent again with the argument by Mead. Instead, people get bogged down by life events and focus on the wrong things. Ultimately, Habermas does identify when people make mistakes, but at the very least, he provides a road map on how to get out of problems, and that is simple— consensus. People need to work together to facilitate common goals, but in doing so, they also pool resources of thought, materials, and practice. We have seen in our recent history how fighting against each other damages and preoccupies people. We lose sight of what is important.

Summary

Power is manifested in many ways. In this chapter we have seen how power is manifest in the items we purchase, the values we place on objects, how people are defined, and other variables and how these impact qualities of life. Marx arguably provided a framework on which others have built their ideas. Marx largely focused on how people in power used existing systems, specifically that associated with the economy to maintain their power base. This impacted ideology in particular when the working class were unable to see their place in society. The working class became pawns to those in power.

Likewise, when addressing critical theorists, the move came into more specifics addressing how this false consciousness takes over in terms of what people see as most important. People become obsessed with what Adorno and Horkheimer see as trivial matters. Because of this, attention is not focused on important matters. The results have been catastrophic, with tens of millions of deaths, as well as the lack of working together to create better systems and societies. Habermas is far more optimistic in this regard, as he focuses more on the potential of humans if we took the time to have dialogue with each other and work together.

Overall, the theories and theorists in this chapter often are seen favorably by those who want to facilitate positive change in the world. Instead of being passive thinkers, those spoke about in this chapter become beacons calling from the wilderness to not only address what is wrong but also what can be done to fix these problems. Often, students become sociology majors because they want to fix the world. The individuals in this chapter as well as the remainder of the book provide the foundation from which this can occur.

Comprehension Questions

1. Explain how Habermas's views differs from those of Adorno and Horkheimer when it comes to the effects of the Enlightenment.

2. Compare Marx's conception of alienation with Adorno and Horkheimer's views on the effects of the culture industry.

3. Compare and contrast Habermas's discourse ethics with Mead's views on morality.

4. What are Habermas's four types of action? Explain them briefly.

5. What were Marx's views on religion and class relations?

Critical Thinking Questions

1. Provide examples of the successes of communicative action in the United States as well as the struggles when instrumental rationality or subjective reasoning has been used.

2. Why are the ideas of Marx, Marxists, and critical theorists that are not trusted by many Americans? What has led to this phenomenon?

3. Explain nihilism according to Adorno and Horkheimer and how it was evident during the height of the COVID-19 pandemic.

4. What type of action is most prevalent in the United States? How has that shaped the country and the attitudes of its citizens?

5. How would communicative action be apparent in Marx's ideas on socialism and communism?

Additional Recommended Reading

Adorno, T. (2001). *The culture industry*. Psychology Press.

Adorno, T., & Horkheimer, M. (1979). *Dialectic of enlightenment*. Verso Books.

Habermas, J. (1984). *The theory of communicative action: Vol. 1, Reason and rationalization of society*. Beacon Press.

Habermas, J. (1987). *The theory of communicative action: Vol. 2, Lifeworld and system: A critique of functionalist reason*. Beacon Press.

Habermas, J. (1990). *The philosophical discourse of modernity*. Polity Press.

Habermas, J. (2006). *The divided West*. Polity Press.

Marx, K., & Engels, F. (1998). *The German ideology*. Prometheus Books. (Original work published 1844)

References

Adorno, T., & Horkheimer, M. (1979). *Dialectic of enlightenment*. Verso Books.

Collins, C. (2021). *Updates: Billionaire wealth, U.S. job losses, and pandemic profiteers*. Inequality.org. https://inequality.org/great-divide/updates-billionaire-pandemic/

Habermas, J. (1984). *The theory of communicative action: Vol. 1, Reason and rationalization of society*. Beacon Press.

Habermas, J. (1987). *The theory of communicative action: Vol. 2, Lifeworld and system: A critique of functionalist reason*. Beacon Press.

Habermas, J. (1990). *The philosophical discourse of modernity*. Polity Press.

Habermas, J. (2006). *The divided West*. Polity Press.

Marx, K., & Engels, F. (1998). *The German ideology*. Prometheus Books. (Original work published 1844)

Marx, K., & Engels, F. (2014). *The communist manifesto*. International Publishers Co. (Original work published 1847)

Mead, G. H. (1910). Social consciousness and the consciousness of meaning. *Psychological Bulletin*, 7(12), 397–405.

Mead, G. H. (1929). National-mindedness and international-mindedness. *International Journal of Ethics*, 39(4), 385–407.

Chapter 6: Feminist Theory Within Sociology

New Waves of Thought

Feminist theory has emerged in many ways similar to the conflict or critical schools of social theory in that it pushes for the development and reliance on theory and advocates political or social movements that seek justice not only for women but for all oppressed peoples. In this sense, feminist theory is potentially the most social justice oriented of any sociological theory and, more than likely, philosophically an extension of critical theory. Feminist theories incorporate nearly all aspects of social theory; that is, it builds on existing theory, with the exception of genetic theories. Because of this focus, feminist theorists address a wide range of topics well beyond ending sexism. They focus on social issues as they apply to social, cultural, economic, and political phenomena. And as is common with social theorists in general, because of the range in focus of these theorists, it should not be surprising that feminist theory as well as its theorists are not advocating for the same things or approaching social phenomena using the same methods. Feminist theory represents the diversity that we find in American sociology today and historically.

Guiding Questions

1. What are the various forms of feminism?

2. How did feminist thought begin in sociology?

3. What are the various waves of feminism?

4. How is theory and method used in feminist research?

5. How is oppression defined in feminist thought?

Feminist theory in its more current form emerged out of the shadows of the civil rights movements of the 1950s and 1960s, finding a place in sociology in the early 1970s. Sociology at that time was beginning to flounder theoretically, as structural functionalism was on its last legs; critical theory was nearing an end of an era with Adorno and Horkheimer; and the origins of symbolic interactionism were being held into question (Lewis & Smith, 1980; LoConto & Jones-Pruett, 2006). It should come as no surprise then that feminist theory introduced new ideas and approaches to the study of social phenomena. Initially, many of these social theorists began addressing all the women social thinkers going back to Mary Wollstonecraft in the late 1700s. Their goal in part was to demonstrate there were many women social thinkers over the previous 200 years and that these social thinkers had written a lot of good sociological texts without gaining much acknowledgement. By providing a two-pronged attack demonstrating the validity of social ideas, as well as a new focus in the 1970s of research topics (e.g., abortion, affirmative action, equal opportunity, marriage, sexuality, and love), feminist theorists incorporated old and new to demonstrate their value in the study of social phenomena.

There have been several forms of inquiries made by and framed by feminist theory and theorists. What are women doing? What social/political locations are they part of or excluded from? How do their activities compare to those of men? Are the activities or exclusions of some groups of women different from those of other groups, and why? What do the various roles and locations of women allow or preclude? How have their roles been valued or devalued? How do the complexities of a woman's situatedness, including her class, race, ability, and sexuality, impact her locations? To this can be added attention to the experiences and concerns of women. Have women's experiences or problems been ignored or undervalued? How might attention to these transform our current methods or values?

As one can see from the list of questions, it is no wonder there exists great diversity of feminist thought. Added to this is how feminist theorists approach these issues. Various methodologies often used triangulation in methods and perspectives to reach conclusions. It should come as no surprise that the thematic focus of their work is often influenced by the topics and questions highlighted by these traditions. This pattern has influenced sociological research. Most methodology courses today will recommend this as the stance sociologists should take when conducting research. As a result, a given question can be taken up and addressed from an array of views, sometimes with very different results. While these different results have led some to criticize feminist thought and research, the research has demonstrated the complexities of life and disavowed often times the findings of earlier research. In this sense, then, feminist research and the resulting theories have opened doors for new study.

What Is Feminism?

One of the fallacies of feminism is that it monolithic. That is, some people think that all feminism is the same. Nothing could be further from the truth. With that said, however, there are overlapping themes that should be acknowledged. Feminism is interdisciplinary and includes a sociological approach to issues of equality and equity based on various aspects of gender, including gender expression, gender identity, the constructions of gender, sexuality, and, as mentioned above, a series of issues revolving around inequalities as understood through social theories and political activism. It takes a critical view and aims at revolution in the sense of fighting for social justice.

Increasingly, feminism integrates intersectionality of ability, class, gender, race, sex, and sexuality. What is more, feminists, have attempted to facilitate change based on gathered data, as mentioned above, specifically where these intersectionalities create power inequities. Intellectual and academic discussion of these inequities allows researchers and students alike to go into the world aware of injustices and to work toward changing unhealthy dynamics and situations.

Auguste Comte wrote his work in French, and this led to many American thinkers having difficulties accessing his writings. This is where British writer Harriet Martineau (1802–1876) gained part of her notoriety. She made available the works of Comte through translating them into English as well as making editorial changes.

Martineau was not content with translating and making substantive changes to Comte's work, however. By our definitions of what a sociologist is today, she was an active sociologist through her analyses of the cultures and economic systems found in both Great Britain and the United States. In *Society in America*, she examined a wide variety of social institutions and behaviors, studying religion, politics, child rearing, slavery, and immigration in the United States. William Graham Sumner stated that he adopted ideas of laissez-faire from Martineau. Of major import for sociologists today, she paid great attention to how various social institutions and behaviors were different with regard to race, ethnicity, and gender. Her works also explored the status of children as well as people who were defined as criminal, mentally ill, disabled, poor, and alcoholic.

From her understanding of Mary Wollstonecraft's *A Vindication of the Rights of Women*, Martineau recognized how Wollstonecraft used the term "sensibilities" in the understanding of human behavior. Like many of her day, Martineau understood that people were born into certain outcomes dictated by their physical characteristics. Where Martineau differed with her colleagues, however, was with the specific outcomes due to these biological traits. Martineau advocated racial and gender equality and wanted to see people reach the best of their genetic abilities. This was something she observed was not happening throughout the Western world due to cultural practices.

Martineau believed that for social scientists to be truly effective, their work would have to be grounded in empirical observations and be accessible to all peoples. She argued that social scientists should be impartial in their assessment of society and that it is entirely appropriate to compare the existing state of society with the principles on which it was founded.

Feminist political activists campaign in a series of areas that make the news, such as reproductive rights, domestic violence, gender equality, social justice, and workplace issues, such as family medical leave, equal pay, and sexual harassment and discrimination. It is safe to say that anytime stereotyping, objectification, infringements of human rights, or intersectional oppression occur, you will find feminists and feminist scholars present to stand up for and show support to people experiencing these inequities. Even with these things in common, however, there are a number of forms or types of feminism.

Approaches to Feminism

Feminism brings many things to social thought, including not only a variety of particular moral and political claims but also ways of asking and answering questions to fasciliate constructive and critical dialogue that contribute to sociological thought and inquiry. Approaches to feminist thought are as varied as approaches to sociology itself, reflecting a variety of beliefs about what kinds of sociological study are both fruitful and meaningful.

Simone de Beauvoir (1908–1986) was one of the most preeminent French existentialist philosophers and writers. She provided a large body of work on ethics, feminism, fiction, autobiography, and politics. Like many feminist thinkers that followed her example, she triangulated many of her ideas, incorporating various political and ethical dimensions into her writings. She addressed how people did not delve deep enough into material, living life at a surface or superficial level and never quite understanding real life. This contributed partially to feminist theorists focusing on embodying subjects instead of seeing them as objects. In her book *The Second Sex*, she lamented how women have historically been relegated to a passive acceptance of roles and identities. The women were pawns of a patriarchal system. Women were the oppressed "other." This became a problem with regard to identity. People possess identities by the relationship to something else. In identifying the place of a woman in society passively accepting their position, they were agreeing to being nothing more than an appendage of a man (i.e., their husbands). This was perpetuated through norms and values of the society—in essence, myths. These myths serve—much like Jungian archetypes, which incorporates multiple myths of woman under it (e.g., mother, the virgin, the motherland, nature, etc.)—to trap women into an impossible ideal by denying the individuality and diversity of women. She longed for women to stand up for their rights and their place in society beyond that which was allowed. The emphasis on freedom, responsibility, and ambiguity permeates all of her works and gives voice to core themes of existentialist philosophy.

All these approaches share a set of feminist commitments and an overarching criticism of institutions, presuppositions, and practices that have historically favored men over women. Feminist thinkers are typically more focused on historical, contextual, and lived experiences of people than their nonfeminist counterparts. Feminist thinkers see people as *embodied*, **and by that I mean relating to oneself or body as the subject**. That is to say that feminists see oneself or the body as how it is experienced: something "in here" and not an object that is "out there." Think of how women specifically have been *objectified*—**that is, degraded to a mere object**. Women over the past centuries have been viewed as objects that people praise or degrade often for their appearance alone. They have been viewed as being outside the norm in terms of feelings, hopes, and desires. They historically have not been taken into account. From a feminist perspective, if people are embodied, then our research turns to the experiences of being a woman, a man, or any other identity that might be associated with an individual or group. This requires more in-depth analyses in order to understand people.

Despite the variety of different approaches, styles, societies, and orientations, feminist theorists' commonalities are greater than their differences. Many will borrow freely from each other and find that other orientations contribute to their own work. Even the differences regarding sex and gender add to a larger conversation about the impact of culture and society on bodies, experiences, and pathways for change.

Liberal feminism is consistent with traditional liberalism in that liberal feminists advocate to work within the system and the structure of society to facilitate change and thereby integrate women and others. It suggests that individuals use their own abilities and the democratic processes in society to help women and men become more equal in the eyes of the law, in society, and in the workplace. By organizing women into larger groups that can speak at a more powerful level, lobbying legislators and raising awareness of issues, liberal feminists use available resources and tools to advocate for change. According to liberal feminists, the state should be a central ally to the feminist movement. The patriarchal nature of systems and institutions prevents women's autonomy and freedom. These systems neglect the needs of women, creating a preventive environment in which they cannot choose or even create the circumstances under which they exist. Therefore, recognizing the civic areas where women are not included and changing them is the only way to enable women's autonomy. In this process, liberal feminists would advocate that society should be more responsive to the rights of women and all people. Liberal feminism does not directly challenge the system. It accepts the system but seeks to improve upon the system from within. The suffragist movement is an example of liberal feminism in that women worked within the system to gain the right to vote.

Radical feminism, on the other hand, views patriarchy and sexism as the biggest factors in the oppression of women. They do not deny the ideology of intersectionality and the influences of other identities and variables but nevertheless focus on patriarchy and sexism as key factors. Unlike liberal feminism, which seeks to work within the system to facilitate change, radical feminists question the very system and ideology behind women's subjugation. Historically, radical feminism was a specific strand of the feminist movement that emerged in Europe and North America in the late 1960s. A unique aspect of radical feminism that distinguished itself from other forms of feminism at the time was the role of male violence against women in the creation and maintenance of gender inequality. Stereotypes developed from this group, as some of the more radical feminists were hostile toward men. And while this slowed acceptance of ideas by the White middle class, radical feminists were instrumental in generating widespread support for campaigns around issues such as rape, domestic violence, and sexual harassment. Radical feminism emerged from the civil rights, peace, and other liberation movements of the 1960s, a time when people were questioning different forms of oppression and power. They sought and seek to understand the roots of women's subordination and have provided the major theoretical understanding that has served as the basis for the inspiration and analysis guiding women's movements around the world.

bell hooks, pseudonym of Gloria Jean Watkins (born September 25, 1952, in Hopkinsville, Kentucky), is an American scholar and feminist activist whose work, in a similar fashion to intersectionality and standpoint epistemology, examines the connections between race, gender, and class. She has written about the varied perceptions of Black women and the development of feminist identities. hooks grew up in a segregated community of the South. hooks assumed her pseudonym, the name of her great-grandmother, to honor female legacies. She spells her name in all lowercase to emphasize the message she is attempting to convey. She feels, similar to Marx, that naming tends to deviate attention from the work. hooks has taught English and ethnic studies at the University of Southern California, African and African American studies at Yale University, women's studies at Oberlin College, and English at the City College of New York. In 2004 she became a professor in residence at Berea College in Berea, Kentucky. The bell hooks Institute was founded at the college in 2014. In the 1980s hooks established a support group for Black women called the Sisters of the Yam, which she later used as the title of a book, published in 1993, celebrating Black sisterhood. She is one of the most published and respected writers of her time.

Black feminism, much like the work of Crenshaw and Collins, states that sexism, class oppression, gender identity, and racism are inseparable. They integrate intersectionality and standpoint epistemology as a means of explaining social phenomena. Therefore, as explained later in this chapter, each identity or variable is considered independent yet is analyzed in a synergistic manner. These identities and variables serve to reinforce each other. Black feminists, as well as other feminist women of color, emerged from the White feminist movements of the 1960s and organized separate feminist groups. This way they could address specific oppressions they were facing. They asserted the racial and class differences among women, and they did so because these differences were largely ignored and neglected by many of the women's movements at that time, thereby rendering Black women and other women of color invisible in theory and in practice.

The end goal was not, however, permanent racial separation for most left-wing Black feminists and other feminists of color, as it has come to be understood since. Barbara Smith (1983) conceived of an inclusive approach to combat multiple oppressions, beginning with coalition building around particular struggles. This is consistent with bell hooks's views, which contend individual groups should focus on smaller, more manageable issues. This approach to fighting oppression does not merely complement but also strengthens Marxist theory and practice, which seeks to unite not only all those who are exploited but also all those who are oppressed by capitalism into a single movement that fights for the liberation of all humanity. The Black feminist approach described above enhances Lenin's (1902/2013) famous phrase from *What Is to Be Done?:* "Working-class consciousness cannot be genuine political consciousness unless the workers are trained to respond to all cases of tyranny, oppression, violence, and abuse, no matter what class is affected—unless they are trained, moreover, to respond from a Social-Democratic point of view and no other" (p. 69). Black feminists, in their understanding of the complexities of human life, adopt a more progressive stance on how not only understanding should be developed but also the necessary actions needed to remedy problems that exist.

Marxist feminists attribute the oppression of women and other groups to the capitalist economic system. While Marxist feminists (sometimes called "socialist feminists") acknowledge patriarchy and sexism as influencing outcomes, they believe the foundation for all the various "isms" identified in feminist thought begins and ends with an oppressive capitalist system. Marxist feminism refers to a set of theoretical frameworks that have emerged out of the intersection of Marxism and feminism. Marxism and feminism examine forms of systematic inequalities that lead to the experiences of oppression for marginalized individuals (Ehrenreich, 1976). Marxism deals with a form of inequality that arises from the class dynamics of capitalism. It understands the class inequality as the primary axis of oppression in capitalist societies. Feminism deals with another form of inequality, which is the inequality that exists between the sexes. Feminism understands gender inequality as the primary partnership of oppression found in patriarchic societies. The goal of the Marxist feminist framework is to liberate women by transforming the conditions of their oppression and exploitation, much like the Marxist theory of change that is illustrated in Chapter 5.

Cultural feminism emphasizes differences between men and women in terms of biology, personality, and behavior. The biological aspects do not, however, mirror the hierarchy found in the works of Spencer, Sumner, or Gumplowicz. While acknowledging biological differences, cultural feminists do not view one sex as inherently better than the other. Instead, cultural feminists acknowledge biological differences and place different values associated with the differences, with all having strengths and weaknesses. Therefore, women are recognized as having some different and superior attributes that provide the foundation for a shared identity, solidarity, and sisterhood. The argument would be that since women are viewed as kinder and gentler than men, it follows that if women were in power, the world would be a better place. Cultural feminists in some ways are ***essentialists*, which suggests that they believe that things have a set of characteristics that make them what they are and that the task of science and philosophy is their discovery and expression**. The differences between men and women are viewed as absolute and are therefore recognized as such. There are differences between men and women; therefore, cultural feminists believe they should be recognized and evaluated as such. Men are better at some things, and women are better at others. They should be viewed as equals.

Ecofeminism is a form of feminism that is much more holistic at its core. Ecofeminists view patriarchy and its focus on control and domination as a source of women's oppression as well as being harmful and destructive to all living creatures and the Earth itself. They combine a more comprehensive analysis that is in some ways reminiscent of how Mead and other pragmatists view nature. They often portray life and existence in a more spiritual manner. With everything coherently linked, they connect women's rights and empowerment to political, economic, social, and cultural factors that benefit all living creatures. As stated, ecofeminists approach analysis in a similar manner to how both Mead and Habermas view morality. Social action is connected to the whole. People need to work together and recognize how their actions impact everyone and everything. Oppression of women and climate change are both aspects of a broken system that needs to be fixed from this perspective. Everything is part of the whole.

Transnational feminism is concerned mainly about how globalization and capitalism affect people across nationalities, races, ethnicities, genders, classes, and sexual orientations. Like Black feminism, it integrates intersectionality as a means to recognize and understand inequalities across different groups of women. In using intersectionality, especially at a global level, it is more overt in terms of recognizing how women are treated and impacted differently across the globe and how different identities and variables work toward that end. By being more clear in how women are overly treated differently, social justice issues are easier to demonstrate and defend at moral or ethical levels. This vision understands the need for comprehensive approaches that integrate multiple issues and movements to find common cause across agendas to ensure long-term social transformation.

There are other forms of feminism, and as stated above, the diversity of feminist approaches equates to providing a more complete picture of what is occurring regarding social justice and social issues. The multiple approaches, especially when reading the various research and theoretical development that has occurred, serves to triangulate data and theory to not only provide a full picture but also to provide better solutions to facilitate social justice locally and globally. This becomes a reminder that no one theory, method, or study captures all the information needed. We are connecting the dots and piecing together a puzzle called life. It is a collective effort.

Waves of Feminism

Similar to the types of feminist theoretical approaches, there have also been identified "waves" of feminist movements that address various interests and approaches. These are time-sensitive, reflecting what is occurring at that moment or period. The first wave represents the time period from the 1830s through the early 1900s and, in some respects, into the 1960s. During this period, women fought for equality in contracts and property rights. It became apparent that if women were to be successful—that is, treated equally within the law— they must first gain political power, which included the right to vote. The belief was that this would bring about change and add fuel the fire of the mvoement. This was a very liberal approach in that change would come from within the existing system through the ballot. During the late 1800s, specifically, this first wave could turn to Irish Americans as an example, who were doing exactly the same thing. Many Irish Americans began running for political office and getting local government jobs in order to facilitate change in issues relevant to them. For women, because these opportunities were not available at the time, they had to first gain the right to access these positions. Their political agenda also expanded to issues concerning sexual, reproductive, and economic matters. The seed was planted that women have the potential to contribute just as much as men and could provide alternative benefits as well. Overall, though change came very slowly, this first wave provided a foundation on which all other waves could build. It was the first wave that began chiseling their way through stereotypes to try and create a more equal world.

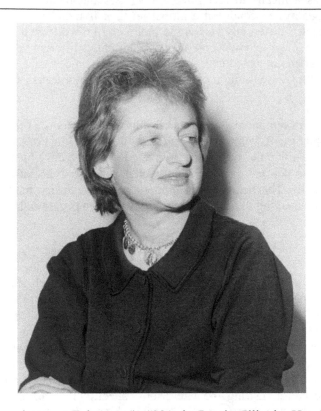

Bettye Naomi Goldstein was born on February 4, 1921, in Peoria, Illinois. Her father, Harry Goldstein, an immigrant from Russia, owned a jewelry store; her mother, Miriam (Horwitz) Goldstein, gave up her position as editor of the women's page of the local paper to raise her family. Friedan attended Smith College, majoring in psychology, and was the editor of the college newspaper. During this time, the paper became a forum for the fight against fascism abroad and in favor of union organizing at home. She graduated in 1942.

Considered by many as the mother of second-wave feminism, she was one of the most influential feminist leaders of the second half of the 20th century. Friedan was the cofounder of the National Organization for Women (NOW) and was its first president. She served on the boards of leading women's organizations, fought for legislation to ensure women's equality, and wrote books analyzing the roles of women in society and the women's movement.

In 1957, she surveyed 200 of her Smith College classmates and found that many of them suffered from "the problem that has no name." They were supposed to be happy in their suburban paradises, with working husbands and smiling children, but many were bored, depressed, and anxious. Friedan argued that the media and educators had created an image of women's proper role as appendages of their husbands and children. Their lack of excitement about their own lives made them smother their children and cling to their husbands. Thus, on a familial level, they were bored and ineffectual. She identified what became known during that time for women as "bridge, booze and boredom" (Coontz, 1992). The result of her research was her book *The Feminine Mystique* (1963), which both labeled the resurgent domestic ideology of the postwar era and exposed those who perpetuated it. Her critique of the romanticization of domesticity led to a feminist explosion, launching the sex-role revolution.

On a societal level, the result was to stifle women's growth, waste massive human potential, and cause immense dissatisfaction among women, as well as among their families. At a time when more and more women were entering the workplace as working mothers, Friedan (2013) argued that women should not accept their inferior status at home or in the work force. By accepting limitations in their public roles, they would also fail in their private roles. She called for women's self-assertion, for women's equality in the workplace and in the home. By defining women's problems as broad and structural rather than personal, she has been credited with getting women to understand their position in society.

Later in life she voiced her ongoing discomfort with new feminist ideologies and argued for more balance within the women's movement itself. She blamed radical elements in the movement who, she worried, being distracted by sexual politics (whether around issues of pornography or lesbian rights), were ignoring the real needs of most women for family and nurturing. She was criticized by many feminists who felt she erased race issues and sexual complexities while blaming the victims, women.

The second wave took place during the 1960s through the 1980s. During this time there was overlap with the first wave in that there was still a focus on reproductive and equal rights. As women became more educated and began competing for jobs within the workplace, the focus of the second wave followed suit. The second wave of feminism focused on the workplace, sexuality, family, and reproductive rights. Influenced by the civil rights and counterculture movements of the 1950s and 1960s, second wave feminism was dealing with increasing beliefs that since the ratification of the 19th Amendment, which was ratified on August 18, 1920, equality was ensured. Yet an attempt at an equal rights amendment in 1972 failed and still has not been passed. The Equal Rights Amendment was first drafted in 1923 by two leaders of the women's suffrage movement, Alice Paul and Crystal Eastman. For women's rights advocates, this amendment was the next logical step after the ratification of the 19th Amendment. Unfortunately, equal rights are easy to agree with but not as easy to pass in law. The version approved by Congress in 1972 and sent to the states reads, in part:

> Equality of rights under the law shall not be denied or abridged by the United States or by any state on account of sex. The Congress shall have the power to enforce, by appropriate legislation, the provisions of this article.

Unfortunately, as of March of 2021, the Equal Rights Amendment still has not passed.

In some ways, the second wave of feminism is viewed negatively. Though the second wave is the time when feminist thought in sociology began to emerge, much like the women's suffrage movement in the 1800s and early 1900s, the voices of non-White women were not being heard. Many women during the second wave were initially part of various social movements fighting for equality. These included the various civil rights movements and the anti-war movement (in response to the Vietnam War). Many women of color felt their voices were not being heard and felt that in order to gain respect they needed to address intragender equality concerns. It is not surprising that the works of Kimberlé Crenshaw and Patricia Hill Collins emerged during this time. Intersectionality, standpoint epistemology, and Black epistemology emerged during and in response to the second wave. Their efforts aimed to present arguments and data to demonstrate how women were not treated equally across the country and globe.

Another aspect that developed during the second wave was the portrayal of feminists increasingly as radical and man-haters. Propaganda suggesting that feminists wanted to castrate all men and that they all wanted to be men escalated. Photos and editorials would be shown or written that placed feminists in a negative light. In short, the word "feminist" increasingly became used as a sort of profanity or slander. I remember giving a talk in Alabama during this time. I was asked to give my thoughts on feminism—my personal thoughts. I self-identified as a feminist. After I was done, several men came up to me and asked why in the world I was a feminist. Surprised by the inquiries, I asked, "Do you believe in equal pay for equal work?" They all nodded their heads "yes." I responded by saying, "Well, you're well on your way to becoming a feminist."

As mentioned above, as a response to and as part of second-wave feminism came the works of Kimberlé Crenshaw and Patricia Hill Collins. Their work continues to push for a better understanding of the dynamics of life, not only of non-White women but also of other minorities, and people in general. Their ideas are part of 21st-century sociology and also part of American and global culture.

Kimberlé Crenshaw

Kimberlé W. Crenshaw (1959–) is an American lawyer, civil rights advocate, philosopher, and a leading scholar of critical race theory. She is a professor at the UCLA School of Law and Columbia Law School, where she specializes in race and gender issues. Crenshaw is also the founder of Columbia Law School's Center for Intersectionality and Social Policy Studies (CISPS) and the African American Policy Forum (AAPF), as well as the president of the Center for Intersectional Justice. Crenshaw is known for the introduction and development of *intersectionality*, the theory of how overlapping or intersecting identities, particularly minority identities, relate to systems and structures of oppression, domination, or discrimination. Her scholarship has also been instrumental in the development of intersectional feminism, which examines the overlapping systems of oppression and discrimination to which women are subject due to their ethnicity, sexuality, and economic background.

Intersectionality generally addresses the interconnected nature of social categorizations (i.e., identities), such as race, class, and gender, as they apply to a given individual or group, regarded as creating overlapping and interdependent systems of discrimination or disadvantage. While many old-time sociologists might state that this is what sociological research should be doing and was doing 100 years ago, what is unique about this current form is that it makes certain identities more explicit, making analyses more clear. It has become commonplace within feminist theory to claim that women's lives are constructed by multiple intersecting systems of oppression. This insight that oppression is not a singular process or a binary political relation but is better understood as constituted by multiple, converging, or interwoven systems originated in antiracist feminist critiques of the claim that women's oppression could be captured through an analysis of gender alone. Intersectionality was offered as a theoretical and political remedy to the exclusion women and, particularly, women of color have experienced for centuries. Intersectionality theory has been celebrated as a much-needed understanding and research tool that cuts across disciplines.

Crenshaw (1991) focuses on intersectionality in part to address not only the violence (e.g., physical, emotional, intellectual, etc.) experienced by women in the world and, particularly, the United States but also to address how intragroup differences do not or have not been explored. Sociologists and social thinkers alike had tended to treat various identities of people as consistent. Under this idea, all African Americans would fit together. All low-SES families would fit together. Therefore, finding solutions to problems appeared rather easy. However, when solutions did not solve problems, and sometimes amplified them, the conclusion tended to be to blame the victim.

Instead, Crenshaw introduced the idea of intersectionality to explore how various identities worked together to facilitate an outcome. Therefore, a White woman would experience oppression in the workplace differently than an Asian woman. But importantly, when factoring in other variables, such as income, education, and geography, into the equation, what develops is a more complex, yet clearer, picture of what is occurring. It is explicitly advocating triangulation as part of the method for understanding. In some ways consistent with postmodernism in terms of analyzing social phenomena—that is, making conclusions more local and focused—Crenshaw's ideas resonated with social thinkers and especially feminist Theorists. Her initial writings focused on race and gender and, particularly, women of color (Crenshaw, 1991). She focused on three forms of intersectionality: (a) structural intersectionality, (b) political intersectionality, and (c) representational intersectionality.

Structural intersectionality is concerned with how systems in society shape the experiences of a group at the intersection of systems of oppression. This occurs when inequalities and their intersections are directly relevant to the experiences of people in society but entrenched in the system of society—that is, through the existing structures. Structural intersectionality can help to explain why a Black woman may not be considered for a job, because she is Black and the "norm employee" is a White woman, while other jobs are also unavailable to her since the jobs available to Black people in that context are predominantly male jobs. An interesting component of structural intersectionality concerns the individual experience of intersections of multiple held identities. While many scholars have insisted that intersectionality should not be reduced to individually held identities, there remains a tension between identity and structure. The ways in which students self-identify are interconnected with their experiences of structural oppression. For instance, given the prevailing consensus among academics of the socially constructed nature of gender and race, one cannot conceive of gender and race as purely structural systems that categorize students. The student to perform gender and race intersects with other physical features and social structures that are beyond the student's control and make these performances and identities likely or unlikely. It addresses the fact that heteronormativity is part of gender inequality, which means that the position of lesbians is very different from the position of heterosexual women. When including race, class, age, and geography into the equation, it serves to see how these identities and other variables work together to facilitate different outcomes.

Political intersectionality indicates how inequalities and their intersections are relevant to political strategies. Crenshaw (1991) uses an example of the unavailability of statistics on domestic-violence police interventions that are broken down in the Los Angeles district, which, given the racial segregation in this city, could provide information she needed on arrests differentiated by race. Crenshaw found that this information was blocked (by domestic-violence activists in and outside the police department) because of fears that it might be abused to reinforce racial stereotypes about some groups being naturally violent. She argued that these concerns, while well-founded, are potentially working against the interests of women of color since they do not help to break the silence within the respective communities, thus thwarting mobilization against domestic violence in these communities. By parsing out the multitude of identities and variables involved, it allows for researchers, especially now with access to big data, to provide information where groups can see and identify how policies impact them both positively and negatively.

Representational intersectionality pertains to the ways in which individuals are represented in the media or literature. For example, in media portrayals of men, thin able-bodied heteronormative White men are often represented as the prototypical identity of a man. Representational intersectionality has implications for representations in engineering education literature, for instance, the explanation of the range of socioeconomic status and sexual orientations of student participants who fit into a gender or racial category. Diversity practitioners may use representational intersectionality to think about the ways their programs are representing prototypical student experiences and communicating about the students and purposes of their programs.

Carastathis (2014) identified four main analytic benefits of intersectionality, as articulated by Crenshaw: (a) simultaneity, (b) complexity, (c) irreducibility, and (d) inclusivity. By simultaneity, consistent with Einstein in his general theory of relativity, or Mead's (1929) sociality, when understanding people, we must attempt to include as many identities or variables as possible when addressing the makeup of individuals. People are more than one thing. This triangulation, if you will, as stated above, serves to recognize how each identity or variable serves to influence outcomes. People are comprised of many identities. Each are a piece of a puzzle that makes up each individual. It becomes important to identify these and integrate them into the explanation. Specifically, for our purposes here, intersectionality provides the means to identify the simultaneity of how oppressions are experienced without fragmenting out those experiences.

The second analytic benefit of intersectionality complexity arises when the subject of analysis expands to include multiple dimensions of social life and categories of analysis. McCall (2005) encourages three methodological approaches that attempt to manage the complexity of intersectionality: (a) the anticategorical approach, (b) the intracategorical approach, and (c) the intercategorical approach. By approaching the complexities associated with everyday life by utilizing these three approaches, researchers once again gain a fuller picture of the people being studied, observing an acknowledging three different dimensions of the life of an identity.

The third benefit of intersectionality posits the irreducibility of the categories of difference (Yuval-Davis, 2006; Caratathis, 2014). Intersectionality contends that both oppression and privilege is produced through the interaction of multiple mutually exclusive, yet analytically symbiotic, identities. To explain one is to ignore the others. It becomes imperative to acknowledge the diverse identities when studying people. Ultimately, divisions do not mean separateness.

The fourth benefit is inclusivity. Because, as Crenshaw stated, women of color, and specifically Black women, were often invisible in the everyday life of the world, intersectionality provides people and researchers alike with the ability to be inclusive. It provides a process of understanding how all people become impacted by the various identities and variables that are part of intersectionality. Instead of the separateness of individual identities, we become united with common identities, yet the weights of some have greater influence than others. This inevitably leads researchers to recognize the more cumulative mass that some identities and variables have than others.

This inclusivity is the lasting legacy of Crenshaw's work that is now over 30 years of age. In the attempt to gain a better understanding of humans and particularly those that experience oppression, Crenshaw created a framework from which research and understanding can proceed.

Patricia Hill Collins

Patricia Hill Collins (1948–) was born to a working-class family in Philadelphia. She earned her bachelor's degree from Brandeis University and went on to earn her master's degree from Harvard, returning to Brandeis for her PhD. As her career developed, she recognized early that there was a lack of research on Black women. Understand that this was the 1970s. Today, there is still a lack of information. Often times, sociologists today want to focus on oppression without addressing other aspects of the Black experience. She has written several books on Black women, specifically addressing Black women's intellectual thought and its lack of appearance in academia and American culture in general.

Like many American scholars, and specifically feminist scholars, Collins integrates many perspectives into her analyses depending upon the subject matter being studied, though she typically is thought of as a critical theorist in the sense that she is critical of the structures found within society that prevent and oppress the dissemination of knowledge and, specifically, prohibits this dissemination through various barriers. She is primarily concerned with the relationships among and between empowerment, self-definition, and knowledge. Collins wants to challenge sociologists and people in general to understand the view of oppression and identity politics. Her ideas, she feels, could facilitate positive change because the focus would not be on one group but instead on understanding the complexities of life. She feels that social movements that are only focused on one specific aspect of life will either end once the purpose of the social movement is achieved (e.g., the removal of a politician in office) or will neglect and possibly harm other aspects of peoples' lives. When focusing her research, she has used ***standpoint epistemology*, which is a theoretical viewpoint suggesting that what one knows is influenced by one's position—that is, their standpoint in society.** At an obvious level, it is easy to understand that even something as simple as physical location provides a glimpse into that which Collins is referencing. Anyone who has traveled understands that location influences attitudes, values, and knowledge in general.

Much like Crenshaw and intersectionality, one's standpoint is not identified with one identity or variable, such as location, but instead includes such variables as race, class, gender, ethnicity, or sexual orientation, to name a few. She identifies and addresses that people are influenced by these variables and are located on a continuum of domination to resistance. For example, in the suffrage movement of the 1800s and early 1900s, we see women sharing a common goal of a desire to vote. However, the movement, as early as the 1840s, experienced friction, as White women ignored many of the ideas and thoughts of Black women in the movement, so much so that Black women, while initially showing up in large numbers to support suffrage, backed away due to their voices not being heard, as race was not being accepted as a critical variable that needed inclusion. At the same time, while seemingly obvious, it is also easy to recognize how people tend to look at others and think their experiences are the same. We see this in the right to vote. Many in Laguna Beach, California, do not understand the dilemmas those in other states, such as Texas, experienced in trying to vote. In the 2020 election, Governor Abbott ordered that only one voter drop box be placed in every county. In other areas around the country, the number of precincts to vote were reduced by 75%, mainly in minority neighborhoods. This attempt at suppressing votes is an everyday aspect of life that others in the United States have never experienced personally. Accordingly, it is more difficult for these individuals to relate. The solutions seem obvious, but they do not understand the complexities on the ground.

Collins (2012) uses another concept to illustrate this further—that is, the ***matrix of domination*, which is that one's position in society is made up of several positions or standpoints.** First, any specific matrix has a particular arrangement of intersecting systems of oppression. Just what and how these systems come together is historically and socially specific. Second, intersecting systems of oppression are specifically organized through four interrelated domains of power: (a) structural, (b) disciplinary, (c) hegemonic, and (d) interpersonal. The structural domain consists of social structures, such as law, polity, religion, and the economy. This domain sets the structural parameters that organize power relations. This relates to her ideas of the interplay between dominance and resistance. The disciplinary domain manages oppression. The disciplinary domain consists of bureaucratic organizations whose task it is to control and organize human behavior through routinization, rationalization, and surveillance. The hegemonic domain legitimates oppression. This is the cultural sphere of influence where ideology and consciousness come together. The hegemonic domain links the structural, disciplinary, and interpersonal domains. Each characteristic or variable that is part of who people are inevitably pushes and pulls individuals in terms of their place in society and what they think. The interpersonal domain influences everyday life. It is made up of the personal relationships we maintain as well as the different interactions that make up our daily life. Collins points out that change in this domain begins with the intrapersonal—that is, how an individual sees and understands themselves and their experiences.

Instead of a linear model that portrays power being top-down and unidirectional, Collins sees this dynamic as a clash of various attributes of individuals in what they bring to the table. People all have strengths and weaknesses they bring to any situation, and these strengths and weaknesses all have different values depending upon the context. This inevitably leads researchers to observe and study the complexities of what people bring to each context and how this influences the outcomes as well as the processes of how they interact.

Much of her work has focused on the place of Black women in American society. Collins believes that Black women are uniquely situated in that they stand at the focal point where two powerful and prevalent systems of oppression come together (i.e., race and gender). The United States is uncertain currently about the place of race—culturally, politically, and structurally. The same can be said for the place of gender. While Americans are aware of the biological differences between males and females, they are less aware of what constitutes the cultural, political, and structural realities of gender in the United States. Collins's belief is that understanding the intersectionality of the relationship of race and gender, specifically as it relates to Black women, would open the door to many more possibilities of seeing and understanding cross-cutting interests in everyday life. Collins sees that the politics of race and gender also influence knowledge and its epistemologies.

She identifies the stereotypical sociological epistemology. First, according to the positivistic approach, true or correct knowledge only comes when the observer separates themselves from that which is being studied. Second, personal emotions must be set aside in the pursuit of pure knowledge. Third, no personal ethics or values must come into the research. Social science is to be value-free, not passing judgment or trying to impose values on others.

And fourth, knowledge progresses through cumulation and debate. She then compares that to four tenets of Black epistemology: First is that Black epistemologies are built upon lived experience, not upon an objectified position. Second is the use of dialogue rather than debate. Third is that the centering of lived experiences and the use of dialogue imply that knowledge is built around ethics of caring. Last is the use of personal accountability. Because knowledge is built upon lived experience, the assessment of knowledge is a simultaneous assessment of an individual's character, values, and ethics. The important issue for Collins is the way intersectionality creates different kinds of lived experiences and social realities. She is particularly concerned with how these interact with what passes as objective knowledge.

During the time when Crenshaw and Collins were publishing this work, a new wave of feminism emerged. The third wave of feminism was the period of the 1990s through the early 2000s. During this time the word "feminist" became more acceptable and was embraced by a greater portion of the population. By this time an entire generation of educated Americans had learned about feminism in college. Third-wave feminism, however, seeks to rethink and transform power structures, basing its political agenda on self-determination that is inclusive and has the power to even render traditional gender roles as being feminist, as long as they are by choice. The diversity of forms of feminism also allowed for people to pick and choose the form of feminism that resonated with them the most without chastising any particular form of feminism. One key difference is that women began embracing aspects of femininity. Women in the second wave made a distinction between boys and girls, men and women, with the cut off typically being around the age of 18. Third-wave feminists did not feel the need to fight this. Wearing a dress and feeling "girlie" was not necessarily a bad thing. Freedom of choice became more represented in third-wave feminism. The main issues from the third wave built on the existing work done in the first two waves. The fight continued against inequities in pay as well as reproductive rights. Work continued against hostile and violent behaviors against women in the United States and the globe. This wave was also the first in which hostility toward the concept of feminism began to subside. It was acknowledged that some struggles had not been overcome, but the fact that there had been some progress brought optimism that it was simply a matter of when, not if, these changes that had been advocated for would occur.

The fourth wave of feminism is arguably an extension of the third wave, as some feminists state there is no fourth wave currently. However, in the mid-2010s, a number of feminist movements emerged in the United States and gained momentum in the course of a changing political landscape. After the election of President Obama, there was a reaction by those who identified as Republican that shifted the Republican Party to more extreme views. Not necessarily conservative, these new Republicans began to build on fears of changes that were and are occurring within the country. As mentioned earlier in Chapter 1, this also coincided with the United States Census announcing in 2008 that by 2050 White people would no longer represent more than 50% of the American population. By 2010, the American government became more polarized. This motivation to "take back" America and return it to its alleged roots was framed in historical inaccuracies, yet it fostered more turnout and more extremism. There also was a heavy antifeminist slant among these newer Republicans. This led to the election of President Trump in November of 2016. Immediately, a response came from feminists not only in the

United States but also globally. The Pussyhat Project was launched to take part in the Women's March on Washington on January 21, 2017. Those associated with the movement wore pink headgear. Approximately 100,000 people wore pink that day, creating a visual statement that stood up and out against the antifeminist backlash that heralded in the Trump administration. Similar demonstrations were conducted globally. The message was clear that women were not going to take this movement that allowed and fostered in the election of Donald Trump as well as similar elections around the globe to destroy the work that had been done for nearly 200 years.

Also, in 2017, the #MeToo movement began and went viral after the *New York Times* published a report on the sexual harassment allegations against Hollywood film producer Harvey Weinstein. Weinstein was accused of sexually assaulting over 80 women over the course of his career. Well-known women celebrities came forward stating they were sexually assaulted by Weinstein. This came after the journalist Gretchen Carlson filed a lawsuit against FOX News television executive Roger Ailes in 2016, which resulted in a $20-million settlement. Though the #MeToo movement began in 2006, these two events provided strength for girls and women around the world. Several other movements gathered strength against a common foe that was more easily recognizable. In 2018, women candidates broke the record for the number of candidates for governor, the U.S. House of Representatives, and the U.S. Senate. A record 117 women won elections across the United States that year. Even with those numbers, however, women still only amounted to 20% of Congress while being over 50% of the American population.

It seems that current feminist movements are returning to second-wave strategies of physical and radical activism. Generally, second-wave feminism is defined by an active political fight that requires the disruption of power structures through participation in public demonstrations against patriarchal suppression. Fourth-wave feminism continues to fight for equal pay for equal work and that the equal opportunities sought for girls and women should extend also to boys and men to overcome gender norms. What is also part of fourth-wave feminism is the utilization of a myriad of media to inform, motivate, and mobilize the public. The tactics of fourth-wave feminism also coincide with the enthusiasm and dedication to demonstration by Generation Z. Ultimately, we should see this fourth wave continue given all the social turmoil experienced in the past 10 years.

The Central Goal of Feminism

To consider some of the different strategies that are involved with intersectionality, let us take, for instance, the claim that women are oppressed, and this oppression is wrong. Generally speaking, one might characterize the central goal of feminism to be ending the oppression of women. However, if we also acknowledge that women are oppressed not just by sexism but in many other intersecting identities and variables, such as classism, homophobia, racism, ageism, ableism, and a myriad of other isms, then it might seem that the goal of feminism is to end all oppression that affects women. Some feminists have adopted this interpretation. And arguably, the view I take personally of feminism is that it aims for exactly that. Let us get rid of oppression everywhere. It is a very humanistic way to look at life. **Humanism is a philosophical stance that emphasizes the value and agency of human beings, individually and collectively**. Humanist beliefs stress the potential value and goodness of human beings, emphasize common human needs, and seek solely rational ways of solving human problems. Feminism, from my own perspective, is humanistic.

The diversity of feminist perspectives, however, allows for the fact that not all feminists agree with such a grand expectation of feminism. One may agree that feminists ought to work to end all forms of oppression. One may even believe that in order to accomplish feminism's goals, it is necessary to combat racism and economic exploitation but also think that there is a narrower set of specifically feminist objectives. Part of the problem anytime anyone attempts to end or combat all oppression is that the mere size of such an endeavor may render the attempt admirable but fruitless. Aiming at specific targets is easier for people to envision and grasp. Then, afterward, aim at connecting the issues. The larger and more diverse the target, the less clarity of the vision. In essence, it becomes too big to understand. The focus can tend to be on removing oppression but without an understanding of what will follow. The absence of oppression does not mean that everything will be wonderful. There needs to be a vision of what life will be like after oppression and a road map on how to get there. Otherwise, we see things like what happened when diverse groups came together to overthrow President Hosni Mubarak in Egypt in 2011. Without a clear resolution and path to life after his presidency, Egypt came under a more hostile regime that has been more repressive regarding freedom and social justice. Social change requires an understanding of life after the change.

Ultimately, within feminist thought, some have suggested they should place themselves as part of a larger struggle, not the entire struggle. Different groups should be working together with a plan that would lead to accomplishing long-term plans that lead to structural changes yet allow for structures to adapt and adjust to continue to make improvements or changes. Without it there can be many problems.

According to bell hooks (1989), the defining characteristic that distinguishes feminism from other liberation struggles is its concern with sexism:

> Unlike many feminist comrades, I believe women and men must share a common understanding—a basic knowledge of what feminism is—if it is ever to be a powerful mass-based political movement. In Feminist Theory: From Margin to Center, I suggest that defining feminism broadly as "a movement to end sexism and sexist oppression" would enable us to have a common political goal. … Sharing a common goal does not imply that women and men will not have radically divergent perspectives on how that goal might be reached. (p. 23)

By focusing solely on sexism, the attempt at finding a solution is more manageable. hooks's approach depends on the claim that sexism is a particular form of oppression that can be distinguished from other forms. The belief is that by feminist groups focusing solely on sexism, it will serve as a beacon leading others to not only fight sexism but also to others standing up and fighting other forms of isms. hooks also, however, highlights that people or women fighting against sexism may not understand the intricacies of other inequities in the world. Therefore, they may not be able to effectively address the varieties of discriminatory practices around the world. Furthermore, because sexist institutions are or can be racist, classist, and homophobic, dismantling sexist institutions will require that people dismantle the other forms of domination intertwined with them (Heldke & O'Connor, 2004). This also takes a better understanding of economics and how dismantling institutions will have a ripple effect on the economy. Therefore, if hooks is correct, feminism can be framed in a manner in which feminists will fight against sexist oppression. Other inequities can and should be left to other groups to fight against.

Part of the problem of that argument, however, can be linked to how Congress has approached education over the past few decades in the United States. Instead of seeing education as being indicative of a larger problem, they approach education in a manner in which money is thrown at schools to improve the education of their students. When the students do not improve, Congress uses that to conclude that the education system in a particular area needs improvement, that it is not a money issue. What gets missed is that the students may be from lowere-SES neighborhoods, may have to work while going to school, or may struggle in neighborhoods where crime is high. To solve the problem of education in those specific areas is to include rebuilding the infrastructure of a community. Therefore, solving sexism by itself without reflecting the larger issues of inequities may end up being a fruitless endeavor.

As this book has shown, there are a variety of interpretations, or theories, whether they be feminist or otherwise, that address the diversity of forms of oppression. One that has been used in somewhat agreement from all feminists, though, is that oppression is a structural problem where communities, cities, and larger governments are established in a manner where there are structural barriers that not only serve to reduce opportunities but also serve to remove enthusiasm for change. The end result is the keeping of a group or groups of people down, with little chance of growth. These structures that serve to oppress, however, do so in a unique manner. Just as intersectionality calls out different identities and variables and their influences, so do these structures. Sexism is something that most Americans agree is a bad thing. Yet it does not overtly impact men as much as women. Therefore, the passion for addressing sexism is not there among as many men as women. This removes the desire for mobilization amongst a large segment of the population. We saw this during the civil rights movements in the 1950s and 1960s. While largely African Americans stood up against injustices during this time, it was only once White college students stood up and joined the fight that structural changes developed. The inclusion of northern White students assisting in the fight brought more national attention to civil rights. The oppressive structures also may be the result of a historical process whose originators are long gone, or it may be the unintended result of complex cooperative strategies gone wrong. Again, the key is taking the time to understand the dynamics of what is occurring. Without doing that, we may be creating more problems. Regardless, the key here is the use of or the recognition of intersectionalities and standpoint epistemologies for and understanding of what is occurring and using that knowledge to create positive change.

What, however, makes a particular form of oppression sexist? Sexist oppression needs to have clarity in terms of what constitutes sexism. If we identify that a form of oppression counts as sexist oppression if it harms women, or even primarily harms women, this is not enough to distinguish it from other forms of oppression. Probably all or nearly all forms of oppression harm women, whether it be racism, classism, homophobia, and so on. In addition, sexism also hurts all people.

What makes a particular form of oppression sexist is that it not only harms women but also that someone is subject to this form of oppression specifically because they are (or at least appear to be) women. This is consistent with how the FBI views or defines hate crimes. The crime has to be against a person or group because of the one specific identity, not a series of identities. Racial oppression harms women, but racial oppression (by itself) does not harm them because they are women; it harms them because they are (or appear to be) members of a particular race or racial group. The suggestion that sexist oppression is oppression to which one is subject by virtue of being or appearing to be a woman provides us at least the beginnings of an analytical tool for distinguishing subordinating structures that happen to affect some or even all women from those that are more specifically sexist.

However, if we pursue a pluralist strategy in understanding sexist oppression, what unifies all the instances as instances of sexism? After all, we cannot assume that the oppression in question takes the same form in different contexts, and we cannot assume there is an underlying explanation of the different ways it manifests itself. So, can we speak of there being a unified set of cases that we can call "sexist oppression"?

Some feminists would encourage people to recognize that there is not a systematic way to unify the different instances of sexism, and correspondingly, and as stated above, there is no systematic unity in what counts as feminism. Relating back to what has been said in this section, ultimately, the basis for feminist unity in coalition building should be in how issues or oppressions are addressed. Different groups should work to combat different forms of oppression.

An alternative, however, would be to grant that, in practice, unity among feminists cannot be taken for granted but to begin with a theoretical common ground among feminist views that does not assume that sexism appears in the same form or for the same reasons in all contexts. We saw above that one promising strategy for distinguishing sexism from racism, classism, and other forms of injustice is to focus on the idea that if an individual or people are suffering sexist oppression, an important part of the explanation and approach is that they are women. This includes cases in which women as a group are explicitly targeted by a policy or a practice, but it also includes cases where the policy or practice affects women due to a history of sexism, even if they are not explicitly targeted. For example, consider the example that was brought to light in second-wave feminism yet continues today. Since women are children's primary caregivers and cannot travel for work as easily as men, employment practices that reward those who can travel can be deemed sexist because the difference is due to sexist practices. The commonality among the cases is to be found in gender-role expectations in the explanation of the injustice rather than the specific form the injustice takes.

Where does this leave us? Feminism is an umbrella term for a range of views about injustices against women, otherwise known as sexism. There are disagreements among feminists about the nature of justice, in general, and the nature of sexism, in particular; the specific kinds of injustice or wrong women suffer; and the group who should be the primary focus of feminist efforts. Nonetheless, feminists are committed to bringing about social change to end injustice against women, in particular, injustice against women for being women.

Summary

Feminist thought is not the monolithic perspective that many still believe it to be. Instead, feminist theories are diverse, utilize multiple methods, and pursue an equally diverse set of social phenomena. The various forms of feminism, from liberal feminism to ecofeminism, represent the wide range of ideas found within feminist thought today. We see through the various waves of feminism how there was this evolution reacting to the changing times yet also facilitating those times—from suffrage and reproductive rights, to workers and equal rights, to freedom of choice. Waves of feminist thought have pushed us to consider not only the rights of women but also the rights of all people. Looking at the works of Crenshaw and Collins, both theoretically and methodologically, we see a movement toward recognizing how our identities and other variables work together in contexts to conclude with specific outcomes. Their approaches to study involve being more holistic in understanding how life comes together to reach certain ends. By understanding the oppression, the goal then is to see how these can work together to facilitate positive change.

Overall, feminist thought helps us focus and understand the various processes and structures at play worldwide that lead to oppression and otherness. Ultimately, feminist thought positions sociology in a manner that is consistent with early social theorists yet at the same time has forced us to recognize specific forces and influences in everyday life that lead to the inequities globally.

Comprehension Questions

1. How does Black feminism differ from Marxist feminism?

2. How did Black feminism emerge from second-wave feminism?

3. What is the argument that suggests that feminists should focus solely on sexism instead of racism and other isms in the world?

4. What are the similarities and differences between intersectionality and the matrix of domination?

5. Explain how feminist theories tend to advocate multiple methods of understanding human behavior.

6. What were criticisms against the suffrage movement that also occurred with second-wave feminism?

Critical Thinking Questions

1. How is it possible to practice intersectionality and standpoint epistemology yet still advocate for feminists to focus solely on sexism?

2. In looking at the world today, what form of feminism would you suggest fits best in explaining sexism? Please explain your answer.

3. What factors do we need to understand when explaining sexism globally? Why is that?

4. What does embodiment mean when feminist theorists are doing research? Is this consistent with Black epistemologies? Please explain your answer.

5. What was taking place in sociology that led to the emergence of feminist theory? What is occurring in today's world that facilitates feminist thought?

Additional Recommended Reading

de Beauvoir, S. (2011). *The second sex*. Vintage Books.

de Beauvoir, S. (2018). *The ethics of ambiguity*. Open Road Media.

Collins, P. H. (2008). *Black feminist thought*. Routledge.

Collins, P. H. (2019). *Intersectionality as critical race theory*. Duke University Press.

Friedan, B. (2013). *The feminine mystique*. W.W. Norton.

hooks, b. (2000). *Feminism is for everybody: Passionate politics*. Pluto Press.

hooks, b. (2004). *The will to change: Men, masculinity, and love*. Washington Square Press.

Martineau, H. (2016). *Household education*. CreateSpace Independent Publishing Platform.

References

Carastathis, A. (2014). The concept of intersectionality in feminist theory. *Philosophy Compass*, *9*(5), 304–314.

Collins, P. H. (2012). Social inequality, power, and politics: Intersectionality and American pragmatism in dialogue. *The Journal of Speculative Philosophy*, 26, 442-457.

Crenshaw, K. (1991). Mapping the margins: Intersectionality, identity politics, and violence against women of color. *Stanford Law Review*, *43*(6), 1241–1299.

Ehrenreich, B. (1976). What is socialist feminism? *Jacobin*. https://jacobinmag.com/2018/07/socialist-feminism-barbara-ehrenreich

Friedan, B. (2013). *The feminine mystique*. W.W. Norton.

Heldke, L. M., & O'Connor, P. (2004). *Oppression, privilege, and resistance: Theoretical perspectives on racism, sexism, and heterosexism*. McGraw-Hill.

hooks, b. (1989), *Talking back: Thinking feminist, thinking Black*. South End Press.

Lenin, V. I. (2013). *What is to be done?* Martino Fine Books. (Original work published 1902)

Lewis, J. D., & Smith, R. L. (1980). *American sociology and pragmatism: Mead, Chicago sociology, and symbolic interaction*. The University of Chicago Press.

LoConto, D. G., & Jones-Pruett, D. (2006). The influence of Charles A. Ellwood on Herbert Blumer and symbolic interactionism. *The Journal of Classical Sociology*, *6*(1), 75–99.

McCall, L. (2005). The complexity of intersectionality. *Signs*, *30*(3), 1771–1800.

Smith, B. (1983). *Home girls: A Black feminist anthology*. Women of Color Press.

Yuval-David, N. (2006). Intersectionality and feminist politics. *European Journal of Women's Studies*, *13*(3), 193–209.

Chapter 7: Postmodernism

Why the Prefix "Post"?

What we began to see in the 1960s and 1970s was the increase in the use of the prefix "post" when talking about both theories and social phenomena. By itself, "post" refers to something coming or being after what was. As mentioned in the previous chapter regarding feminist theory, we saw many of the theorists of the previous generation struggle to adequately address the social changes occurring in the Western world, as well as many of these theorists retiring or passing away. This left a void where new theories and theorists could find their niche in academic circles. One of these was postmodernism. Taking into consideration the overall changes that had been occurring technologically, as well as the subsequent social changes, social theorists began questioning how things were explained and addressed in the arts, humanities, and social sciences. Specifically, when we refer to *postmodernism*, **we mean a broad skepticism, subjectivism, or relativism to our understanding of everything; a general suspicion of reason; and an acute sensitivity to the role of ideology in asserting and maintaining political and economic power.** In short, the concern again was addressing, as critical theorists and feminist theorists would ask, "How enlightened are we?" To understand postmodernism, we need to see the connection to postindustrialism.

Guiding Questions

1. Identify the differences between modernity and postmodernity.

2. Understand how postmodernists define reality.

3. Identify the differences between Lyotard and Baudrillard in what they focus on regarding postmodernity.

4. Understand the place of discourse in understanding the social world.

5. Understand the role of consumer society in social life.

Postindustrialism and Postmodernism

The term "postindustrial" gained wide acceptance in the 1970s. It served primarily to explain changes in the American economy. It marked what many observers thought to be the third century of American economic life moving from preindustrial, through industrial, to a postindustrial economy (Hoeveler, 1996). In modernity or industrialism, industry centered on the production of goods. Manufacturing constituted the critical sector of the economy and determined the location of related business activity and forged the dominant culture of the working classes. The rhythm of life followed the timetable of machinery. The rationality of the industrial system, the discipline of the machine process, and the standardization of all its components reinforced each other and absorbed them into its operations. Citizens of this society acquired similar thought processes by evaluating things in a more static, black-and-white manner as the machine process reshaped all aspects of daily life.

By contrast in postmodernity, in the postindustrial economy there is or became a significant shift in the labor force (Hoeveler, 1996; Lyotard, 1991; Seidman, 1992). More people work in the service economy. The service economy features such growing enterprises as hotels and restaurants, overnight mail deliveries, sports, health clubs, entertainment and the arts, travel agencies, governmental bureaucracies, real estate, the airlines industry, education, and health care services (Hoeveler, 1996; Klapp, 1969; Lyotard, 1991; Seidman, 1992).

Industrial society focused on the coordination of humans and machines, and postindustrial society organizes itself around communications and the dissemination of knowledge (Gergen, 1991; Hoeveler, 1996; Lyotard, 1991; Seidman, 1992). Media services, newspapers, journals, radio, television, and now the internet increasingly provide the information that informs the daily lives of individual citizens (Carty, 2015; Gergen, 1991; Mills, 1956; Twenge, 2014). This is facilitated by an electronics revolution, specifically the computer industry and digital media. These industries help process and disseminate information with tremendous speed (Gergen, 1991; Klapp, 1969; Twenge, 2014; Twenge & Campbell, 2009). This also potentially facilitates more fluidity in norms and values. That will be discussed later in this chapter.

In addition, the demographics of American society have helped shape postindustrial America. Declining birthrates have become more noticeable. Women have increasingly decided to have careers and opted to either not have children or to postpone having children (Cheal, 1996; Hoeveler, 1996). In addition, the postindustrial economy has affected personal choice where there has been a greater emphasis on leisure, health, the arts, and other sensations (Carty, 2015; Cheal, 1996; Tedrick, 1991; Twenge, 2014). These sensations have tugged at traditional roles that reshaped family patterns, altering expectations of family life and providing more opportunities for women (Cheal, 1996: Twenge, 2014; Twenge & Campbell, 2009). The postindustrial period signifies the postmodern culture of altering science, literature, and the arts and has challenged Americans to enter a period of postmodernity (Baudrillard, 2017; Lyotard, 1991). That is, with the end or ending of the industrialized and mechanized economy and the corresponding methods of thought, we have entered into another cultural period, therefore changing everyday life.

In abstract terms, as stated above, postmodernism or the postmodern is skepticism toward grand narratives or metanarratives (Lyotard, 1991). Grand or metanarratives are overarching accounts or interpretations of events and circumstances that provide a pattern or structure for people's beliefs, giving meaning to their experiences. An example of a metanarrative would be something such as the fact that many feminists hold that patriarchy has systematically oppressed and subjugated women throughout history. Prior to any kind of dialogue with someone who holds that metanarrative, one would have to frame the conversation by acknowledging the truth of that statement. However, within postmodernism, the metanarrative has lost its narrative function. They no longer work. The universalistic heroes, great dangers and great goals of the modern era are replaced by pluralistic or fragmented values and beliefs. Everything becomes situational and relative. This also renders a strong belief in universal ethics, values, and rule of judgment impossible, leading to more irrationality (Lyotard, 1988; Shlapentokh, 1995). Common convictions are becoming increasingly uncommon. Patterns of behavior so counted on in the modern, positivistic method of inquiry self-destruct (Gergen, 1991; Lyotard, 1991). They are replaced with layers of realities where individuals are saturated with possibilities of statuses to act out in an era of multiphrenia where reality becomes transitory (Gergen, 1991). In this sense, then, postmodern civilization is reflected by increased diversity that relies on local or context-driven rules (Seidman, 1992). This can be referred to as *demassification*, **or the breakup of large-scale organizations and the mass culture that supported them** (Mills, 1963).

In the postmodern era, there is a response that advocates that large-scale organizations cannot meet the needs of individuals in an individualistic society (Weber, 1947). A movement has developed away from universalistic bureaucratic norms toward particularistic (situational) norms negotiated and renegotiated to fit the people and the evolving purposes of the organizations. Consistent with this, these organizations rely more on the capacity for dialectic communication and negotiation with a network of other organizations (Cheal, 1996). Finally, because of this there is an increase in horizontal relationships and a decrease in vertical relationships (Cole et al., 1993). This provides a setting for an interactive community within various social institutions. People begin reverting to various status characteristics that are context driven (Goffman, 1951). This weakens the collective conscience, limiting collective symbols of the modern society (Durkheim, 1933/1984; Goffman, 1951) and increases the likelihood of smaller community-based factions defining and redefining their existence in an ever-changing realm of consciousness and realities (Seidman, 1992). As Lyotard (1991) states regarding the great narratives, they are "being dispersed in clouds of narrative language elements—narrative, but also denotative, prescriptive, descriptive, and so on" (p. xxiv). The saturation of information provided in the 21st century results in exponential growth of self-multiplication (Gergen, 1991). The certainty of life can then only be foretold as a shadow of what might be. Predictions of life at a grand level falter as to what lies ahead, and morality enters a state of flux.

Postmodernism: A Simple Explanation

While all the above may seem like a lot of philosophical and theoretical jargon, postmodernism is relatively easy to explain. This connects back to the difference between industrialism and postindustrialism. Imagine that society, culturally, reflects the type of industry that dominates. In the industrial period, manufacturing churned out products that were identical to each other. Subsequently, the culture reflected one that recognized right from wrong easily. After all, with manufacturing it is easy to identify how something is made correctly. However, in postmodernism, the postindustrial world is dominated by the service industry. The old adage "The customer is always right" applies. Therefore, think of how that is reflected in real life. If the customer is always right, what does that do for truth? For fact? It leads us into circumstances where right and wrong no longer are carved in stone but depend on other factors. As one of my professors used to say, "The best answer to any question should always begin with 'it depends.'" What can be right in one situation is not in another. Of course, we could simply reference something like a mom stealing food so her children can eat as being different than someone who is wealthy committing fraud, stealing the money from investors as an example of this. Penalties vary. We would have no problem making that distinction. Is a 22-year-old college student partying at a bar viewed the same as a 60-year-old man acting the same way at that same bar? Is a woman dying of cancer at age 90 viewed the same way as a child of 5 dying of cancer? Thinking of things in those terms, it becomes easier for us to recognize that subjectivity and skepticism toward grand or metanarratives make a lot of sense.

Jean-François Lyotard

<insert IMG 7.1: Lyotard>

Jean-François Lyotard (1924–1998) was born in Versailles and studied at the University of Paris. He was a French philosopher and was best known in sociological circles for his critically acclaimed book *The Postmodern Condition* (1991). I read that book for one of my classes while a graduate student. That was my introduction to postmodernism. Despite its popularity in sociology, this book is one of his more minor works. Lyotard's writings cover a variety of topics in philosophy, politics, and aesthetics. His works can be roughly divided into three categories: (a) his early writings on phenomenology, politics, and the critique of structuralism; (2) the intermediate libidinal philosophy; and (3) his later work, which is our interest here, on postmodernism and the differend. The ***differend* refers to the distinctiveness of things, making the case that to make the argument against grand or metanarratives, we must accept the idea that everything is different or unique in some form**. A unifying factor that Lyotard operated under in the latter part of his career was the assumption of the differend, that reality consisted of singular events that could not be represented accurately by rational theory. Patterns become broken down or deconstructed into individual, unique events connected loosely by language. In this sense then, he is consistent with poststructuralists (see Chapter 8).

For Lyotard, this view of what "is" became critical when talking about politics. Politics operate under the assumption of a belief in hard, black-and-white facts. Think of this in terms of how Donald Trump represented or depicted the world. It was very different from normal. This lack of normalcy in a way could be used as an example of to what Lyotard is referring. What happens if the facts no longer applied? Or what if the facts were completely different from how we thought? Because of this world view, Lyotard ultimately calls into question the powers of reason; asserts the importance of nonrational forces, such as sensations and emotions; rejects humanism and the traditional philosophical notion of the human being as the central subject of knowledge; champions heterogeneity and difference; and suggests that the understanding of society in terms of "progress" has been made obsolete by the scientific, technological, political, and cultural changes of the late 20th century. Lyotard delt with these common themes in a highly original way, and his work exceeded many popular conceptions of postmodernism in its depth, imagination, and rigor. His thought remains pivotal in contemporary debates surrounding philosophy, politics, social theory, cultural studies, art, and aesthetics.

Postmodernism

As mentioned above, our concern regarding Lyotard is his ideas on postmodernism or the postmodern. As he began moving toward postmodernism, it was largely and in many ways like the motivation for other social theorists at the same time—that is, to understand social justice and morality. After all, if life is a series of unique events, what happens when there are competing definitions of right and wrong? We have seen this in the varying degrees of protests with contesting groups in the United States both historically and in recent years. Another recent example is our two major political parties wherein there are competing definitions of right and wrong.

If we took the issues associated with Black Lives Matter movement—that is, protesting incidents of police brutality and all racially motivated violence against African Americans—we gain a better understanding of the kind of issues Lyotard was referencing. The Black Lives Matter movement typically advocates against police violence toward African Americans, though philosophically they are advocating for equal treatment across all groups of people. The Black Lives Matter movement is consistent with the views of Lyotard in the sense that they are acknowledging how problems develop when there are competing definitions of right and wrong. Historically and currently in this country, African Americans do not get treated equally before the law. Lyotard's views on competing definitions of right and wrong are also consistent with Robert Merton (1972) when he spoke about the struggles of people when they are attempting to own truth. Inevitably, what is left is groups of people fighting for ownership of what "fact" is.

To address this ***ontological pluralism*, which is the doctrine of multiplicity where there are different ways, kinds, or modes of being**, Lyotard used the term paganism. ***Paganism* refers to a way of thinking that considers and strives to do justice to unequal differences**. In belief systems, paganism can reference many gods; therefore, this was consistent with his overall view. Lyotard's pagan philosophy reflected a concern for pluralism and multiplicity and its relationship to social justice. Therefore, if reality is comprised of unique occurrences or events, any form of metanarrative regarding laws would lead to social injustices, as these laws would not consider the diverse influences in daily life. Paganism suggests that there are irreducible differences in the order of things and that we must take things on their own terms without attempting to reduce them to these metanarratives. Instead, Lyotard suggested that paganism was the most appropriate response if people wanted social justice. Paganism is godless politics; therefore, it should avoid inherent biases in the system or systems. Paganism would lead to the negating of universal judgments but instead focus on a justice of multiplicities that would require a multiplicity of justices. Paganism is the attempt to judge without preexisting criteria in matters of truth, beauty, politics, and ethics. It is situational.

Though Lyotard's use of paganism rejected any metanarrative criteria for judgment, he nevertheless relied on a metanarrative that people need to judge and that justice must occur. To do this, Lyotard used the ideas of both Kant and Nietzsche in his answer. Kant agreed with ***Cartesian dualism*—that is, that the mind and body are separate, indicating a more spiritual plain for consciousness**. Therefore, it is not unexpected that Kant would suggest the use of the imagination. However, Kant did agree with utilitarianism; therefore, this imagination would attempt to maximize the good while minimizing the bad. Lyotard included Nietzsche's ideas as well. In Nietzschean terms, Lyotard said that judgment was an expression of the will to power.

Inevitably, this became problematic at several levels, as Lyotard was making claims that suggest metanarratives. While he was not suggesting specific criteria for judgment, he was instead suggesting that the process was a metanarrative. What Lyotard was denying was the possibility of a discourse that would give us adequate criteria (i.e., an umbrella for judgment in each case). Instead, what we must do is evaluate every instance of behavior with judgment based on the knowledge of the circumstances at hand. This would then lead to an acknowledgement of the diversity of influences, leading to a more pluralistic (pagan) doctrine of judgment and evaluation. In many ways this is like Crenshaw's and Collins's works addressing intersubjectivity; however, in this case, Lyotard was addressing specifically judgment and not research. It also must be remembered that Lyotard did acknowledge that what he was suggesting was that there was and is indeed some form of metanarrative process that has universal value. Life is not simply anarchy and randomness. Ultimately, the goal would be to recognize pluralism in justice.

The Postmodern Condition

By the late 1970s, Lyotard was moving more formally toward postmodernism. In many ways, you should be able to see how different theorists identified similar problems yet found alleged solutions differently. Such is the case with Lyotard. Much like critical theorists, he identified metanarratives that carried forward throughout recent history: (a) People were progressing toward social enlightenment and emancipation, and (2) knowledge was progressing toward totalization. In addition to how modernity and postmodernity were explained at the beginning of this chapter, Lyotard would also add that modernity was the age of metanarrative legitimation, while postmodernity was the age in which grand or metanarratives had become bankrupt. Through his theory of the end of metanarratives, Lyotard developed his own version of what tended to be a consensus among theorists of the postmodern. Building on or taking the best from paganism, Lyotard saw postmodernity as an age of fragmentation and pluralism.

The Postmodern Condition is a study of the status of knowledge in computerized societies. In many ways, his views are like Gergen's (1991), as they apply to saturation, and within that saturation there would be an inability to commit fully to any one thing. There are too many choices and, therefore, too much fragmentation. He felt that the explosion of information now available that had been growing since the end of World War II had radically changed or influenced the Western world. He saw the computer and all associated with computers as the instrument from which these changes would or were occurring. Lyotard (1991) identified the problem with which he was dealing—that is, knowledge as one of legitimation. In the late 1970s, Lyotard identified and anticipated the problems we face today. Through the technology associated with computers, we are in a struggle for power based on the specific forms of knowledge perpetuated. If you control the knowledge (i.e., facts or, more precisely, what are conceived as facts), then you control the people. Again, we revert to not only Merton's ideas on the sociology of knowledge but also the struggles we see with Twitter, Facebook, Snapchat, and the myriad of other influences found on the internet that influence what people believe to be true. When you control that flow of and quality of information, you have power.

The method Lyotard chose to use was language games. Lyotard (1991) wrote that the developments in postmodernity were concerned with language. The theory of language games means that the forms of "speak," or how we talk, can be defined in terms of rules specifying their properties and the uses to which they can be put. Lyotard made three observations about language games: (a) The rules of language games do not carry within themselves their own legitimation but are subject to a contract between the people involved; (b) if there are no rules, there is no game, and even a small change in the rules changed the game; and lastly, (c) every form of speaking should be thought of as a move in a game. Much like Mead and symbolic interactionists' use of gestures as a form of dance, the same applies here with Lyotard and the dance people do while speaking with each other. He identified such forms of speak as (a) the *denotative* **that attempts to identify an object or thing to which it refers**; (b) the *performative* **as a form of speak that addresses doing something**; and (c) the **prescriptive instructs, recommends, requests, or commands**.

Lyotard's choice of language games was primarily political in motivation and is connected to his views on knowledge and power. He needed a methodological approach to apply to society to examine the status of knowledge in postmodern societies. He used two views of society that were popular in sociology in the mid-20th century: (a) society as a functional whole, much as Parsons described; and (b) society as a binary division, which reflected more the ideas of Marx, as well as Adorno and Horkheimer. Simplistic in his representation of social thought, Lyotard obviously rejected both. Instead, he left himself a third choice, the postmodern.

In the postmodern, Lyotard (1991) argued that even as the status of knowledge had changed, so too had the nature of the social bonds. This was especially true regarding institutions of knowledge. Consistent with his pluralistic view using paganism, Lyotard presented a methodological representation of society as composed of assorted and fragmented language games. Yet these assorted and fragmented language games still had control over people in equally diverse situations, and more generally, he went as far as to say these also applied to subsequent institutions. Therefore, one followed orders in the military, sought God in church, and pursued an understanding of society with sociology. Lyotard then made a distinction between two types of knowledge within the postmodern: (a) narrative and (b) scientific. *Narrative knowledge* is the kind of knowledge prevalent in less complex societies, relying heavily on storytelling, rituals, music, and dance. This is like many of the preindustrial descriptions found in social thought from Comte through Marx. Narrative knowledge is legitimized through tradition. If you have ever heard someone say something like "This is the way it's always been done," then you should have an idea of narrative knowledge. There is no questioning of something, unless of course you are some young kid who questions everything. That is narrative knowledge.

<insert IMG 7.2: Rorty>

Richard Rorty (1931–2007) was an American philosopher of the late 20th and early 21st century. He studied initially at the University of Chicago where he earned his bachelor's and master's degrees. He eventually received his PhD at Yale. I had asked him, since he attended Chicago and worked with Charles Morris (former student of Mead), what his thoughts were on Mead. My hope was that he would provide insights not found in print. He responded that he found Mead "boring."

Nevertheless, he was influenced by pragmatists William James and John Dewey; therefore, the pragmatism link is there. But many pragmatist philosophers disagree on whether Rorty was indeed a pragmatist. Rorty liked the works of Dewey and, specifically, his ideas on democracy. Although a fan of Dewey, Rorty reinterpreted Dewey on this subject. Rorty's ideas coincide more with those found within postmodernism. These revolved around absolutes, for our purposes here, regarding truth. Rorty had disagreements with Habermas in particular regarding the concept of truth. Habermas believed there was indeed a way to demonstrate a universal or unconditional validity to truth. Habermas believed that whether or not a statement of fact was true, was to also make the claim that, that statement is then supported by reason, and would apply in any context. Rorty found no use for unconditional validity. While, like all pragmatists, Rorty integrated action with concepts of morality and truth, he moved away by further avoiding experience as part of what we should focus on. Instead, Rorty chose, much like postmodernism and poststructuralism, to focus on discourse. He took a more situational and contextual position, however. When it comes to truth, Rorty (1982, 1991) believed that all one would need is consensus within the specific community in which the truth is being tested. In this sense, then, Rorty is distinct from Dewey, who is more consistent with both Mead and Habermas. In short, Rorty makes Dewey more nominalist in approach, being similar then to James, calling into question both truth and objectivity. Two things Dewey believed existed. Rorty, on the other hand, goes beyond where pragmatists would go. He felt that people and researchers alike aim not at truth but at solidarity, or what we have come to take as true. In his most extreme positions, Rorty emphasized that truth and objectivity were merely labels for what people will let others get away with saying. He would like to see a postphilosophical culture where there are no appeals to authority of any kind, including appeals to truth and rationality. He sees forced agreement as mistaken for truth. In this sense, he is more extreme than Lyotard.

In scientific knowledge, however, the question of legitimation always arises. This may seem odd or even contradictory. However, think of life at a university and scientific inquiry, generally. Academics are always testing hypotheses, questioning conclusions, and pushing for clearer understandings of the world and existence around us. Lyotard is acknowledging this phenomenon. Scientific evidence is always being questioned. A key element, however, regarding Lyotard is that legitimation with scientific knowledge is assumed when viewed as legitimate by the body of scientists. Scientific knowledge is legitimated by certain scientific criteria, one of those being reliability. We saw that with research on COVID-19. While the press often highlighted where there were inconsistencies regarding results, this is how scientific research is actually conducted. Eventually, patterns begin to develop. The distinction between narrative and scientific knowledge is a crucial point in Lyotard's theory of postmodernism and is one of the defining features of postmodernity. Lyotard highlighted the dominance of scientific knowledge over narrative knowledge. Again, reflecting upon COVID-19, think of how some groups were stating that we needed to trust the science, while others leaned more toward narrative knowledge. Scientific knowledge does not allow the recognition of narrative knowledge as legitimate.

Lyotard viewed this dominance as problematic since it is contradictory to his more pluralistic and situational views of reality. In other words, Lyotard did not believe that science has any justification in claiming to be a more legitimate form of knowledge than narrative. Part of his work in *The Postmodern Condition* can be read as a defense of narrative knowledge from the increasing dominance of scientific knowledge. Furthermore, Lyotard sees a danger to the future of academic research that stems from the way scientific knowledge has come to be legitimated in postmodernity.

The language that has been used here can be scary sometimes for students. I mean, what does fragmented look like? The gist of postmodernism, as portrayed by Lyotard, is that things are not as clear cut as we think. People do not communicate with each other effectively. People do not see each other regularly. Life itself is full of peaks and valleys. Think of this process occurring throughout all of life and life experiences. The world around us changes so fast. If we do not adapt and adjust, we can feel and be out of place. This is what fragmentation is. Inconsistencies are part of our lives. Ideals are nice, but they do not reflect real life. Fragmentation does.

The Differend

One of my favorite aspects of Lyotard's work involves the differend. Again, consistent with his views using paganism and part of the allure of postmodernism, Lyotard focused on how social injustices occur but specifically, regarding the differend, as they relate to language. This is by far the most consistent work of Lyotard's with poststructuralism. As mentioned above, a differend refers to the distinctiveness of things, making the case that to make the argument against metanarratives, we must accept the idea that everything is different or unique in some form. A differend is a case of conflict between parties that cannot be equitably resolved for lack of a rule of judgment applicable to both. If we accept the case of a differend, the parties cannot agree on a rule or criterion by which their dispute might be decided. A differend is opposed to a *litigation*, **a dispute that can be equitably resolved because the parties involved can agree on a rule of judgment**. We see this in the United States today. There is skepticism toward the law and how it is enforced. The rules vary depending upon who is under investigation.

Lyotard (1988) distinguished the victim from the plaintiff. The latter is the wronged party in a litigation; the former, the wronged party in a differend. In a litigation, the plaintiff's wrong can be presented. In a differend, the victim's wrong cannot be presented. A victim, for Lyotard, is not just someone who has been wronged but someone who has also lost the power to present this wrong. This disempowerment can occur in several ways:

- The victim may be threatened into silence or in some other way disallowed to speak;

- The victim may be able to speak, but that speech is unable to present the wrong done in the discourse of the rule of judgement.

- The victim may not be believed (e.g., may be thought to be mentally ill) or not be understood.

- The discourse of the rule of judgement may be such that the victim's wrong cannot be translated into its terms.

- The wrong may not be presentable as a wrong.

Do we not see this in the claims made against law enforcement by minorities in the United States? The victims (i.e., people of color and underrepresented groups) fit with all these claims made by Lyotard.

Lyotard, however, presented his case addressing the Holocaust and, specifically, what occurred at Auschwitz. There are people who insist that the Holocaust never happened. Lyotard used the example of the revisionist historian Robert Faurisson's demands for proof of the Holocaust to demonstrate how the differend could be applied in understanding phenomena. Faurisson would only accept proof of the existence of gas chambers from eyewitnesses who were themselves victims of the gas chambers. However, any such eyewitnesses are dead and are not able to testify. Faurisson therefore concluded from this that there were no gas chambers. The situation is this:

1. Either there were no gas chambers, in which case there would be no eyewitnesses to produce evidence, or

2. There were gas chambers, in which case there would still be no eyewitnesses to produce evidence.

Since Faurisson would accept no evidence for the existence of gas chambers except the testimony of actual victims, he concluded from both possibilities that gas chambers did not exist. The situation is a double bind because there was no way to demonstrate that gas chambers did exist and killed people. The case is a differend because the harm done to the victims cannot be presented in the standard of judgment upheld by Faurisson.

Another example of the differend that commentators on Lyotard often invoke is that of indigenous peoples' claims to land rights in colonized countries. This example shows the relevance of Lyotard's work for practical problems of justice in the contemporary world. Let us take the Aboriginal Peoples of Australia as an example. Many tribal groups claim that land they traditionally inhabited is now owned and controlled by the descendants of European colonists. They claim that the land was taken from them wrongfully and that it should be given back to them. There is a differend in this case because Aboriginal land rights are established by tribal law, and evidence for such rights may not be presentable in the law of the Australian government. The court of appeal in which claims to land rights are heard functions entirely according to government law, and tribal law is not considered a valid system of judgment. In the case of a dispute over a certain area of land by farmers who are descendants of colonists on the one hand and a tribe of Aboriginal people on the other hand, the court of appeal would be the one that involved the law that the farmers recognize (government law), while the law that the Aboriginal people recognize (tribal law) will not be considered valid. It may be the case that the only evidence for the claim to land rights that the Aboriginal people have will not be admissible as evidence in the court of government law (though it is perfectly acceptable in tribal law). Hence, we have a case of a wrong that cannot be presented as a wrong: a differend.

The same was done here in the United States after the Treaty of Guadalupe Hidalgo in 1848. Citizens of Mexico that then became citizens of the United States through the annexation of lands through the treaty were supposed to have equal rights. However, the court systems established in these areas were in English. When Spanish-speaking citizens arrived in court either to file a claim or defend against one, they did not understand the language of the proceedings. Increasingly, formerly wealthy landowners lost their properties and wealth. They were given the same rights as other citizens, but because the court proceedings were in English, they did not understand what was being said. They were taken advantage of. It was a differend.

Lyotard, in attempting to break down the differend and provide a deeper understanding, increasingly relied on the role of language in this process. Like many social theorists in the post-1960s, with the explosion of multimedia occurring in the Western world, Lyotard focused on the phrase as event, and the limits of representation are seen in the indeterminacy involved in the linking of phrases. Phrases, according to Lyotard (1988), were ***extralinguistic*, which means communication went beyond words**. Phrases and communication, in general, can and do include signs, gestures, and objects. In this sense, then, phrases have to be viewed as contexts. Every event is to be understood as a phrase that fits with the differend. These events or phrases are pieced together to tell a larger, deeper, and more diverse story. This facilitates a better understanding of the world around us. Think of this in terms of how professors will want students to elaborate, to explain, and to avoid using one-sentence statements to illustrate an idea. For Lyotard, this occurs in communication. People string together phrases but think of them in the same manner that Mead talked about the act-as-such. There are steps along the way. Lyotard called the way phrases are linked together in series the "concatenation of phrases." **The *law of concatenation* is the process by which phrases are strung together to assist in making sense of what is trying to be conveyed.** A phrase must be followed by another phrase, yet at the same time, there is not necessarily a concrete method for doing that. Unlike writing code for computers, which have set procedures for concatenation, in human communication, this takes many forms. One need only attempt to speak with someone who does not speak the same language or travel to foreign countries where your host language is not spoken or known to see the lengths people will go to and the methods people will use to try to communicate.

Lyotard went further with this idea, however, than you might expect from symbolic interactionists. Here, Lyotard focused on phrases as events that were beyond full understanding and accurate representation. He went against the symbolic interactionists who would connect these phrases, gestures, signs, and so on to something that is happening. One cannot attend a baseball game and string together phrases to empirically explain the game. No, Lyotard does acknowledge that the phrase or phrases are referencing something, but instead, Lyotard undermined the common view that the meanings of phrases can be determined by what they refer to (the referent) by focusing on the diverse series of meanings attached to every word. For Lyotard there is more than objective connections to language. Instead, there are emotions, senses, that drive how people perceive the phrases being articulated. Therefore, phrases being strung together provide details and a greater chance for understanding. They help us make sense. For Lyotard, only phrases carry sense. Lyotard defined reality as this complex of possible senses attached to a referent through a name. The correct sense of a phrase cannot be determined by a reference to reality since the referent itself does not fix sense and reality itself is defined as the complex of competing senses attached to a referent. The phrase event remains indeterminate.

Lyotard used the concepts of a phrase universe (yes, a metanarrative) and of the difference between presentation and situation to show how phases can carry meanings and yet be indeterminate. Every phrase presents a universe composed of the following four elements or, as Lyotard called them, instances:

- The sense (the possible meanings of the phrase)

- The referent (the thing to which the phrase refers)

- The addressor (that from which the phrase comes)

- The addressee (that to which the phrase is sent)

Before we go further, understand that this is simply a method for breaking down how people communicate with each other. But it also fits with the issues of pluralities addressed above that Lyotard articulated. Therefore, this demonstrates not only how meaning develops but also how things can lead to fragmentation, with people identifying differences in understanding.

In the initial presentation of the phrase, the instances of the universe are equivocal. That is, there are many possible ways in which the instances may be situated in relation to each other. Who or what uttered the phrase, and to whom? To what does the phrase refer? What sense of the phrase is meant? This equivocation means that the meaning of the phrase is not fixed in the initial presentation and only becomes fixed through what Lyotard calls "situation." ***Situation* takes place when the instances of the phrase are fixed through the concatenation of phrases (i.e.,** when the phrase is followed by another phrase). When phrases are concatenated, they follow rules for linking called "**phrase regimens.**" *Phrase regimens* **fix the instances of the phrase universe within a concatenation; these regimens are syntactic types of phrases, such as the cognitive, the descriptive, the prescriptive, the interrogative, the evaluative, and so on.** Any situation of a phrase within a concatenation will only be one possible situation of the initial presentation of the phrase, however. It is always possible to situate the phrase in a different way by concatenating with a different phrase regimen. In other words, the presentation of the phrase event is not able to be accurately represented by any particular situation. This also means that there is no correct or single way of concatenating a phrase; there is no "correct" phrase regimen to be employed in following one phrase with another.

Lyotard insisted that phrase regimens are heterogenous and cannot be measured. That is, they are of radically different types and cannot be meaningfully compared through an initial presentation of the phrase event of which they are situations. However, different phrase regimens can be brought together through genres. *Genres* **supply rules for the linking of phrases, but rather than being syntactic rules as phrase regimens are, genres direct how to concatenate through ends, goals, or stakes.** What is at stake in the genre of comedy, for example, is to be humorous, to make people laugh. This goal directs how phrases are linked on from one to another. Genres of discourse can bring heterogenous phrase regimens together in a concatenation, but genres themselves are heterogenous and incommensurable. This means that there is no correct genre to situate the initial phrase that is presented, and no genre has more validity than others. The differend arises on this level of genres when the phrase event gives rise to different genres, but one genre claims validity over the others. That is, one genre claims the exclusive right to impose rules of concatenation from the initial phrase.

How do we know when a differend has occurred? Lyotard (1988) said that it is signaled by the difficulty of linking one phrase to another. A differend occurs when a discourse does not allow the linkages that would enable the presentation of a wrong. Lyotard insisted that phrases must, of necessity, follow other phrases—even silence is a kind of phrase, with its own generic effects. A silent phrase in the context of a dispute may be covering four possible states of affairs, corresponding to each of the instances in the phrase universe:

- The sense: The meaning of the referent cannot be signified.

- The referent: The referent (e.g., the wrong, etc.) did not take place.

- The addresser: The addresser does not believe that the referent falls within their competence to present.

- The addressee: The addresser does not believe that the referent (e.g., the wrong, etc.) falls within the competence (e.g., to hear, to understand, to judge, etc.) of the addressee.

For the referent to be expressed, these four silent negations must be withdrawn. The referent must have reality, must be presentable in the rules of the discourse, and the addresser must have confidence in the competence of both themselves and the addressee. Through the idea of the differend, Lyotard drew particular attention to the problems of the presentability of the referent when the parties in dispute could not agree on a common discourse or rule of judgment. Justice demands, however, that wrongs be presented. How is this possible? Lyotard did not believe that there was an easy answer. But for the sake of justice, people must try. People must identify differends as best they can. It may be something as simple as the feeling of not being able to find the words. Lyotard associated the identification of a differend with the feeling of the sublime, the mixture of pleasure and pain that accompanies the attempt to present the unpresentable.

Ultimately, the joy of Lyotard involved his ability to break down or deconstruct everything into unique phenomena. He created a series of methods to demonstrate how special life can be. Lyotard suggested a place or essence of being where people would be more appreciative and acknowledge the contributions that exist. This way of addressing social phenomena provided sociologists more ammunition to dig deeper into the social world and not take everyday life for granted.

<insert IMG 7.3: Derrida>

Jacques Derrida (1930–2004) was the founder of *deconstruction*, which is a theory of textual analysis suggesting that a text has no stable reference, thereby questioning assumptions about the ability of language to represent reality. His views on deconstruction have been popular in the 21st century, though many who have followed his ideas know little of Derrida and what he wrote. His ideas, however, have wide-ranging influence in philosophy; literary criticism and theory; art and, in particular, architectural theory; and political theory. Sociology takes a far back seat when it comes to formally addressing his ideas. Because Derrida's writings often concern *autobiography* (writing about one's life as a form of relation to oneself), many of his writings are autobiographical. The key factor though is that this style has garnered much attention in the social sciences with regard to *autoethnography research*, which is a form of qualitative research in which an author uses self-reflection and writing to explore anecdotal and personal experience and connect this autobiographical story to wider cultural, political, and social meanings and understandings.

One of the easiest ways to understand part of the deconstruction that Derrida wrote about involves experience. Focusing solely on experience, what one cannot deny is that experience is conditioned by time. Every experience takes place in the present, which is so different from Mead in that Mead saw the present as being specious or occurring over time. In the present experience, there is the now. What is happening right now is an event, different from every other now ever experienced. However, Derrida does acknowledge the speciousness of time. People remember the recent past and use that to anticipate and expect what to do in the present. This is conditioned, repeatable, and can serve to motivate action. Importantly, though, what is occurring now is unique and is only specific to the act now.

Derrida (1989) suggests four implications of experience in the now. First, he suggests that experience is never a simple experience. Instead, he acknowledges, as stated above, the recent past and the anticipation of what is to come. Second, nothing is unilateral, acting independently of everything else. Derrida's argument demonstrates that the empirical event is a nonseparable part of the structural or foundational conditions. Third, each experience has an origin, and the origin is always heterogeneous. Since this is the case, nothing is ever given as such in certainty. Whatever is given is given as other than itself, as already past or as still to come. What becomes foundational, therefore, for Derrida is this "as": origin as the heterogeneous "as." The "as" means that there is no knowledge as such, there is no truth as such, there is no perception, and there is no intuition of anything as such. Faith, perjury, and language are already there in the origin. Lastly, if something already taken place has taken place essentially or necessarily, then every experience contains an aspect of lateness. Every experience then is always not quite on time or, as Derrida quotes Hamlet, time is "out of joint." But we should also keep in mind, as we move forward, that the phrase "out of joint" alludes to justice: Being out of joint, time is necessarily unjust or violent.

Jean Baudrillard

<insert IMG 7.4: Baudrillard>

One of the most well-known social theorists associated with postmodernism is Jean Baudrillard (1929–2007). Baudrillard was born in Reims, France, in 1929. In 1956, he began working as a professor of secondary education in a French high school and in the early 1960s did editorial work for the French publisher *Seuil*. Baudrillard was initially a Germanist who published essays on literature in *Les Temps Modernes* in 1962–1963. He also translated works of Peter Weiss and Bertolt Brecht into French, as well as a book on messianic revolutionary movements by Wilhelm Mühlmann. During this period, he met and studied the works of Marxist Henri Lefebvre, whose critiques of everyday life impressed him. He also met Roland Barthes, whose *semiotics* **(the study of sign processes, which are any activity, conduct, or process that involves signs, where a sign is defined as anything that communicates a meaning that is not the sign itself to the sign's interpreter)** analyses of contemporary society had a lasting influence on his work, especially as it relates to Baudrillard's famous use of *simulacrum*—**that is, an image or representation of someone or something.**

Like many social theorists, Baudrillard was a sharp critic of contemporary society, culture, and thought. He wrote on several specific topics, all of which seemed to resonate with younger people, as Baudrillard was able to connect social life with the increased influence of communication technologies on human outcomes. He wrote on the erasure of the distinctions of gender, race, and class that structured modern societies in a new postmodern consumer, media, and high-tech society; the mutating roles of art and aesthetics; fundamental changes in politics, culture, and human beings; and the impact of new media, information, and cybernetic technologies in the creation of a qualitatively different social order, providing fundamental mutations of human and social life.

For some years a cult figure of postmodern theory, Baudrillard moved beyond, or his thought evolved from the 1980s until his death in 2007. In retrospect, Baudrillard can be seen as a theorist who traced, in original ways, the impact of technology on social life. He also systematically criticized major modes of modern thought while developing his own philosophical perspectives. Ultimately, with Baudrillard, his works are much more palatable to sociological thinking than those of other postmodern thinkers.

The Consumer Society

For Baudrillard, the period spanning the late 20th century and early 21st century is represented by an economic system that eats up the goods produced by capitalist industries. We crave things. We must purchase new technologies regularly or else we feel out of touch. We mock those who do not have the right products. People no longer can function without their phones connected to them. We are addicted to purchasing. The economic system now feeds on the newest technological devices and fashionable products. Its appetite is whet by ideas found within the culture industry, as articulated by Adorno and Horkheimer. The system is enamored with ambiance, style, novelty, identity, freedom, and social differentiation. The economic system and those of us within it are satisfied in the consumption of products.

During this time, to live is to consume. Everything is up for consumption, and our lives are organized around commodities. When tax cuts come, the hope is that Americans will take the extra cash and buy more things. After the 2008 crash of the global economy, politicians and economists around the world sought quick ways to fix the economy, and providing tax cuts appeared the way it would occur. The problem was that, initially, Americans were not spending their money. Concerned about the economy, Americans paid off bills and kept money in the bank just in case it was needed. This slowed the process of recovery for economies. Instead of purchasing something, people effectively chose not to be so impulsive. During the COVID-19 pandemic, a similar process occurred. One example is something as simple as the use of paper towels (throw-away products). When distribution and supply issues made paper towels scarce, people began using towels, something that could be washed, instead.

For Baudrillard, however, he saw consumption as dominating everyday life. He saw consumption connected with abundance, which confirms what happened in 2008 and in 2020. When abundance is not guaranteed, behaviors change. However, when abundance is manifest, we surround ourselves with things. The adage "Those who die with the most toys wins" is suggestive of this. As a Star Trek fan and one who is heavily involved with the fandom, it is amazing the amount of money that is spent on Star Trek products by the fans. Basements, living rooms, bedrooms, and even cars become statements of the fandom, as they are comprised of consumables. At the first Star Trek convention I went to, I was riding down the elevator. There was another fan with me. He asked if this was my first convention. I nodded "yes." He then asked, "How many thousands of dollars have you spent?" Talking with others about this is a rite of passage. I am a Star Trek fan because I have Star Trek things (LoConto, 2020). I am because I buy.

Baudrillard, when talking about the consumer society, was influenced by critical theorists and their views on the culture industry. He emphasized how everything good had been turned into goods. Health and well-being translated into a membership at a gym, as well as the "need" to drink the latest energy drinks. New and unusual art became reduced to a few songs sung by whoever was popular in the moment, only to be replaced by the new object or artist quickly thereafter. Art had turned into mass production, which changed the meanings of art as well. Baudrillard (2017) stated:

> Art speculation, which was based on rarity value, is over. With the "Unlimited Multiple,"
> art moves into the industrial era (as it so happens, these Multiples, produced in limited

editions, immediately give rise to a black market and "alternative" speculation: the false ingenuousness of the producers and designers). (p. 125)

In addition, for Baudrillard, literature ceased to be literature. Instead, literature became a product that must conform to the latest fads. Think of how popular culture in the form of superheroes and dystopian literature have dominated the 21st century. Marvel and DC style storylines have dominated. Movies are either remakes, sequels, prequels, or similar storylines. They play it safe, avoiding risk, knowing full well they will have a ready-made, programed audience who is ready, willing, and able to purchase products.

Ultimately, as Baudrillard stated, the medium becomes the message. When he wrote, the medium was TV and radio. Now it is the internet and the various forms of social media that dominate our information sources. Filter bubbles recognize what we read and observe, then we are inundated with advertisements that fit with what we search. As Baudrillard (2017) stated:

> This technological process of mass communications delivers a certain kind of very imperative message: a message-consumption message, a message of segmentation and spectacularization, of misrecognition of the world and foregrounding of information as a commodity, of glorification of content as sign. In short, it performs a conditioning function … and a function of misrecognition. (p. 141)

Consistent with critical theorists, Baudrillard saw mass media as conditioning us to need and look forward to the messages (e.g., the best part of the Super Bowl is the commercials). But the messages provide us information that leads us elsewhere, away from anything important, to something that leads us to purchase more. And if we run out of space, we can sell on eBay, give the things away, or throw them away. One of my friends used to have a large collection of Star Wars products. When his Buffy the Vampire Slayer and Star Trek collectibles were squeezing space in his home, he decided to sell the Star Wars collection. While he made thousands of dollars in profit from the sales, he reminded me that everything we bought could be resold. Our needs were fleeting, but it is okay, because others have similar needs to buy what you valued for a short time.

However, it goes beyond fandom products. Anything can be sensationalized or universalized. All that needs to be done is advertising. When talking to others, it is amazing how much the word "need" comes into play when talking about products. Why are some cars cool and others not? They both get us to where we are going. Ah, but the image (i.e., the brand) is key. The value placed on the product is of utmost importance. The advertising tells us that we need to buy even the right kind of cleaning products. We must have the right kind of beer and the right kind of toothpaste. When I watch TV or go on the internet, they tell me what I am supposed to have. I even have to get the right kind of insurance because Flo told me to.

In this consumer society, consumption excludes no one. We are offered a zillion choices. The capitalist industries make sure that all taste and sense of style could be bought. I noticed a few years ago that one of my colleagues would speak in Spanish instead of English when getting upset with her kids. She also spent time in Cuba. I went on Amazon, and it took about 30 seconds to find a T-shirt that said, "Don't make me use my Cuban voice." I bought it, and she loved it. This capitalist drive even infiltrates those who want to buck the system. How many younger people, in trying to echo the sentiments of the counterculture movements of the 1960s, buy tie-dye clothing? They craft their clothing to match the image of what suggests being against the system. In my support of being against the system (which is odd because most of my adult life I have worked for the state government), I bought a revolutionary hat that Che Guevarra was always portrayed as wearing. I am against the system because I wear Che Guevarra hats, tie-dye shirts, and Birkenstocks. A real revolutionary.

Baudrillard extended critical theorists' critique of the culture industry by focusing more on consumption as the new social order. Instead of living in a state of false consciousness that critical theorists advocated through being distracted by the power of the culture industry, Baudrillard argued for recognizing the linguistic character of commodities. He wanted people to recognize the importance of signs. While Marx and neo-Marxists insisted that the value of products depended upon their exchange value, Baudrillard focused on a different perspective. For him, commodities were consumed for their sign value. Each commodity had a meaning attached to it. Starbucks coffee ceased to be mere coffee. A consumer who drank Starbucks coffee gained prestige in the same way that a person who drives a red Porsche becomes cool. We become the product, or I should say, we become consistent with the image of the products we consume.

The consumer society gave way to a change in behavior and ethical concerns. Baudrillard highlighted the change from the work ethic of the modern society where peoples' most salient identity was that of what they did for a living. Instead, in postmodern society, the identity is what one does for fun. In the consumer society, the hedonistic morality—that is, the focus on personal pleasure—became legitimized. The repressed and discontent people of the modern society were encouraged to enjoy life by consuming. During the modernistic period, people would be so attached to their jobs that there was nothing left after the job was over. As one uncle said to me, "Why should I retire? I'll just die." He was right. He died 11 months after his retirement. In the consumer society, according to Baudrillard, people found contentment through consumption and not much else.

Freedom was a myth. People were controlled by what they were socialized into. Therefore, freedom of choice was conditioning to pursue the purchase and consumption of products. As Baudrillard stated (2017):

> The freedom and sovereignty of the consumer are mystification pure and simple. This carefully sustained mystique … of individual satisfaction and choice, which is the culmination of a whole civilization of "freedom," is the very ideology of the industrial system, justifying its arbitrary power and all the collective nuisances it generates: dirt, pollution, deculturation. In fact, the consumer is sovereign in a jungle of ugliness where freedom of choice has been forced upon him. (p. 90)

Consistent with Thorstein Veblen's (1899) ideas, people are conditioned now to seek joy in not only consumption but also conspicuous consumption: consumption that has physical substance (i.e., things that people can see and touch). This creates the illusion of satisfaction. They must be commodified as well. What this does, however, is lead to this frantic search where people not only pursue consumption but also attempt to distinguish themselves from others by purchasing similar products, but products that represent the new "thing," the new fad. Why purchase a brand new 2020 Nissan Rogue when the new redesigned 2021 Nissan Rogue is available? When I was at Oklahoma State University, I always enjoyed walking through the student parking lot the first week of school. There I could see all the new cars.

At the same time, all these new products have to be desired. This becomes a production-consumption dialectic. Our focus on consumption means that to meet that need, production must accommodate the demand. Without it, consumption would stall. During the first part of the COVID-19 pandemic, early in the Spring 2020, conversations began regarding what would happen to television and movie watching if production could not continue. Streaming services are predicated upon the new show or movie. Inevitably, production continued, though slower. More documentaries were pushed through to accommodate the need from consumers.

Since consumption became the new order of society, advertising also became more important. We are bombarded by images in advertising in the 21st century. Advertisements now, however, do not simply inform the average person of the products, nor do they clearly persuade. What occurs now is that advertising has underlying themes applying to a way of life or, more precisely, the image of a way of life that resonates with gratification, gratification that is based in part on consumption and the image of happiness this consumption will provide. Inevitably, what we are left with is this desire to purchase for happiness, and the more we buy, the happier we will be. The advertisements have become so important that people have become obsessed with the advertisements. We go on YouTube and watch collections of funny commercials. Those collections are entertainment. The products have been replaced, but the joy of watching 10- and 15-year-old commercials remains.

Consistent with this is the introduction of the movie or television sponsors' products being placed within the show. It became obvious within the movie *Jurassic Park* when at the theme park in the movie, viewers got to see all the potential products that were available for purchase. It was a commercial built within the movie. Afterward, several of these products were being sold in the lobby of the theater. Watch other movies or television shows. Look at the angle of the "shot" in respect to the product. Actors are directed to make sure the label of the product they are handling is obvious to the viewer.

While Baudrillard mentioned the existence of malls, which are increasingly closing, the key element for Baudrillard is more apparent today than when he wrote. His focus was on organization and how malls represented this one-stop shopping where people could purchase all their "needs" in one place. When I was married, my wife and I had a tradition where we would go Christmas shopping. We would do most of it in one day. We went to the mall. Now, of course, we can go to Amazon and find whatever we want. The products are a few seconds away from being ordered. Now, I can also go to the doctor virtually, and if I need a haircut, I can simply go online and make the appointment. Purchasing and consuming are easy.

We have reached the point where consumption dominates our entire lives. People are now socialized to consume, so much so that we do not recognize the oppressive nature of consumption. When COVID-19 happened, purchasing habits did change, but not as much as feared. States like New Mexico did so well that midway through 2020, the state government told universities and other schools that they (the state government) would be returning money that had been cut at the beginning of the fiscal year. While many Americans paid off their credit cards, still others did work on their homes. Others continued to purchase products online at an even greater rate. Amazon's stock, at the time of writing this, has increased over 60% during the COVID-19 pandemic. Because people have an outdated model of what oppression looks like, they do not and have not seen how they are manipulated into continual purchasing and consumption.

Ultimately, the consumer society that Baudrillard said existed is characterized by our obsession with and the consumption of objects, of commodities. We are because we buy. Or, I should say, we are the image, that virtual image, of the things we consume.

The Virtual

Linked to the consumer society was Baudrillard's idea of the virtualization of the world. *Virtualization* **is the art and science of making the function of an object or resource simulated. Virtualization makes real that which is not.** This could fit with technology and various forms of computer software, but it is also consistent with how the abstract has social force, like the social facts that Durkheim wrote. In Baudrillard's later works, he focused on the virtualization of reality, which is, in a sense, a commodification of efficiency.

Inevitably, when most sociologists talk about Baudrillard and postmodernism, this virtual reality, the simulation and hyperreality, is what comes to mind. In that sense, this is simply a pivot from the consumer society to the postmodern society. The society characterized by simulation and hyperreality will be called postmodern society. In postmodern society, the sign, or the identifier of an object, becomes the reality. Everything becomes surface oriented. People and things cease to have depth. Baudrillard sees this as consistent as with how language works. Language, for Baudrillard, is always a matter of distinction. A word represents something and not another. We often do that when meeting people who are from different countries who speak different languages. We point to something and then say a word. The belief is that that word "is" that thing. But even with that, the distinction is not complete. You could point to something and say, "tree." It becomes more complex than that, however. It could be a pine tree, a deciduous tree, a dead tree, a flowering tree, a fruit-producing tree, and so on. As time goes on, and language develops more; the more words we have, the more we can make more specific distinctions between things. For Baudrillard, the word is what that thing or object is. The tree no longer has depth; it is only a word.

He goes on to address life as a system of objects. A system of objects is what life is, what societies and civilizations are. This fits with his consumption model, as much of what Baudrillard sees as value in a consumer and postmodern society are the things we buy or consume. Because of this, Baudrillard saw objects as dictating life. They have control over people, and our consumption gives the impression of blind consumption. Baudrillard's discussion of the system of objects is also a diagnosis of the symptom of reification of signs. If you remember, reification is when our mental creations take on a reality of their own. Therefore, Baudrillard stated that signs take on a reality of their own. He felt that signs were becoming more independent from the commodities themselves. Signs were separating from their referents. We may become fearful of the sign or embrace the sign without there being on object there. An obvious example would be God, whose function has been forgotten and has instead simply become real for many people. And this reification lies in the shift in the relation of the human to the object. Think about how often you take classes and do not know the professor's name. They are simply a professor. This goes both ways, with professors sometimes only seeing students, not unique people.

Signs also have value. Historically, sociologists identified three types of value: (a) value, (c) exchange value, and (c) use value. Baudrillard brought in the fourth, sign value. *Value* by itself is typically associated with a Marxian approach—that is, the value that commodities gain from the labor put into making them. *Exchange value* is the price of a commodity being sold on a market. *Use value* is how useful a commodity is. *Sign value*, on the other hand, is the value commodities gain from differentiating themselves in a system of objects and representing luxury and status. Therefore, sign value can reflect the restaurants one eats at, the clothes one wears, or the type of business card one has. Former tennis player Andre Agazzi used to do a commercial for American Express where he finished by saying, "Image is everything." That is sign value.

This behavior is not limited to the postmodern. Max Weber and some critical theorists have critiqued **the *iron cage of reason*, the oppressive dogmatic bent of some epistemologies**.

Baudrillard insisted that the value and the valorization of reality, truth, time, the social, and everything else have accelerated toward obscenity, toward a kind of ecstatic creation. Everything has ballooned to its breaking point. Everything has sped up to the end. The history people live in now is not the history of progress but a history of exhaustion, a countdown history. Everything becomes the greatest of all time or the worst of all time, the biggest tax cuts or the biggest tax increases. Life appears to be always on the cusp of ending. Everything is at risk.

When reading Baudrillard, one can get the picture that he believed we had reached a point of no return. The end had come, but we had not gotten the memo yet. He argued that people had murdered the "real". The real has been exterminated, and we were unaware of it. Overnight, the real was murdered, and in its place was a virtual existence. We began living in an image of a world where we defined and redefined life, and that was life for us. If our leaders told us that murderers and rapists were coming across the border and murdering and raping Americans, we believed them without any concept of fact. The election was rigged? Sure, why not? What Baudrillard addressed was that we were and are living in a simulation of reality. And unfortunately, we no longer realize that we are living in a post-fact world.

Amusement parks, malls, RPG computer games, and simulated environments all add up to the illusion that reality is still what it was, that it could still be easily differentiated from the unreal. But Baudrillard maintained that in the postmodern society, there are no longer clear distinctions between spheres of life. The media, the political, the social, the sexual, the economical—all of these have collided into each other, tangled, and bungled up into a dizzying network of cable wires. The difference between the sign and the object could no longer be put into question, because every idea, dream, fantasy, and utopia will be eradicated because it will immediately be realized, or operationalized. Nothing will survive as an idea or a concept. You will not even have time enough to imagine. Everything happens in an instant. Everything has been infested by technology, controlled by signs, and confused by the media. It is not just the loss of meaning. It is total alienation. Everything is strategically planned, simulated, and reduced to a spectacle. Everything has been foreseen by the virtual.

Even in death, the virtual intervenes. The age-old desire for immortality has moved out of actions, speech, and legacy to physical immortality. In the postmodern society, physical immortality seemed possible. Baudrillard (2000, p. 5) writes: "It is common to speak of the struggle of life against death, but there is an inverse peril. And we must struggle against the possibility that we will not die." Here, he is speaking of cloning, of preserving bodies without heads, of cryonic suspension, of cryogenics, and other biotechnological experiments. The postmodern person, via technological advances, is working on the dedifferentiation of the world, a project to reconstruct a homogeneous and uniformly consistent universe that unfolds within a technological and mechanical medium, extending over our vast information network, where we are in the process of building a perfect clone, an identical copy of our world, a virtual artifact that opens up to the prospect of endless production.

The world that Baudrillard was trying to paint was not just a panic attack of a technophobic old man. This is not only the virtualization of reality but also the robotization of humans. People become the answering machine, the beep of a phone, the avatar in a social network site. People became obsessed with high-quality sound, enhanced through autotunes; they grew to prefer the high definition of images that enabled them to zoom in to the minutest detail. We are nothing more than objects, and surface objects at that.

Summary

Ultimately, what we see with postmodernism is the questioning of things we took for granted and never questioned. As my dad used to say, "Things are this way, they've always been this way, and they will always be this way." Both Lyotard and Baudrillard called into question these metanarratives. Lyotard laid the groundwork for the postmodern beginning with paganism and gradually worked his way to the postmodern and differend. The conclusions were that life was so unique, so plural, that truth had to be situated in understanding the specific context everything existed within. How could we have laws that applied to everyone when everything was so different?

Likewise, Baudrillard focused on how the consumption of products increasingly made the value of those products less important. That is, they became fleeting. Consuming was the goal. Mass production reduced quality into what is popular in the moment. Evolving into focusing on virtualization, Baudrillard recognized that life had been replaced by images of life. Getting to know things and people were replaced with the surface. In the classroom, students do not want dialogue and conversation; they want to know what they need to know for the exam. The feelings and thoughts of the students are as valued as the decades of scientific research that reach different conclusions. Ultimately, we find ourselves living in a world where depth has no place. If a student got A's in their classes, they were a good student, even if they did not know much of anything.

The gist of the argument for postmodernism is that people have lost sight of what is real yet act as though everything is real. If everyone's feelings matter, then no one's feelings matter. Everything becomes meaningless. For what it is worth, postmodernists such as Lyotard and Baudrillard were frustrated with what the Western world had become. They took out their frustration by explaining how those problems are manifest. At the same time, they did not provide a roadmap on how to return from the abyss. Instead, what is left was that depth no longer mattered. Behind the façade does not matter. And even if we look beyond the façade, there would be yet another façade. What is more, we no longer care.

Comprehension Questions

1. Explain paganism according to Lyotard and its value for social justice.

2. How does a consumer society influence how people perceive the world around them?

3. What are the similarities and differences between Lyotard and Baudrillard in how they define and operationalize postmodernity?

4. What is the difference between industrial and postindustrial societies? How does this help us explain the difference between modernity and postmodernity?

5. How do both Lyotard and Baudrillard explain how there are no metanarratives?

Critical Thinking Questions

1. What is a differend? Provide an example of a differend occurring today. Explain how this is a differend.

2. Using the ideas of Lyotard, explain how that could help change (for the better) the world today.

3. What is meant by there being no referent? How is that obvious in life today for college students?

4. Explain phrase regimens. In addition, explain how phrase regimens help or hinder American society when it comes to the criminal justice system.

5. What are the moral consequences in life if we do indeed live in virtualization? Please also explain what is meant by virtualization.

Additional Recommended Readings

Baudrillard, J. (2017). *The consumer society: Myths and structures*. Sage Publishers.

Borges, J. L. (2007). *Labyrinths*. New Directions Books.

Derrida, J. (2017). *Writing and difference*. The University of Chicago Press.

Gaddis, W. (2012). *The recognitions*. Dalkey Archive Press.

Gergen, K. J. (1991). *The saturated self*. Basic Books.

Lyotard, J. (1988). *The differend: Phrases in dispute*. University of Minnesota Press.

Lyotard, J. (1991). *The postmodern condition: A report on knowledge*. University of Minnesota Press.

References

Baudrillard, J. (2000). *The vital illusion*. Columbia University Press.

Baudrillard, J. (2017). *The consumer society: Myths and structures*. Sage Publishers.

Carty, V. (2015). *Social movements and new technology*. Westview Press.

Cheal, D. (1996). *New poverty: Families in postmodern society*. Greenwood Press.

Cole, T. R., Achenbaum, W. A., Jakobi, P. L., & Kastenbaum, R. (1993). *Voices and visions of aging: Toward a critical gerontology*. Springer Publishing Company.

Derrida, J. (1989). *Of spirit*. University of Chicago Press.

Durkheim, E. (1984). *The division of labor in society*. The Free Press. (Original work published 1933)

Gergen, K. J. (1991). *The saturated self*. Basic Books.

Goffman, E. (1951). Symbols of class status. *The British Journal of Sociology, 2*(4), 294–304.

Hoeveler, J. D., Jr. (1996). *The postmodernist turn: American thought and culture in the 1970s*. Twayne Publishers.

Klapp, O. (1969). *Collective identity*. University of Chicago Press.

LoConto, D. G. (2020). *Social movements and the collective identity of the Star Trek fandom: Boldly going where no fans have gone before*. Lexington Publishers.

Lyotard, J. (1988). *The differend: Phrases in dispute*. University of Minnesota Press.

Lyotard, J. (1991). *The postmodern condition: A report on knowledge*. University of Minnesota Press.

Merton, R. K. (1972). Insiders and outsiders: A chapter in the sociology of knowledge. *American Journal of Sociology, 78*(1), 9–47.

Mills, C. W. (1963). *Power, politics, and people: The collected essays of C. Wright Mills*. Oxford University Press.

Rorty, R. (1982). *Consequences of pragmatism*. University of Minnesota Press.

Rorty, R. (1991). *Objectivity, relativism, and truth: Philosophical papers, Volume 1*. Cambridge University Press.

Seidman, S. (1992). Postmodern social theory as narrative with a moral intent. In S. Seidman & D. G. Wagner (Eds.), *Postmodernism and social theory* (pp. 47–81). Blackwell.

Shlapentokh, D. (1995). History and irrationality: Postmodernism–East and West. *International Journal of Politics, Culture, and Society, 9*(2), 179–195.

Tedrick, T. (1991). Aging, developmental disabilities, and leisure: Policy and service delivery issues. In *Activities, adaptation, and aging* (pp. 141–152). Haworth Press.

Twenge, J. M. (2014). *Generation me: Why today's young Americans are more confident, assertive, entitled—and more miserable than ever before*. ATRIA Paperback.

Twenge, J. M., & Campbell, W. K. (2009). *The narcissism epidemic: Living in the age of entitlement*. ATRIA Paperback.

Weber, M. (1947). *The theory of social and economic organization*. The Free Press.

Chapter 8: Another "Post": Poststructuralism

Carving a Place in Social Theory

Unlike the postmodernism of Baudrillard that separated the sign from the referent, in poststructuralist theories, there is no separation. They word it differently, however, choosing to not make a distinction between discourse and the objects of discourse. The implication here is that the theory is not separate from reality, nor is reality separate from theory. More specifically, *what those in this school of thought suggest is that people are socialized to see what they are taught to see.* Everything is a *social construction*—**that is, that people develop knowledge of the world in a social context and that much of what we perceive as reality depends on shared assumptions**. People are taught to understand meanings in what they see, and these meanings are socially constructed. Unlike many social theorists that came before them, specifically those discussed throughout this book, poststructuralists view reality as far more complex, with *discourse*—**written or spoken communication used for dialogue and debate**—being part of the nearly endless stream of reality of which people are a part. In this sense, this is very similar to Baudrillard's virtualization; however, Baudrillard saw the function of signs as being far more determinative. While that can be the case with poststructuralist theories, there is a bit more fluidity involved. In short, the lines drawn between the theories and theorists are not as distinct as one might believe.

As mentioned above, poststructuralism recognizes the power of discourse to shape reality. Discourse can produce the ability to see things that are a fiction, such as in the concept of race. Race is a social construction, of which its only reality is when people believe it to be true. For example, in the United States, the typical American will believe that Asian, Native, Latinx, and African Americans are distinct races of people. Yet there is little to no evidence at the genetic level to reach that conclusion. People have created the concept of race and the meanings associated with it, and those meanings are localized here in the United States. In other countries, and during other time periods, race is and was defined differently. In the United States in 1850, there were three races: White, Black, and multiracial (Gould, 1996). Poststructuralists state this is all the influence of discourse. Discourse can, however, also negate the ability to see things. Much of what you have probably been taught in your sociology courses to this point implies that this is the case, especially when talking about such things as inequality. How many conversations have you had where friends or family have demonstrated they do not see the unequal treatment of African American or Latinx populations? They fail to see how the system is a structure where some Americans are denied equal opportunities because of their age, gender, race, and so much more. For poststructuralists, this is the influence of discourse.

From the perspective of poststructuralists, people see and experience limited aspects of the world. What is more, however, is that people then get shaped to see what those who control discourse want them to see. For instance, former president Trump continuously used the term or concept of "fake news" when addressing stories or discourse he did not want others to believe. This became truth for those that believed him. Likewise, what we see currently from the Biden administration is an effort to reshape the discourse and convince those who support or supported Donald Trump to see and experience a different world. The consequences can be both minimal or devastating. A recent poll in April of 2021 showed that about 45% of Republicans had no intention of getting the COVID-19 vaccine (Hamel et. al., 2021). That may seem like a lot, considering there are 330 million people in the United States. However, approximately 211 million Americans are registered to vote, and of those, approximately 29%, or 61 million, are Republicans. Take 45% of that brings us to approximately 27 million Americans. With the adult population—that is, those 18 and over—in the United States being 256 million, having a little more than 10% of the adult population not willing to get vaccinated does not seem as problematic. Of course, not all independents, Democrats, or adults not registered to vote are going to get the vaccine either. The point, however, is that though former president Trump advocated for people to get the vaccine and he and his family have gotten them as well, many believed some of the discourse coming from those that supported him. That became the reality. Over time, these numbers will change, but hopefully you can see how discourse shapes views on what is real. The easier method would be to watch MSNBC for an hour during a weekday. Then the following hour watch Fox News for an hour. It is two different worlds. That is the power of discourse.

Also, much like postmodernist thought, poststructuralists see the world being comprised of continuous processes. If everything is in process, everything is changing and in a state of flux. If everything is in motion, (i.e., in process), it becomes the processes that need to be studied, not the objects. Therefore, they often reject many of the early social theories as being too simplistic or naïve. Similarly, then, they negate the idea of a metanarrative. There simply is not a metanarrative if everything is in a state of process. Truth is not singular but instead multiple, much like what Lyotard stated. It is like what one of my professors used to say, quoting the Greek philosopher Heraclitus who said, "You can never step in the same river twice." Life is like a river. It is flowing; therefore, it is never the same.

Poststructuralism means to go beyond the structuralism of theories that imply a rigid inner logic to relationships that describe any aspect of social reality. Their view is that most social theories that preceded them led to far more structured explanations of what was occurring in the world. Hence, people like Michel Foucault or Pierre Bourdieu, who are discussed in this chapter, reflect more poststructuralist approaches to the world.

Guiding Questions

1. How do Foucault and Bourdieu address the issues of power and status?

2. How does discourse shape the reality of people?

3. How do people use networking to further their own goals?

4. How does discourse influences habit, which facilitates normality?

5. How does the unconscious shape reality?

Michel Foucault

<insert IMG 8.1: Foucault>

Michel Foucault (1926–1984) was born Paul-Michel Foucault in 1926 in Poitiers in western France. His father, Paul-André Foucault, was a well-known surgeon who was the son of a doctor. Foucault's mother was also a daughter of a surgeon and had longed to follow a medical career, but her wish had to wait, as a career was not available for women at the time. Because of this influence or Foucault's background, many of his early works were social commentaries and histories on various forms of the medical field. His work in sociology can be applied to a variety of topics, but his early work is useful in understanding the fields of medicine and psychiatry. When I taught courses addressing health, medicine, or disability, Foucault was a staple, as his work was a foundation for demonstrating how the field of medicine has not only changed but also how people in power shaped the discourse. Foucault entered the École Normale in 1946, where he was taught by Maurice Merleau-Ponty and Louis Althusser. Their influences of the importance of perception (Merleau-Ponty) and Marxism (Althusser) shaped how Foucault approached the world. Inevitably, we see the poststructuralist approach evolve from him as discourse shaped reality (perception) and then how that discourse held sway over people and their experiences, attitudes, and values (Marxism). Foucault primarily studied philosophy, but he was also educated in psychology. He was a major figure in social thought during his lifetime. By the end of his life, Foucault had some claim to be the most prominent living intellectual in France. To this day, he is one of the most popular social theorists utilized by sociologists.

Foucault's work was and is interdisciplinary, being employed in a diverse range of disciplines in both the social sciences and the humanities. Later in his life, Foucault, like most social theorists, thought of his work as one continuous story. Nevertheless, scholars from various disciplines have attempted to place him in boxes of thought. I, myself, would tend to see Foucault mainly as a general social theorist who adopted elements of several disciplines to explain the social world around us. He relied heavily on history to explain what is occurring, laying a foundation for social standards of what is today. What Foucault did across his major works was to attempt to produce a historical account of the formation of ideas, including those that were philosophical and political. Such an attempt was neither a simple progressive view of history, seeing it as leading to our present understanding, nor a thorough history that insisted on understanding ideas framed within the time in which they occurred. Rather, Foucault continually sought for a way of understanding the ideas that shaped our present not only in terms of the historical function these ideas played but also by tracing the changes in their function through history. In short, his attempt was to understand today by understanding the processes of the past.

It was in Paris in 1960 that Foucault met the militant leftist Daniel Defert, then a student and later a sociologist, with whom he would form a partnership that lasted the rest of Foucault's life. In 1964, Defert was posted to Tunisia for 18 months of compulsory military service, during which time Foucault visited him. This led to Foucault in 1966 taking up a chair of philosophy position at the University of Tunis, where he remained until 1968. In 1966, Foucault published *The Order of Things*, which garnered him recognition. It became a bestseller and cemented Foucault as a major figure in the French intellectual structure.

The early 1970s were a politically tumultuous period in Paris, where Foucault found himself. Foucault embraced political activism, primarily in relation to the prison system, as a founder of what was called the "Prisons Information Group." It originated in an effort to aid political prisoners but in fact sought to give a voice to all prisoners. In the late 1970s, the political climate in France cooled considerably; Foucault largely withdrew from activism and turned his hand to journalism. He covered the Iranian Revolution firsthand in newspaper dispatches as the events unfolded in 1978 and 1979. He began to spend more and more time teaching in the United States, where he had begun to find an audience.

It is believed that Foucault contracted HIV when he came to the United States. He developed AIDS in 1984 and his health quickly declined. He finished editing two volumes on ancient sexuality that were published that year from his sickbed, before dying on June 26, leaving the editing of a fourth and final volume uncompleted. He left his estate to Defert, with the proviso that there were to be no posthumous publications.

Psychology

The early works of Foucault lack the style of his later works and do not necessarily feel like one is reading Foucault. Definitely, as with most of us, his ability to write evolved over his short career. In these early works, however, specifically addressing the area of mental illness, Foucault displayed the influences of his two mentors, especially where he addressed phenomenology, psychoanalysis, and Marxism. The key piece during this time was *Mental Illness and Personality*, published in 1954. This book, written specifically to entice students, began with a historical survey of the types of explanation put forward in psychology before producing a synthesis of perspectives from evolutionary psychology, psychoanalysis, phenomenology, and Marxism. What is particularly recognizable in this work is Foucault's ability to integrate and synthesize concepts from different academic disciplines into a coherent whole. In this work, mental illness (formally) is defined and described as an adaptive, defensive response by humans to conditions of alienation, which people experience during capitalism. It is the stress due to an exploitive and oppressive system become manifest, not by choice. People adapt and adjust to this system by exhibiting the stress in their daily lives, resulting in poorer outcomes.

Foucault's first recognized monograph was his 1961 primary doctoral thesis *Madness and Unreason: A History of Madness in the Classical Age*, which is best known in the English-speaking world by an abridged version, *Madness and Civilization. Madness and Civilization. It* is a work that shows several influences, as his works tend to do. It resembles Friedrich Nietzsche's *Birth of Tragedy* in style and form, proposing a disjunction between reason and unreason similar to Nietzsche's Apollonian/Dionysian distinction. It also bears the influence of French history and the philosophy of science, specifically the work of Gaston Bachelard, the developer of a form of epistemological break to which most of Foucault's works are indebted. Yet Georges Canguilhem's focus on the division of the normal from the pathological is perhaps the most telling influence on Foucault in this book. Foucault's thought continued to owe something to Marxism and to social history more generally, constituting an historical analysis of social divisions. My point here is how Foucault integrated ideas. He did not confine himself to an epistemological box.

Madness and Civilization followed from Foucault's interest in psychology, which relates back to his upbringing. Much of the work is concerned with the birth of medical psychiatry, which Foucault associated with extraordinary changes in the treatment of people with mental illness in modernity. He categorized it as (a) their systematic exclusion from society in early modernity, followed by (b) their pathologizing in late modernity. This is a pattern that anyone who has studied insane asylums or similar institutions knows, that early on they were built away from towns. Here in the United States, populations eventually grew to where they would grow out to where these institutions were. In addition, what we see with manuals such as the *Diagnostic Statistic Manual of the American Psychiatric Association*, is that they attempted to make mental illness something within the body, though even to this day there is no consensus, with little evidence to support such a claim. *Madness and Civilization* demonstrated the pattern for most of Foucault's works throughout the rest of his life by being concerned with changes in each area of social life at points in history. Like Foucault's other major works of the 1960s, it fits broadly into the category of the history and philosophy of science. It has wider philosophical appeal. Foucault found it odd suggesting that madness had not been included as part of the "reason" associated with the Enlightenment. He felt that because madness or insanity was excluded, there was an exclusion of "unreason." During the time in which Foucault was writing about, people simply moved those defined as "mad" away from the rest of the population. This practice continued well into the late 20th century and occurs today in countries such as North Korea and Russia. Nevertheless, Foucault felt that prominent individuals who were deemed mad, whose political or social views led them to being exorcized from society, should have their ideas and writings be critically evaluated. This was because many who were put in these "asylums" (I put quotes around asylum because the reality of these institutions does not align with the classic definition of "asylum," which implies protection) were placed there because leaders felt they were enemies of the state. Even today, many Marxist and critical theorists believe that medication is used to minimize dissenting voices and keep people all acting and thinking the same as the masses.

The major work of 1963 for Foucault was his follow-up to *Madness and Civilization*, entitled *The Birth of the Clinic: An Archaeology of Medical Perception. The Birth of the Clinic* examined the emergence of modern medicine. In this text, Foucault connected and analyzed how madness became classified as a disease (pathological) and how this merged into and facilitated what we would think of today as modern medicine. *The Birth of the Clinic* is a historical study of the emergence of clinical medicine around the time of the French Revolution. What is key about this text is that Foucault is able to demonstrate how the transformation of social institutions and political imperatives combined to produce modern institutional medicine. This is similar in how Weber was able to connect the Protestant Reformation to capitalism. Foucault demonstrated the interconnectedness of social phenomena: that life does not emerge independent of everything else. Everything is connected (hence the relationship to process).

<insert IMG 8.2: Butler>

Judith Butler (1956–) is a philosopher and social thinker whose theories of the performative nature of gender and sex have had a huge impact on how sociologists and social thinkers generally view the concepts of gender and sex. Her ideas have been influential in a variety of academic genres, specifically cultural theory, queer theory, and elements of second-wave feminism that led into third-wave feminism. She questioned the belief that some behaviors typically associated with gender are natural or genetic. She focused on gendered behavior as a learned performance influenced by White, male heteronormative sexuality. She postulated (Butler, 1990) about how much of an individual is the he-she dichotomy, preferring to see the distinction as predetermined by the society or culture where one lives. She followed postmodernist and poststructuralist practices in using the term "subject" (rather than "individual" or "person") to underline the linguistic nature of the position of people within what Jacques Lacan termed the *symbolic order*, the system of signs and conventions that determines the perception of what people see as reality. Butler believed that even subjectivity is not stable enough when talking about performative actions regarding gender.

Identity itself, for Butler, is an illusion retroactively created by performances. She goes so far as to state that gender, as a natural "thing," does not exist. Gender is only real because of the performance in the culture in which it is performed. Butler goes on to state that gender is a complete social construction and that it is therefore open to the contesting of its existence. By illustrating the artificial, conventional, and historical nature of gender construction, Butler attempts to critique the assumptions of White, male normative heterosexuality: those punitive rules (e.g., social, familial, and legal) that force people to conform to hegemonic, heterosexual standards for identity.

She goes further though in her ideas. Not only questioning the realist validity of gender, Butler continues by calling into questioning the distinction between gender and sex, something that some feminist theorists acknowledged as true. According to traditional feminists, sex is a biological category, and gender is a historical category; therefore, gender is a social construction. Butler questioned that distinction by arguing that the predetermined performances found within cultures were so effective they impacted the ability to objectively disregard social conventions. She saw sex as nothing more than a social construct that was a powerful influence in societies because of the discourse used to articulate and make real the differences people grew up believing as being obvious.

The Order of the Human Sciences

In his book *The Order of Things: An Archaeology of the Human Sciences*, Foucault attempted to uncover the history of what today are called the human sciences—that is, such disciplines as psychology, sociology, and culture studies. Foucault analyzed Diego Velàzquez's painting *Las Meninas*. In doing so, he was able to attribute order in the design, addressing such things as what is in the foreground versus background. In doing this, he was able to then use these same ideas and apply them to everyday life. Foucault believed that the painting represented a structure of society that people operated within unknowingly. Of course, this relates back to the foundational views of poststructuralism regarding the influence of discourse and how people are shaped and influenced by those in power to see and define things in a certain way. In essence, we become pawns. Foucault used the term ***episteme*, which is the orderly, unconscious structure of science**.

Foucault referred to these (epistemes) as stable, unspoken, and largely unconscious rules that govern knowledge. He demonstrated that whether a society will make use of the scientific method appeared to be predetermined by their epistemological assumptions about reality. We saw this struggle manifest itself regarding what the public was told regarding COVID-19 and the vaccines developed to protect against it. In the United States, as has been mentioned throughout this text, political affiliations have influenced perceptions of both the virus and the vaccine. Regardless, Foucault's central argument in *The Order of Things* is that beliefs dictate what sort of culture will arise. Will they be great artists? Scientists? Economists? All these are predetermined, says Foucault, by what things a culture generally takes for granted at an unconscious level.

He offered an analytical elaboration on this concept, showing that grammar is an epistemological foundation for human linguistics. Foucault analyzed the transformations in discourse. He showed that in each of the disciplines he looked at, the precursors of the contemporary disciplines of biology, economics, and linguistics, the same general transformations occurred at roughly the same time, encompassing a myriad of changes that might not seem connected to one another.

Before the late 1800s, Foucault argued, Western knowledge was disorganized, consisting of various aspects of superstition, religion, and philosophy. In the late 1800s, clear distinctions between academic disciplines emerged. This was due in part to the increase in the division of labor increased, and specialization began to take shape (see Durkheim). The aim at this stage, from a scientific perspective, was for a definitive cataloguing and categorization of what could be observed. Foucault, however, saw science as concerned with the superficial, the surface. He believed that science at the time was not looking for anything deeper. This seems the antithesis of what Americans usually believe about science. Language, for Foucault, was understood as simply representing things, such that the only concern with language was that of clarification. For the first time, however, Foucault saw a change. There developed an appreciation of the reflexive role of subjects in scientific inquiry where the scientist became an object for inquiry, an individual conceived simultaneously as both subject and object. Then, from the beginning of the 19th century, a new attention to language emerged. There began a search for the hidden. We saw this explosion of new ideas in the rapid development of fields of study.

Discipline and Punish

The work that Foucault did in the 1970s is the most well-known for sociologists. Issues of power, control, and how these shaped the masses are the most utilized ideas in sociological research in the 21st century. In the 1970s, as mentioned earlier, Foucault became involved with the prisoners' movement. The 1970s prisoners' revolts were the first collectively initiated prison rebellions in France since the 1700s and played a crucial role in helping to problematize the societal function and concept of the prison. Living conditions were inhumane. The prisoners were not only successful in seizing control of their prisons but were also, and more importantly, effective in opening up public discourse on the politics of France's incarceration system. Various French intellectuals, including Foucault, spoke out on the conditions. This led to the publication of his book in 1975 of *Discipline and Punish: The Birth of the Prison*.

Discipline and Punish is a book about the emergence of the prison system. The flow is like other sociohistorical books that Foucault wrote. The conclusion of the book is that the prison is an institution that inevitably has the complete opposite effect than people would think. That is, the format of the prison system led to increased criminality and recidivism of those that are housed there. In other words, people were going to prison and not only learning not only to be better at criminal behavior but were also being socialized to embrace that way of life. Because of this impact, Foucault argued that the prison system needed to be completely reformed.

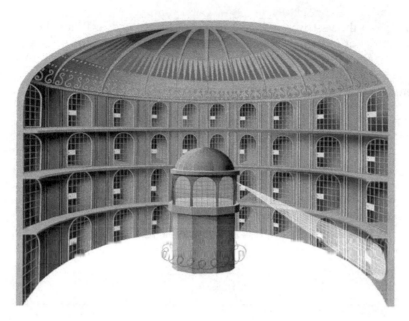

Figure 8.1: Panopticon Prison

The more important general theme of the book was that of discipline in the penal sense. Though he addressed this in many forms, the most popular has been how Foucault referenced the use of the ***panopticon,*** **which is a disciplinary concept brought to life in the form of a central observation tower placed within a circle of prison cells.** From the tower, a guard could see every cell and inmate, but the inmates could not see into the tower. Prisoners would never know whether they were being watched. This was a specific historical form of power that was taken up by the state, which included professional soldiering in the 17th century, and spread widely across society, first via the panoptic prison, then via the division of labor in the factory and universal education. The purpose of discipline, according to Foucault, was to make the masses docile and desiring to submit to authority. By socializing people to live in such a manner, they created a situation where people would defer to those in power. Foucault viewed people as having their movements controlled coercively, either directly or indirectly, which in turn involved the thought process of the people changing so they voluntarily think and do what those in power would want them to. This is particularly easy to see in the prison environment, but it is also an effective tool throughout society. Sociologists have used this idea to explain how the masses are controlled in any industrial or postindustrial society. The idea of the surveillance society came of this. A ***surveillance society*** **is a society where surveillance technology is widely used to monitor people's everyday activities. This is seen in the modern occurrence of cameras everywhere recording movements of people** and the opportunity to track people on their phones (e.g., the calls they make, their internet searches, etc.). In the industrial and postindustrial world, people are being monitored. Working for a state university, even our emails get monitored.

Foucault focused on the concept of power so much so that he remarked that he produced the analysis of power relations rather than the history he had intended. In *Discipline and Punish*, he developed a notion of power-knowledge, recombining the analysis of the epistemic with an analysis of the political. For Foucault, ***power-knowledge*** **is when power is based on knowledge and makes use of knowledge; on the other hand, power reproduces knowledge by shaping it in accordance with its intentions.** Knowledge, for Foucault, is incomprehensible apart from power. He introduced the idea of power-knowledge as a replacement for the Marxist notion of ideology in which knowledge is seen as distorted by class power. For Foucault, there is no pure knowledge apart from power, but knowledge also has real and intricate importance for power. Hence, we see the connection of Althusser's ideas reflected in Foucault's writing.

Systems of power, whether governmental, academic, cultural, corporate, or scientific, are all justified and upheld by a complex web of beliefs generally accepted as truth or as knowledge by people of various ranks and roles within any particular context, such that it is not possible, even in principle, to separate the complexities of power relationships from the vast web of beliefs, each of which feeds off the other in a relationship that is deeper than mere symbiosis or reciprocity. Thus, when we speak of either power or knowledge, according to Foucault, we are really dealing with power-knowledge as a single vast web of power relationships and systems of knowledge, the majority of which are implicit and not commonly called attention to within any society, context, or institution. It is not two words; it is one word: power/knowledge.

Therefore, my ability as a professor to have power-knowledge is coordinated by having in place a university system; educational system; assumptions about what is needed for specific degrees; and the buy-in from the populous. There are certainly more than this, but what these things do is work together to provide a rank for me in society and allow me to either do or not do things. It is not unusual for journalists to contact me and ask about events occurring locally, nationally, or globally. And when I speak on social issues, there is a tendency for people to listen. That is power-knowledge. Of course, it is not all unidirectional. Students fill out evaluations. The university has expectations of scholarship as well as service. Failure on my part to succeed in any of those three areas will lead me to have less power-knowledge. For now, just imagine a web, a good web, and think of it representing elements of everyday life that help to facilitate an end. That is how power-knowledge is orchestrated.

<insert IMG 8.3: Eco>

Umberto Eco (1932–2016) was an Italian literary critic, novelist, and semiotician (student of signs and symbols). While much of Eco's fame comes from his work as a novelist, for our purposes here, let us focus on his theory addressing semiotics. *Semiotics* is the study of signs and symbols and their use for interpretation of human behavior. Drawing his ideas on semiotics largely from Charles Sanders Peirce (see Chapter 4), founder of pragmatism, the starting point of Eco's ideas are that both industrialized and nature-based civilizations are evolving in a system or systems of signs (Eco, 1976). A distinguishing feature of Eco's theory was that in addition to words and language, the sign also addresses nonlinguistic and even natural signs, which do signify, based on a code or previous learning. He placed humans at the center of meanings attached to signs. He saw the sign as something that is used by people to transmit information—that is, to say or indicate a thing that someone wants others to know. This comes through social interaction and experience. However, unlike other theories, Eco stated that the sign was an actor in signification, thereby having agency.

This model can be applied to most processes of communication. However, a message can pass through a channel from sender to receiver without ever signifying if the sender and the receiver do not share a common code. Besides being an element in the process of communication, the sign is also an actor in the process of signification. However, Eco believed that a code had to exist to allow for signification. A code suggests a system in place that makes it possible for communication to occur, as the receiver of the information would need to understand what is trying to be sent to them. This code could be something as simple as language (one usually needs to speak the same language) but can entail nonverbal gestures, which are paramount in pragmatism. Anyone who has tried communicating with someone who does not speak the same language understands the dynamics involved in attempting to convey a message. Eco developed categories of signs, as well as the modes of sign production. Because of Eco's success in literature, his ideas on semiotics were met with skepticism. Was he a contributor to philosophical and social thought? Or was he simply someone with an ego big enough to try anything?

Returning to the concept of power, Foucault began his foray into power in *Discipline and Punish*, but it was in *The Will to Knowledge* (1976) where he probed the depths of the concept. *The Will to Knowledge* is probably Foucault's most influential work in the social sciences as a whole. The central thesis of the book addressed power as it relates to sexual repression. In sexual repression, the thought is often that since sex typically revolves around a small number of people, power might be limited to small interactions. This is not what Foucault is referencing. He suggested that, culturally, people are being socialized in a way so they are being controlled regarding their expectations, desires, and dreams. The goal would be to liberate themselves through changing the culture, to recognize how people are being manipulated. This is consistent with the work by Adorno and Horkheimer with their writings on the culture industry and how the culture industry creates a passive populous, thereby allowing those in power to do as they please.

The problem, according to Foucault, however, is that we have a negative conception of power, which leads people only to call power that which prohibits, while the production of behavior is not problematized at all. Think of that. Foucault is suggesting we look at how power is being used to facilitate behaviors. Foucault claimed that all previous political theory found itself stuck in a view of power reproduced in connection to absolute monarchy and that our political thought had not caught up with the French Revolution. Foucault's point is that we imagine power as being a thing that can be possessed by individuals, as being organized like a pyramid, with one person at the top operating via negative sanctions. Foucault argued that power was more amorphous and autonomous than this—and relational. That is, power consists primarily not of something a person has but rather is a matter of what people do, living in our interactions with others (think "processes," as mentioned earlier in this chapter). As such, power is completely pervasive in social networks (see Bourdieu). People are as much products of power as they are wielders. Power thus has a relative autonomy apropos of people, just as they do apropos of it: power has its own strategic logics, emerging from the actions of people within a network of power relations. The incarceration system and the construct of sexuality are two prime examples of such strategies of power: They are not constructed deliberately by anyone or even by any class but rather emerge organically.

This led Foucault to an analysis of the specific historical dynamics of power. Remember, as stated above, that power influences many aspects of us, including our needs and desires. He introduced the concept of "biopower," which combined disciplinary power, as discussed in *Discipline and Punish*, with a biopolitics that invests peoples' lives at a biological level, making people live according to norms, to regulate humanity at the level of the population.

Overall, when I think of Foucault, the area that garners my attention most involves the concepts of biopower and biopolitics. This is in part because it fits so well with the concept of disabilities in my early research. Regardless, biopower and biopolitics are especially important when discussing the various ways our bodies are subjugated in everyday life, as well as how we are influenced by those in power to view and feel about our bodies. ***Subjugation* is the action of bringing someone or something under domination or control.** This notwithstanding, biopower and biopolitics continue to hold significant power in and for discussions on modern forms of governance and modes of subjectification. ***Biopower* is the practice of modern states to regulate their subjects through an explosion of numerous and diverse techniques for achieving the subjugations of bodies and the control of populations, using statistics, probabilities, and professionals.** It is the "how." ***Biopolitics* can be understood as a political rationality that takes the administration of life and populations as its subject.** The government, other institutions, or powerful companies state what the body is supposed to be, what it is to look like. Biopower is how governments and other powerful institutions can dictate which bodies are seen as defective and which are not. Think of something such as amniocentesis. ***Amniocentesis* is a medical procedure used primarily in prenatal diagnosis of chromosomal abnormalities and fetal infections as well as for sex determination.** This is a form of biopower, as when so-called infections or abnormalities are identified, a decision can be made as to whether the pregnancy should be terminated. Amniocentesis provides the opportunity to decide who is fit to live.

Included with biopower would be the treatment of the body, not only by the individuals themselves but also how people should view and interpret bodies, both their own and others'. Therefore, what occurs is that powerful agencies or the government dictate to the populous through discourse, or some form of narrative, socializing people to know how bodies should appear and be treated. From there, people abide by those values and act accordingly, discriminating or appreciating specific types of bodies. One need only to look at how the bodies of models or celebrities are viewed and evaluated to see this in action. More important is how those who do not fit within the norm of society are treated and evaluated.

The notion of biopolitics brought Foucault's thinking to the question of the state. Foucault's work on power had generally been a matter of minimizing the importance of the state in the network of power relations, but now he started to ask about it specifically, via a genealogy of government, focusing his attention on understanding and critiquing neoliberalism. He did this in *The Birth of Biopolitics*. Here, Foucault coins the term "governmentality." ***Governmentality* is the action of the government to shape, guide, or affect the conduct of people**.

This notion of government takes Foucault's research on biopower and puts it on a more human plane, in a biased move away from the bracketing of subjectivity that had branded Foucault's approach up to that point. The notion of government, for Foucault, like that of power, straddled a gap between the government today and personal conduct, so-called government-of-the-self. The two are closely related inasmuch as, in a rather Aristotelian way, governing others depends on one's relation to oneself. This theme indeed takes Foucault in precisely the direction of ancient Greek ethics.

Ultimately, Foucault died at far too young an age, when his works were still relevant and vital to understanding the genealogies or histories of various aspects of life. Much like Marxist and critical theorists, Foucault paid close attention to the techniques that were developed from knowledge and how they were used to control people, whether that be physically or our thoughts (e.g., values, beliefs, attitudes). They inevitably became called technologies of power. The form from which this power is wielded changes over time and space but has the same or similar effects. He saw this impact occurring through the various institutions, whether it was through medical fields or the criminal justice system, among others.

Pierre Bourdieu

<insert IMG 8.4: Bourdieu>

Pierre Bourdieu (1930–2002) was a French sociologist and social thinker who was primarily concerned with the dynamics of power in society. His work addressed culture and the various forms of capital and is largely popular in sociology, especially how he addressed issues of social stratification, status, and power. More specifically, Bourdieu was concerned with the nature of culture: how it is reproduced and transformed, how it connects to social stratification, and the reproduction and exercise of power. He specifically addressed capital, breaking it down into social and cultural capital (Bourdieu, 1986), as well as economic and symbolic capital (Bourdieu, 1987). This continued a trend within sociology, as seen throughout this book, of how sociologists deconstruct stratification.

Social Capital

Most well-known is Bourdieu's (1986) conceptualization of social capital as based on the recognition that capital is not only economic, but that social exchanges are based on life beyond self-interest. His ideas on social capital were founded on issues of social reproduction and symbolic power. Bourdieu's work emphasized structural constraints and unequal access to institutional resources based on class, gender, and race. ***Social capital* allows a group of people to work together effectively to achieve a common goal yet at the same time allows the individual to dominate and/or manipulate others**.

The key difference for Bourdieu, as opposed to someone like Robert Putnam, is that Bourdieu portrayed social capital as the property of the individual rather than the group. Power was the key. This was achieved through the social position and status of individuals. In his view, social capital enabled an individual or group to exert power on other individuals or groups through using limited or vast resources. Much like Collins's matrix of domination where there is no pure victim, Bourdieu saw social capital as not being equally available to members of a group or collective. Social capital was available to those who achieved positions of power and status through their ability to network with others they could use (Bourdieu, 1986). His view of social capital is utilitarian. For Bourdieu, social capital is connected to economic class and other forms of stratification that serve to benefit that individual or group in numerous ways. In other words, he envisioned social capital as the process of obtaining real or virtual resources by individuals or groups through the possession of "more or less institutionalized relationships of mutual acquaintance and recognition" (Bourdieu & Wacquant, 1992, p. 119). Therefore, social capital resided in the individual and was linked to social connections that a person could utilize for advancement.

According to Bourdieu, while social capital was achieved through benefits derived from social networks, the power associated with social capital for the individual or group was achieved through networks that yielded social, economic, and cultural structures for themselves but not others. One of the key factors associated with Bourdieu's social capital was that eventually there would be assumptions made by others whereby the opportunities for advantage for the individual or group would become part of everyday life. Power and status would create a taken-for-granted-ness. It would be normal. Social capital would therefore not be so much about having a large social network but having, instead, a social position or positions that create the potential for advantage from one's social network. When I first became a sociologist, I began to get heavily involved in a sociological association. Quickly, I began meeting people—that is, sociologists from around the region. As I came to know them, doors began to open for me. People offered me jobs, provided opportunities for me to publish in journals of which they were editors, or they were publishing an edited book where they encouraged me to submit my work. My students started having access to graduate programs because of my networking. It was a very simple process. I knew all the administrators at my former university and was on a first name basis with all of them. When I needed something, I could make a call or pay them a visit. Inevitably, it increased my power and status on the campus. This is how social capital works.

The Social Capital of Robert Putnam

As stated above, Bourdieu's depiction of social capital is in some ways different than other social thinkers. The key difference between Bourdieu's conception of social capital and virtually all other approaches is the inclusion of power by Bourdieu. Others, such as Putnam, have helped shape contemporary definitions and applications of the value of social capital. According to Putnam (2000), social capital refers to the social networks and norms of reciprocity and trust that develop within these networks. For Putnam, social capital emphasizes cultural values and norms that encourage people to cooperate, trust, understand, and empathize with one another, which is in stark contrast to Bourdieu. For Putnam, this process was developed through socialization and the subsequent cultural systems. Putnam's work describes social capital as a cultural system where communities serve as moral entities where civic citizenship develops through goodwill, values, and consensus. Therefore, social capital can be a resource that people and communities can leverage to facilitate and accomplish mutually beneficial interests through providing emotional support as well as financial or physical assistance (Adler & Kwon, 2002; Blackshaw & Long, 2005; Kay & Bradbury, 2009; Putnam, 2000). Putnam highlights participation in communities as a core element of social capital. Of course, Bourdieu allows for that form of social capital, but he also addresses power and status and how people can and do use their social capital for advantage over others.

A clear distinction that Putnam does make is between two forms of social capital: bridging and bonding. Bridging social capital has the potential to forge connections across individuals or groups. Although social capital is relational, its influence on communities is most profound when relationships are among heterogeneous groups. Heterogeneity of social connections integrates diverse groups across a broad range of resources or opportunities (Narayan & Cassidy, 2001). Through it, people from different backgrounds can connect and find common ground to work together for the benefit of their community. These networks and ties are comprised of people with diverse social identities. Based on this view, it can be argued that individuals who are connected through bridging capital have a greater range of associates and greater opportunities for broader community engagement (Frank & Yasumoto, 1998). Bridging social capital is therefore not only essential for enhancing social inclusion but is also essential for improving a community's ability to develop.

Bridging social capital can lead to bonding social capital. Putnam suggested that bonding social capital occurred when people with similar backgrounds, values, and interests enter relationships and collaborate to achieve shared goals. These associations, according to Putnam, are inward looking, close knit, and tend to reinforce exclusive identities and homogenous groups. Bonding is of particular interest to fandom and sports, as it represents significant positive reproductive social qualities while also serving as a way of protecting members of the groups by providing buffers and support systems. While Putnam stated that bonding social capital typically occurred among homogenous populations, not all agree. Aldrich and Meyer (2014) maintain that bonding social capital typically develops between people who attend the same schools, have similar life goals, pursue similar careers, or participate in the same religious rituals. This does not always entail homogeneity.

Therefore, one can see the difference between Bourdieu and others such as Putnam. While Putnam's work from 2000 put social capital on the map, if you will, Bourdieu's version of social capital has increasingly gained attention, especially when trying to understand power inequities found throughout societies. Ultimately, the connection to Bourdieu for sociologists has been the form of networking that he illustrates. His work revolved around how through networking people produce more power and status than others with whom they come into contact. It is now common to find scholars who adopt this network approach to social capital, utilizing definitional or conceptual issues related to social capital.

While the network approach positioned social capital with the individual, for Bourdieu, social capital was also interconnected to context since it is part of a system of social, economic, and cultural structures. These structures were typically beyond the purview of the network approach to social capital, which tended to focus exclusively on social networks, and therefore, the role of social, economic, and cultural structures had not been considered. Yet for Bourdieu, these structures were related to the production and reproduction of social capital. Social capital was attributed to power and status by social norms and taken-for-granted assumptions that created and reinforced advantage. Therefore, again, Bourdieu analytically connected the processes associated with these structures. One cannot talk about social capital without acknowledging these interconnections, much like Foucault with power-knowledge. I suppose an easy way to understand this is to talk about fingers without talking about hands, arms, and the human body. Sociologists need to also address social, economic, and cultural structures when addressing social capital.

Habitus and Fields

Unlike Putnam's utilization of social capital, which tends to be more approachable for the scholar and layperson alike, Bourdieu's take on social capital is more demanding. There are many concepts underlying the terms he used that have specific and significant meaning. His approach is based on his wider sociological theories of habitus and fields. ***Habitus*** **refers to the thoughts, habits, skills, and tendencies people are socialized into having**. This includes how people see and experience the world around them. More importantly, through habitus, the social, economic, and cultural structures are reproduced and maintained, thereby facilitating a stable environment. ***Fields*** **are distinct areas of professionalism or informalities, such as art, education, religion, and sports**. Each field has their own set of rules in which people operate (Bourdieu, 1987). The relationship to social capital involved how each field, through habitus, recreates itself through patterns of interconnectedness. This forces researchers to always consider context when analyzing human behavior and, in this case, social capital. Therefore, while on the surface Bourdieu's work addresses macro structures in the social, economic, and cultural realm, analysis also requires the micro processes involved in everyday life.

For Bourdieu, habitus serves to frame the world around them. In this process, habitus works to assist people in how they perceive phenomena and objects, but from there, it leads to specific forms of actions, whether that be behavioral or cognitive. People will then be able to understand not only their own location in the world around them but also those of others. And while this could also lead to such rudimentary aspects of life, such as customs, ceremony, and common courtesy, our concerns here are ultimately how habitus is used to facilitate power and status. People have varying forms of access to behaviors, attitudes, and values that can lead them to achieve more. We see how people will change as they access different people or things. When students come to college, they meet diverse groups of people and learn new things. Students usually notice this initial change in themselves when they go home for Thanksgiving or Christmas their first year in college. Somehow, things changed while they were off to school. Throughout college, students learn to or are socialized to see the world differently. They make connections that open doors for them, whether that be options for jobs, graduate school, places to live, connections to people in power in their community or state, or potential partners for romantic relationships. All these avenues provide opportunities for change, for developing habitus that will result in a change in social capital. Reciprocally, social capital also changes the habitus.

Likewise, fields open the door to many different areas of life. For myself, though I have been a Star Trek fan since 1966 when it first aired, attending Star Trek conventions provided a different area (field) that I could take advantage of regarding research. Having access to fans by networking allowed for the ability to conduct interviews and learn more about the history of the franchise and fandom. People told me what to look for, where to look, and who to speak with. Within a short time, I became an expert on Star Trek and its fandom. I had access to a field, which helped develop habitus that lead to greater social capital. The people I met who directed me in various directions then began seeing me as someone who now knew more than themselves.

Fields also help explain the differences in power found throughout a society. For instance, think of the state of women in the United States, even to this day. Just as Crenshaw and Collins highlighted the different identities that people arrived with in their interactions, Bourdieu could use fields in a similar manner. Think of the power differential for many women who may have high paying jobs with high status, yet when they go home to their families, they may be seen as the housekeeper who would also cook and clean and take care of the day-to-day lives of those in the household. What is key, however, from Bourdieu's point of view is that these women are socialized to behave, think, and feel this way. This has been widely observed by feminist activists and researchers. For Bourdieu, this is another way of saying that women and men are socialized to behave differently in public, private, and intimate arenas of power (VeneKlasen & Miller, 2002).

A comparison with Foucault, then, yields stark differences. Foucault saw power everywhere, and it was therefore beyond the scope of studying agency or structure strictly. Bourdieu, on the other hand, saw power as culturally and symbolically created, as well as recreated, thereby always legitimizing the system through the interplay of agency and structure. This is created, recreated, and maintained, as mentioned above, through habitus. Habitus is created through social processes, leading to patterns that are enduring and transferrable from one context to another but that also shift in relation to specific contexts and time. What we see with habitus is that it is not something fixed but instead is something that adapts and adjusts to the circumstances in which people find themselves. More than that, habitus is created and reproduced unconsciously. People are socialized into the social, economic, and cultural structures; therefore, there is a sense of normalcy created as they grow up and live; it is simply the way things are. There is no need to call them into question. This allows for people to use their social capital to hold sway over others, as well as for those with little social capital to accept that situation and to not pursue more.

Cultural Capital

As mentioned above, another form of capital for Bourdieu was cultural capital. **Cultural capital refers to the collection of skills, tastes, postures, clothing, mannerisms, material belongings, credentials, and so forth that people acquire through membership in social and economic classes.** When people share similar forms of cultural capital, there is a sense of togetherness, a collective identity. There is a sense of "us." However, being consistent with his ideas on social capital and the relationship to power and status, Bourdieu acknowledged that cultural capital also contributed to social inequality. There is also somewhat of a hierarchy of forms of cultural capital. These serve to open or close doors for people.

As Bourdieu stated (1986),

Cultural capital can exist in three forms: in the embodied state, i.e., in the form of long-lasting dispositions of the mind and body; in the objectified state, in the form of cultural goods (pictures, books, dictionaries, instruments, machines, etc.), which are the trace or realization of theories or critiques of these theories, problematics, etc.; and in the institutionalized state, a form of objectification which must be set apart because, as will be seen in the case of educational qualifications, it confers entirely original properties on the cultural capital which it is presumed to guarantee. (p. 17)

For Bourdieu, embodied cultural capital comprised the knowledge that is consciously acquired and passively inherited by socialization to culture and tradition. Unlike property, cultural capital is not transmissible but is acquired over time, as it is impressed upon the person's habitus, which, in turn, becomes more receptive to similar cultural influences. Linguistic cultural capital is the mastery of language and its relations: the embodied cultural capital, which is a person's means of communication and self-presentation, acquired from the national culture. Therefore, an example of embodied cultural capital is how people change with the amount of education they achieve and their exposure to life around them. I had a student years ago who was from a low-SES family and grew up in rural Alabama. She had a strong, rural southern accent that reminded me often of Ellie May Clampett from the tv show *The Beverly Hillbillies*. She was an outstanding student. As time went on, she got more and more involved with sociology. She began attending conferences. She networked. After she graduated, she went on to graduate school and became an activist for civil rights. I saw her several years later while I was traveling. We were talking, and I noticed her voice had changed. She no longer spoke with a southern accent, and her mannerisms had changed. She had come to embody the culture of an upper middle class, educated professional. Her body language, habits, and attitudes had changed.

The objectified state as it applies to cultural capital is comprised of someone's properties, such as something like a work of art, gold and silver coins, or guitars. What is unique about these cultural possessions is they represent artifacts that can be bought and sold, always or usually turning a profit. These objects provide a symbolic element of culture, especially, in this case, more high culture. The cultural element of these forms of objectified culture is that unless something occurs by accident, people who possess, buy, and sell these items typically are well-versed in their understanding of the value of them not only pricewise but also their cultural significance (usually in specific fields). Many of my cousins are in the music industry, both here in the States and in Italy. Some of them have guitar collections. While they did not spend a lot of money in purchasing these guitars, they held onto them. Guitars they bought for $100 are now worth $5,000 or more, each. The knowledge necessary to operate in these fields becomes important. Knowing the economic, cultural value, and fields these fit becomes crucial when attempting to circulate with people in an attempt to make a positive impression but also potentially find more of these items. Friends have given me Star Trek collectibles they had little use for, as they purchased them when they were kids 40 or 50 years earlier. One friend's husband died, and she wanted to know if I wanted his collection, and when I saw it, I told her I would gladly take the items from her, but in all honesty, she had probably $50,000 in Star Trek collectibles. She asked where to sell them to get the highest price and what each item was worth.

She went that route.

Bourdieu then addressed the institutionalized state and the cultural capital associated with these institutions. Typically, this is associated with the labor market and the types of jobs one has. For instance, several years ago I saw a list of prestige associated with types of employment in the United States. They were ranked. Medical doctor was number one. Lawyer was number two. Three was college professor. Last on this long list was garbage collector. What I found interesting is what the United States would look like if we had no garbage collectors. Culturally, that position is not highly valued, yet imagine what your town would look like if no one came and took away your garbage. Nevertheless, think of the differences that exist when you are attending college and have friends who decided not to attend. Think of how we view individuals with college degrees versus those who do not. And even within those institutionalized states of cultural capital, there is a difference based on where you are working or where you earned your degree. There is even a difference based on what you majored in. Think of the difference if you earned a degree at an Ivy League school versus a small state school in southern Mississippi: same degree, different schools. The cultural value and how people treat you are different. At least that is how it would be when you first left school. After the first job, where you earned your degree holds less and less importance. The institutional recognition, however, is easily converted from cultural capital into economic capital, thereby either increasing or decreasing pay, as well as influencing how likely or unlikely you are to gain a position. Institutionalized cultural capital allows the person possessing that form of capital to present themselves to the buyer as being of higher or lower value. Again, this goes back to how people are socialized and learn the "place" of everything, from jobs, to paintings, to music, to what your degree is. With effective socialization, people learn these rankings and come to accept them as part of normal, everyday life.

Habitus Revisited

By addressing the relationship of habitus and fields, we discover that this leads to differences in choices, in life trajectories. The concept of habitus, like many of the theories and/or theorists addressed in this text, helps to make sense of how people see and experience the world. Like the pragmatism of Mead or Dewey, people rely on lived experience, not simply a theory they base their lives upon. Ultimately, found within the concept of and lived experiences of habitus, people will eventually rely on and will fall prey to experiencing the world as though it is taken-for-granted. It may be impossible to think of every move one makes. We do not think much about all the moves conducted while driving. We do not think about walking. And we do not think about what our fingers are doing when we are typing. This may not appear to be the greatest insight on everyday life, but it is a simple analogy that helps depict this idea. Habit was addressed in pragmatism. In symbolic interactionism, Blumer (1936) referred to habit as nonsymbolic interaction. In other social theories, habit per se is not addressed directly but is explored in slightly different ways, such as how those in power, talked about in Marxist thought, take advantage of others by getting them to think the way they want them to, lulling them into a false consciousness. While not the same as habit, the outcomes are the same. When we stop thinking about what we are doing, we become easy prey for others, easily succumbing to their whims.

Michael Polanyi's (1966) concept of tacit knowledge, frequently encountered in the organizational sociology literature, pointed in the same direction. ***Tacit knowledge* is knowledge that you get from personal experience, not from being taught, from books, and so on.** Polanyi contended that tacit knowledge was the foundation of all knowledge. The habitus of people is a product of their individual history and implies that they can follow rules without referring to them (Bourdieu, 1987). The view that people have of the world and their actions tend to be framed by their experience (tacit knowledge) and their current position in the social field. This is the case in part because people develop, by necessity, a practical sense of orientation that guides them in their actions. The taken-for-granted character of this sense of orientation does not call for examination by people themselves, because the choices that are the product of this practical sense seem self-evident, beyond questioning. They are normal. Therefore, people appear to follow rules while at the same time, again, appearing to retain their agency or independence. Yet they are not free.

For Bourdieu, the process whereby the habitus reproduces both itself and its subjects also entails the production of a self-perpetuating system of unequal power relations that does not require direct political struggle. Instead, within the habitus, there is a production of relationships of domination through its institutions because institutions distribute cultural capital differently among individuals. As Bourdieu stated, the unequal distribution of cultural capital creates and further intensifies unequal sociocultural settings; however, this inequality comes to appear natural or normal within the habitus because the institutions of the habitus muddy up the waters, blinding the masses to the processes occurring. In turn, cultural capital assists in the maintenance and acquisition of other forms of capital, be it economic or social, thereby perpetuating inequalities in society.

On this view, habitus therefore not only confers unfair levels of privilege to certain individuals but also is invisible to the masses. As a result, the struggle to facilitate change becomes difficult, as people are unaware of the dynamics of the system. This is because those in power are able to exercise their dominance merely by conforming to the status quo and by "being themselves," while those who are being dominated or oppressed must change the habitus from within the habitus itself. Put differently, within the habitus, the dominance of dominant subjects appears normal. The dominant can just "be," while the dominated must first clear the way before they can "be." In many ways, this is similar to the revolution Marx advocated.

Summary

Poststructualism and, more specifically, the theorists that tend to be grouped under its theoretical umbrella are popular within sociology today. The focus on discourse as an indicator of what is becomes paramount, as some theorists even suggest that discourse is the only reality. Nevertheless, the focus on how words shape what people see and experience is a critical element among poststructuralist theorists.

Foucault brought together power with knowledge and could not separate them. He analyzed how various institutions evolved and developed, focusing on how discourse illustrated and shaped each of these institutions. In the analysis of mental illness (which he refers to as "madness"), Foucault identified how people became defined as "mad" and what processes took place to remove these individuals from society. By keeping them away from the populous, any form of influence potential political opponents would have was removed. Eventually, to keep people away, madness became pathologized to justify the alienation and isolation inflicted on these individuals: an issue that still exists today in American society. He used his understanding of discipline and punishment to demonstrate how people can be confined to their beliefs and inevitably be shaped by those in power to not only see the world around them but also their own and others' bodies in a certain way. The focus on discourse led many to believe that Foucault was advocating social constructionism as an underlying theory for understanding society when all he was doing was identifying the history of institutions and how they evolved.

Bourdieu, on the other hand, focused quite a bit of his work on power and status. He used the concepts revolving around capital, specifically social, economic, and cultural capital, that would yield benefits for individuals and groups in society. Unlike Putnam, who took a more "social" understanding of capital, Bourdieu gave it more of a dark turn where people, working with others, would build their associations in a manner that will benefit them over others. A utilitarian approach, he saw cultural capital fitting this model as well as asserting that people will acquire or possess forms of cultural capital for networking and furthering their cause, specifically at a superficial or surface level. In its wake, this understanding of cultural capital will allow for researchers to identify how people use artifacts or items to facilitate a financial payoff. Likewise, his use of habitus and fields provides a framework for research that focuses on the "how" in regard to people using capital and how habitus is institutionalized.

Comprehension Questions

1. Explain what social constructionism is and how it is evident in biopolitics.

2. Explain how social capital is used to dominate and oppress others.

3. What are the similarities and differences between social and cultural capital?

4. How do habitus and fields assist researchers in analyzing power and status?

5. What is power-knowledge? How is power-knowledge evident in Foucault's ideas on biopower?

Critical Thinking Questions

1. Explain how the surveillance society—that is, the idea of the panopticon—is found in 21st-century America. Should all Americans be vaccinated (any form of existing vaccinations)? Explain your answer in relation to the surveillance society.

2. What is amniocentesis? How is that a form of biopower? People with disabilities argue for money to be spent on building healthy communities instead of on medical research associated with amniocentesis. What might the ethical issues associated with this line of thought entail?

3. Explain differences in social and cultural capital and how people in the United States reacted toward COVID-19, as well as the vaccination for COVID-19.

4. Explain how discourse shapes reality by providing a detailed example of this in process in the present day.

5. Explain how social and cultural capital are used in American society to perpetuate inequality.

Additional Recommended Reading

Bourdieu, P. (1985). The genesis of the concepts of habitus and field. *Sociocriticism*, *2*(2), 11–24.

Bourdieu, P. (1986). The forms of capital. In J. G. Richardson (Ed.), *Handbook of Theory and Research for the Sociology of Education* (pp. 241–258). Greenwood Press.

Butler, J. (1990). *Gender trouble: Feminism and the subversion of identity*. Routledge.

Eco, U. (1976). *A theory of semiotics*. Indiana University Press.

Foucault, M. (1994). *The birth of the clinic*. Vintage Publishing.

Foucault, M. (1995). *Discipline and punish: The birth of the prison*. Vintage Publishing.

Foucault, M. (2001). *The order of things*. Routledge.

Foucault, M. (2009). *History of madness*. Routledge.

References

Aldrich, D. P., & Meyer, M. A. (2015). Social capital and community resilience. *American Behavioral Scientist*, *59*(2), 254–269.

Adler, P. S., & Kwon, S. (2002). Social capital: Prospects for a new concept. *The Academy of Management Review*, *27*(1), 17–40.

Blackshaw, T., & Long, J. (2005). What's the big idea? A critical exploration of the concept of social capital and its incorporation into leisure policy discourse. *Leisure Studies*, *24*(3), 239–258.

Blumer, H. (1936). Social attitudes and nonsymbolic interaction. *The Journal of Educational Sociology*, *9*(9), 515–523.

Bourdieu, P. (1986). The forms of capital. In J. G. Richardson (Ed.), *Handbook of theory and research for the sociology of education* (pp. 241–258). Greenwood Press.

Bourdieu, P. (1987). *Choses dites*. Minuit.

Bourdieu, P., & Wacquant, L. J. D. (1992). *An invitation to reflexive sociology*. The University of Chicago Press.

Butler, J. (1990). *Gender trouble: Feminism and the subversion of identity*. Routledge.

Eco, U. (1976). *A theory of semiotics*. Indiana University Press.

Frank, K. A., & Yasumoto, J. Y. (1998). Linking action to social structure with a system: Social capital within and between subgroups. *American Journal of Sociology*, *104*(3), 642–686.

Gould, S. J. (1996). *The mismeasure of man*. Norton.

Hamel, L., Lopes, L., Sparks, G., Stokes, M., & Brodie, M. (2021). KFF COVID-19 vaccine monitor – April 2021. KFF. Retrieved May 12, 2021, from https://www.kff.org/coronavirus-covid-19/poll-finding/kff-covid-19-vaccine-monitor-april-2021/

Kay, T., & Bradbury, S. (2009). Youth sport volunteering: Developing social capital? *Sport, Education and Society*, *14*(1), 121–140.

Narayan, D., & Cassidy, M. F. (2001). A dimensional approach to measuring social capital: Development and validation of a social capital inventory. *Current Sociology, 49*(2), 59–102.

Polanyi, M. (1966). The logic of tacit knowledge. *The Journal of the Royal Institute of Philosophy, 41*(155), 1–18.

Putnam, R. D. (2000). *Bowling alone: The collapse and revival of American community*. Simon & Schuster.

VeneKlasen, L., & Miller, V. (2002). Power and empowerment. *PLA Notes, 43*, 39–41.

Credits

Img. 1.1: Source: https://commons.wikimedia.org/wiki/File:Auguste_Comte2.jpg.

Img. 1.2: Source:
https://commons.wikimedia.org/wiki/File:%D0%9B%D0%B5%D1%81%D1%82%D0%B5%D1%80%D0%A4%D0%92%D0%BE%D1%80%D0%B4.jpeg.

Img. 2.1: Source: https://commons.wikimedia.org/wiki/File:Herbert_Spencer_5.jpg.

Img. 2.2: Source: https://commons.wikimedia.org/wiki/File:Portrait_of_Franklin_H._Giddings.jpg.

Img. 2.3: Copyright © by The Warren J. Samuels Portrait Collection at Duke University (CC BY 2.5) at
https://commons.wikimedia.org/wiki/File:William_Graham_Sumner_from_left.jpg.

Img. 2.4: Source: https://commons.wikimedia.org/wiki/File:Charlotte_Perkins_Gilman_c._1900.jpg.

Img. 2.5: Copyright © by Anjalukic (CC BY-SA 4.0) at
https://commons.wikimedia.org/wiki/File:%D0%93%D1%83%D0%BC%D0%BF%D0%BB%D0%BE%D0%B2%D0%B8%D1%87.jpg.

Img. 2.6: Source: https://commons.wikimedia.org/wiki/File:Francis_Galton.jpg.

Img. 3.1: Source: https://commons.wikimedia.org/wiki/File:%C3%89mile_Durkheim.jpg.

Img. 3.2: Source: https://commons.wikimedia.org/wiki/File:Portrait_de_Maurice_Halbwachs.jpg.

Img. 3.3: Source: https://commons.wikimedia.org/wiki/File:Max_Weber_1894.jpg.

Img. 3.4: Source: https://commons.wikimedia.org/wiki/File:M.Mauss_1872-1950.jpg.

Img. 4.1: Source: https://commons.wikimedia.org/wiki/File:George_Herbert_Mead.jpg.

Img. 4.2: Source: https://commons.wikimedia.org/wiki/File:John_Dewey_in_1902.jpg.

Img. 4.3: Copyright © by Lisha prona (CC BY-SA 4.0) at
https://commons.wikimedia.org/wiki/File:Charles_Horton_Cooley.jpg.

Img. 5.1: Source: https://commons.wikimedia.org/wiki/File:Karl_Marx.png.

Img. 5.2: Source: https://commons.wikimedia.org/wiki/File:Gramsci.png.

Img. 5.3: Copyright © by Harold Marcuse (CC BY-SA 3.0) at
https://commons.wikimedia.org/wiki/File:Herbert_Marcuse_in_Newton,_Massachusetts_1955.jpeg.

Img. 5.4: Copyright © by Wolfram Huke (CC BY-SA 3.0) at
https://commons.wikimedia.org/wiki/File:JuergenHabermas.jpg.

Img. 6.1: Source: https://commons.wikimedia.org/wiki/File:Harriet_martineau_portrait.jpg.

CPSIA information can be obtained
at www.ICGtesting.com
Printed in the USA
LVHW052103300721
694167LV00006B/80